Ontology: the philosophical study of the nature of reality

Paradigm shift: jargon for step-changes in awareness or understanding such as the Copernican Revolution or Einstein's Theory of Relativity; often used colloquially for any insight that redefines an academic field

Phronesis: one of Aristotle's three intellectual virtues (cf Episteme and Techne) which relates to practical wisdom, value-judgements, and moral choice

Physicalism: the view that everything in existence is physical; nothing else exists

Plea in mitigation: in law, the submissions made by the defendant or their representative as part of the sentencing process, to present any mitigating circumstances that the judge should take into account while sentencing

Predestination: the belief that all the events of your life have already been willed by God

Predetermination: the belief that all the events of your life have been already decided or are already known by whoever or whatever logic it was that designed the world

Psychopathy: a neuro-psychiatric disorder characterised in humans by deficient emotional responses, a lack of empathy, poor behavioural controls, and an absence of conscience or any capacity for remorse. Usually assessed using the Robert D. Hare Psychopathy Checklist.

Qualia: individual instances of subjective, conscious experience (cf Sentience)

Quantum entanglement: Einstein's 'spooky action at a distance' whereby once a particle has interacted with another particle, they will remember that entanglement thereafter, and it will continue to affect their behaviour into the future

Realis: types of grammatical mood which relate to things that are the case, used to portray situations that are real

Recurrent Neural Network: a type of Deep Learning neural network that contains feedback loops to promote the persistence of information over time in order to create 'memory'

Reinforcement Learning: a program that rewards and punishes AI to drive its learning and improvement

Robot: a word first coined in a 1920s science fiction play by the Czech writer Karel Čapek called RUR (Rossum's Universal Robots) and used mainly in literature to describe AI that has been given a physical body which resembles a human person (cf Cognitive and Deterministic Robots)

Robotics: the marriage of computer science and engineering to design machines that can help humans

SF: Science Fiction or Speculative Fiction, used here interchangeably to relate to stories of internally consistent parallel or future worlds that often contain AI and alternative intelligences

Sapience: possessing or having the ability to possess wisdom (cf Sentience)

Savoir: the French verb for knowing that refers to a type of knowing that is objective, like wissen in German (cf Connaître)

Self-awareness: in humans, the ability to have a sense of self; in robots, their existing ability to build a virtual model of their own body in space, and any eventual ability they may develop to build a similar virtual model for their robot 'mind' or artificial intelligence

Sentience: an ability to sense, an ability to perceive, and feel things (cf Sapience; Qualia)

Seven Basic Plots: Christopher Booker's distillation of the world's stories into seven distinct storylines: Overcoming the Monster, Rags to Riches, The Quest, Voyage and Return, Comedy, Tragedy, and Rebirth

Singularity, the: the irreversible point in the future at which AI overtakes human intelligence such that it can no longer be controlled by humankind

Sociopathy: a non-diagnostic term for a neuro-psychiatric disorder that is often confused with psychopathy, except that a sociopath does have a conscience but has managed to suppress it

Sophistry and illusion: David Hume's famous dismissal of metaphysics as an exercise in delusional cleverness

Soul: the idea that we possess an ineffable spirit or vital spark that feels life-giving

Source Code: the basic instructions or design written in text that in programming are then compiled in machine code and operationalised through executable code

Stochastic algorithms: algorithms that include learning functionality, which makes the behaviour of the AI into which they are programmed ultimately unpredictable

Stoicism: an ancient philosophy that teaches the development of self-control and fortitude and the overcoming of destructive emotions:

which are properly errors of judgement: in order to seek happiness in virtue

Substrate Non-Discrimination: a principle used by Nick Bostrom to argue that if AI had the same functionality and the same conscious experience as a human, then regardless of whether they were made of the same substance as a human, they merit equivalent moral status

Techne: one of Aristotle's three intellectual virtues (cf Episteme and Phronesis) which is about applying intelligence to making things, either through materials like wood or clay, or through media like song and dance

Technomoral virtues: a phrase coined by Shannon Vallor to describe the list of virtues that should govern our interaction with AI

Tragedy: the story genre in which a hero with a fatal flaw (hamartia) and full of arrogant overconfidence (hubris) meets a crisis which leads to their downfall (nemesis)

Transistor: a device made from a semiconductor like silicon used in electronics to amplify or switch electrical signals and power

Turing Test: Alan Turing's 1950 suggestion that a computer could be deemed to be 'thinking' if it were able to fool a person into thinking it was a fellow human being, which has become the standard benchmark in AI

UNESCO: the United Nations Educational, Scientific and Cultural Organization, a specialised agency with aims to promote world peace and security through international cooperation in education, arts, sciences, and culture

Uncanny Valley: the hypothesis that humans react in indirect proportion to the verisimilitude of a robot, such that an AI appearing too human will repel rather than attract a human

Utilitarianism: the school of morality often summarised as 'the greatest good for the greatest number' which prioritises outcomes over intent

Vale of soul-making: a phrase coined by the poet John Keats in 1819 and adopted in theodicy by John Hick to describe the formation of moral character through the vicissitudes of life

Veil of Ignorance: John Rawls' 1971 idea that those designing a society should design blind to their own potential status, assuming they might be the losers as well as the winners in any scenario, on the view that this would result in a design that would be fair for everyone

Virtue Ethics: the school of morality that draws on Aristotle to argue for an approach to ethics that focuses on the formation of a person's character rather than the rules governing their individual decisions

Wissen: the German verb for knowing that refers to a type of knowing that is objective, like savoir in French (cf Kennen)

Zero-shot learning: the human capacity to tackle something new, for instance to size up an unfamiliar object and then move it, because of pre-existing spatial self-maps and a general knowledge of how to address such challenges

References

Adams, Douglas (2002) *Life, the Universe and Everything*, London: Picador

Almeida, Patricia, Santos Jr, Carlos & Farias, Josivania (2021) 'Artificial intelligence regulation: a framework for governance,' *Ethics and Information Technology* 23:10

Anderson, Michael & Anderson, Susan Leigh (2011) *Machine Ethics*, Cambridge: CUP

Antognazza, Maria Rosa (ed) (2021) *The Oxford Handbook of Leibniz*, Oxford: OUP

Ariely, Dan (2009) *Predicably Irrational*, London: Harper

Asaro, PM (2012) 'A body to kick, but still no soul to damn: legal perspectives on robotics,' in Lin, P, Abney, K & Bekey, GA, eds, *Robot Ethics*, London: MIT Press, 169–186

Asimov, Isaac (2018) *I Robot*, New York: Harper Voyager

Asimov, Isaac (2018) *Robots and Empire*, New York: Harper Voyager

Avila Negri, Sergio MC (2021) 'Robot as legal person: electronic personhood in robotics and artificial intelligence,' *Frontiers in Robotics and AI*, Volume 8. DOI: 10.3389/frobt.2021.789327

Babiak, Paul & Hare, Robert D (2007) *Snakes in Suits*, New York: HarperCollins

Bakan, Joel (2004) *The Corporation*, London: Constable & Robinson

Bakhtin, A, Brown, N, Dinan, E, Lewis, M et al (2022) 'Human-level play in the game of diplomacy by combining language models with strategic reasoning,' *Science*, 378:6624, 1067–1074

Bash, Anthony (2020) *Remorse*, Eugene, OR: Cascade

Beames, Simon, Mackie, Chris & Scrutton, Roger (2020) 'Alumni perspectives on a boarding school outdoor education programme,' *Journal of Adventure Education and Outdoor Learning*, 20:2, 123–137.

Beck, Richard (2021) *Hunting Magic Eels*, Minneapolis, MN: Broadleaf

Biggar, Nigel (2009), 'Saving the "Secular" – the public vocation of moral theology,' *Journal of Religious Ethics* 37:1, 159–178

Boden MA (1988) *Computer Models of Mind*, Cambridge: CUP

Bok, Sissela (1999) *Lying*, New York: Vintage

Booker, Christopher (2004) *The Seven Basic Plots*, London: Continuum

Bostrom, Nick (2002) 'Existential risks: analyzing human extinction scenarios and related hazards,' *Journal of Evolution and Technology*, 9:1, 15–31

Bostrom, Nick (2013) 'Existential risk prevention as global priority,' *Global Policy* 4:1, 15–31 at https://existential-risk.org/concept.pdf

Bostrom, Nick & Yudkowsky, Eliezer (2014) 'The ethics of artificial intelligence,' in Ramsey W & Frankish, K, eds, *The Cambridge Handbook of Artificial Intelligence*, Cambridge: CUP

Bostrom, Nick (2017) *Superintelligence*, Oxford: OUP

Brand, P & Yancey, P (2010) *Fearfully and Wonderfully Made*, Grand Rapids, MI: Zondervan

Breithaupt, Fritz, Li, Binyan & Kruschke, John (2022) 'Serial reproduction of narratives preserves emotional appraisals,' *Cognition and Emotion* 15, 1–21

Brown, Dan (2017) *Origin*, London: Penguin

Brown, S, Davidovic, J, & Hasan, A (2021) 'The algorithm audit: scoring the algorithms that score us,' *Big Data & Society* 8:1, 1–8

Brown, ZC, Anicich, EM, & Galinsky, AD (2020) 'Compensatory conspicuous communication: low status increases jargon use,' *Organizational Behavior and Human Decision Processes* 161, 274–290.

Bungay, Stephen (2011) *The Art of Action*, Boston, MA: Nicholas Brealey

Burns, JM & Swerdlow, RH (2003) 'Right orbitofrontal tumor with pedophilia symptom and constructional apraxia sign,' *Archives of Neurology* 60:3, 437–440

Carr, M, Curd, J & Dent, F (2005) *MBTI Research into Distribution of Type*, Berkhamsted: Ashridge Business School

Carroll, Lewis (1910) *Through the Looking Glass and What Alice Found There*, London: Macmillan

Caruso, Gregg D (2022) 'The public health-quarantine model,' in the *Oxford Handbook of Moral Responsibility*, Nelkin, D & Pereboom, D, eds, New York: OUP, 222–246

Cattell, RB (1963) 'Theory of fluid and crystallized intelligence: a critical experiment,' *Journal of Educational Psychology* 54, 1–22

Chen, B, Kwiatkowski, R, Vondrick, C & Lipson, H (2022) 'Fully body visual self-modeling of robot morphologies,' *Science Robotics*, 7:68, eabn1944

Chiang, Ted (2002) *Stories of Your Life and Others*, London: Picador

Chiang, Ted (2019) *Exhalation*, London: Picador

Christian, Brian (2020) *The Alignment Problem*, London: Atlantic Books

Coates, JM, Gurnell, M, & Sarnyai, Z (2010) 'From molecule to market: steroid hormones and financial risk-taking,' *Philosophical Transactions of the Royal Society B Biological Sciences* 365:1538, 331–43

Coleridge, ST (1997) *The Complete Poems of Samuel Taylor Coleridge*, London: Penguin

COMEST report on Robotics Ethics at https://unesdoc.unesco.org/ark:/48223/pf0000253952

Corcoran, K, ed (2001) *Soul, Body, and Survival*, Ithaca, NY: Cornell University Press

Cottingham, John (2020) *In Search of the Soul*, Princeton, NJ: Princeton University Press

Criado Perez, Caroline (2019) *Invisible Women*, London: Vintage

Davies, Robertson (1983) *The Deptford Trilogy*, London: Penguin

Dennett, Daniel C (1988) 'Quining qualia,' in Marcel, A & Bisiach, E, eds, *Consciousness in Modern Science*, Oxford: OUP

Dennett, Daniel C (1993) *Consciousness Explained*, London: Penguin

Denno, D (2011) 'Courts' increasing consideration of behavioral genetics evidence in criminal cases,' *Michigan State Law Review*, 967, 967–1047. https://core.ac.uk/download/pdf/144231854.pdf

DeYoung, CG, Hirsh, JB, Shane, MS, Papademetris, X, Rajeevan, N. & Gray, JR (2010) 'Testing predictions from personality neuroscience: brain structure and the Big Five,' *Psychological Science*, 21:6, 820–828

Dickins, Rosie (2015) *Computers and Coding*, London: Usborne

Dorobantu, Marius (2021) 'Cognitive vulnerability, artificial intelligence, and the image of god in humans', *Journal of Disability & Religion*, 25:1, 27–40

Dreyfus, Hubert L (1992) *What Computers Still Can't Do*, Cambridge, MA: MIT press

Dreyfus, Hubert L (2007) 'Why Heideggerian AI failed and how fixing it would require making it more Heideggerian,' *Artificial Intelligence* 171:18, 1137–1160

Ekman, Paul (1999), 'Basic emotions,' in Dalgleish, T, & Power, M, eds, *Handbook of Cognition and Emotion*, Chichester: Wiley

Fine, G (1983) 'Plato and Aristotle on form and substance,' *Proceedings of the Cambridge Philological Society*, 29, 23–47

Fjeld, Jessica, Achten, Nele, Hilligoss, Hannah, Nagy, Adam, & Srikumar, Madhu (2020), 'Principled artificial intelligence: mapping consensus in ethical and rights-based approaches to principles for AI,' Berkman Klein Center for Internet & Society

Flyvbjerg, Bent (2002) *Making Social Science Matter*, Cambridge: CUP

Foster, Charles (2021) *Being A Human*, London: Profile

Foster, Claire & Newell, Edmund, eds (2005) *The Worlds We Live In*, London: Darton, Longman & Todd.

Frankl, Viktor E (2004) *Man's Search for Meaning*, London: Rider

Fuegi, John & Francis, John (2003) 'Lovelace & Babbage and the creation of the 1843 "notes,"' *IEEE Annals of the History of Computing* 25:4, 16–26

Fukushima, K (1980) 'Neocognitron: a self-organizing neural network model for a mechanism of pattern recognition unaffected by shift in position,' *Biological Cybernetics*, 36, 193–202

Furnham, A, Moutlafi, J, & Crump, J (2003) 'The relationship between the revised NEO-personality inventory and the Myers-Briggs type indicator,' *Social Behavior and Personality*, 31:6, 577–584

Gaita, Raimond (2002) *A Common Humanity*, London & New York: Routledge

Gambetta, Diego & Hertog, Steffen (2016) *Engineers of Jihad*, Princeton, NJ: Princeton University Press

Gawdat, Mo (2021) *Scary Smart*, London: Bluebird

Geraci, RM (2006) 'Spiritual robots: religion and our scientific view of the natural world,' *Theology and Science*, 4:3, 229–246.

Giorgi, S, Le Nguyen, K, Eichstaedt, JC, Kern, ML, Yaden, DB, Kosinski, M, Seligman, MEP, Ungar, LH, Schwartz, HA, & Park, G (2021) 'Regional personality assessment through social media language,' *Journal of Personality* 90:3, 405–425

Gladwell, Malcolm (2006) *Blink*, London: Penguin
Glattfelder, James B (2019) *Information—Consciousness—Reality*, New York: Springer
Goetz, S & Taliaferro, C (2011) *A Brief History of the Soul*, Chichester: Wiley-Blackwell
Goleman, Daniel (1996) *Emotional Intelligence*, London: Bloomsbury
Gooder, Paula (2016) *Body*, London: SPCK
Gosling, SD, Rentfrow, PJ & Swann, WB Jr (2005) 'A very brief measure of the Big-Five personality domains,' *Journal of Research in Personality* 37; 504–528.
Graziano, Michael (2018) *The Spaces Between Us: A Story of Neuroscience, Evolution, and Human Nature*, New York: OUP
Guiso, Luigi, Sapienza, Paola & Zingales, Luigi (2003) 'People's opium? Religion and economic attitudes,' *Journal of Monetary Economics* 50:1, 225–282
Gunkel, David J (2018) *Robot Rights*, Cambridge, MA: MIT Press
Hallie, Philip (1985) 'Classical scepticism—a polemical introduction,' in Hallie, Phillip, ed, *Sextus Empiricus: Selections from the Major Writings on Scepticism, Man, and God*, Indianapolis, IN: Hackett
Haraway, Donna (1985) 'A manifesto for cyborgs: science, technology, and socialist feminism in the 1980s,' *Socialist Review* 80
Harris, Sam (2012) *Free Will*, New York: Free Press
Hick, John (1991) *Evil and the God of Love*, Basingstoke: Macmillan
Hicks, RD (1907) *Aristotle's De Anima*, Cambridge: CUP
Hinton, GE, Osindero, S, & Teh, Y-W (2006) 'A fast learning algorithm for deep belief nets,' *Neural Computation*, 18:7, 1527–1554
Hobbes, Thomas (2017) *Leviathan*, London: Penguin
Hodges, Andrew (2014) *Alan Turing: The Enigma*, London: Vintage
Hood, Robert E (1994) *Begrimed and Black*, Minneapolis, MN: Fortress Press
Hume, David (1999) *An Enquiry Concerning Human Understanding*, Oxford: OUP
Inglehart, Ronald F (2021) *Religion's Sudden Decline: What's Causing It, and What Comes Next?* New York: OUP
Ishiguro, Kazuo (2021), *Klara and the Sun*, London: Faber & Faber
James, Oliver (2007) *Affluenza*, London: Vermillion
James, Oliver (2008) *The Selfish Capitalist*, London: Vermillion
Kahneman, Daniel (2012) *Thinking Fast and Slow*, London: Penguin
Keats, John (2009) *Selected Letters*, Oxford: OUP
Koenig-Robert, R, Pearson, J (2019) 'Decoding the contents and strength of imagery before volitional engagement,' *Scientific Reports* 9, 3504
Konadu, DD, Mourão, ZS, Allwood, JM, Richards, KS, Kopec, G, McMahon, R, & Fenner, R (2015) 'Land use implications of future energy system trajectories' *Energy Policy* 86, 328–337
Kramm, Matthias (2020) 'When a river becomes a person,' *Journal of Human Development and Capabilities* 21:4, 307–319
Larkin, Philip (1964) *The Whitsun Weddings*, London: Faber & Faber
Layard, Richard (2005) *Happiness*, London: Penguin
Lewis, CS (2002) *Mere Christianity*, London: Harper Collins
Lodge, David (2002) *Thinks*, London: Penguin

Logg, JM, Minson, JA & Moore, DA (2019) 'Algorithm appreciation: people prefer algorithmic to human judgment,' *Organizational Behavior and Human Decision Processes* 151, 90–103

Loiacono, D, Lanzi, PL, Togelius, J, Onieva, E, Pelta, DA, Butz, MV, Lonneker, TD, Cardamone, L, Perez, D, Saez, Y, Preuss, M, & Quadflieg, J (2010) 'The 2009 simulated car racing championship,' *IEEE Transactions on Computational Intelligence and AI in Games*, 2:2

MacAskill, William (2015) *Doing Good Better*, London: Guardian Books and Faber & Faber

MacDougall, Duncan (1907) 'Hypothesis concerning soul substance together with experimental evidence of the existence of such a substance,' *Journal of the American Society for Psychical Research* 1:5, 237–275

Machiavelli, Niccolo (1995) *The Prince*, trans George Bull, London: Penguin

Martinón-Torres, M, d'Errico, F, Santos, E et al (2021) 'Earliest known human burial in Africa' *Nature* 593, 95–100

McEwan, Ian (2020) *Machines Like Me*, London: Vintage

McGilchrist, Iain (2009) *The Master and His Emissary*, New Haven, CT: Yale University Press

McGilchrist, Iain (2021) *The Matter With Things*, London: Perspectiva

Millbank, Paul (2022) 'A society without imagination: A lament,' *The Kenarchy Journal* 3:1. https://kenarchy.org/starting-points-health-and-wellbeing/

Moravec, Hans (1988) *Mind Children*, Harvard, MA: Harvard University Press

Morse, SJ (1994) 'Culpability and control,' *University of Pennsylvania Law Review* 142, 1587–1660

Morse, SJ (2011) 'Genetics and criminal responsibility,' *Trends in Cognitive Science*, 15:9; 378–380

Moser-Wellman, Annette (2002) *Five Faces of Genius*, New York: Penguin

Myers, IB, McCaulley, MH, Quenk, NL, & Hammer, AL (1998) *MBTI Manual* 3rd Edition, Palo Alto, CA: CPP

Nagel, Thomas (1974) 'What is it like to be a bat?' *The Philosophical Review* 83:4, 435–450

Nagel, Thomas (2012) *Mind and Cosmos*, Oxford: OUP

Nietzsche, Friedrich (1997) *Thus Spake Zarathustra*, trans Anthony Common, Ware: Wordsworth

Nixon, Matt (2016) *Pariahs*, Farringdon: Libri

Onen, M, Emond, N, Wang, B, Zhang, D, Ross, FM, Li, J, Yildiz, B, del Alamo, JA (2022) 'Nanosecond protonic programmable resistors for analog deep learning,' *Science* 377:6605, 539–543

Palmer, FR (1973) *Grammar*, Harmondsworth: Pelican

Palmer, FR (2001) *Mood and Modality*, Cambridge: CUP

Papadopoulos, Renos K, ed (2006) *The Handbook of Jungian Psychology*, London: Routledge

Pasquale, Frank (2020) *New Laws of Robotics: Defending Human Expertise in the Age of AI*, Harvard, MA: Belknap Press

Perline, IH & Goldschmidt, J (2004) *The Psychology and Law of Workplace Violence*, Springfield, IL: Charles C. Thomas

Perolat, J, De Vylder, B, Tuyls, K et al (2022) 'Mastering the game of Stratego with model-free multiagent reinforcement learning' *Science*, 378:6623, 990–996

Picard, Rosalind (1997) *Affective Computing*, Cambridge, MA: MIT Press

Poetry House (2020) *150 Most Famous Poems*, Springville, UT: Vervante

Poole, Eve (2009) 'Organisational spirituality,' *Journal of Business Ethics* 84:4, 577–588

Poole, Eve (2015) *Capitalism's Toxic Assumptions*, London: Bloomsbury

Poole, Eve (2017) *Leadersmithing*, London: Bloomsbury

Poole, Eve (2018) *Buying God*, London: SCM Press

Prinzing, M, Van Cappellen, P, & Fredrickson, BL (2021) 'More than a momentary blip in the universe?' *Personality and Social Psychology Bulletin* 49:2

Rawls, John (2005) *A Theory of Justice*, Harvard, MA: Harvard University Press

Rhodes, Richard (2012) *Hedy's Folly*, New York: Vintage

Riddell, Patricia (2017) 'Reward and threat in the adolescent brain: implications for leadership,' *Leadership & Organization Development Journal*, 38:4, 530–548

Roux, L, Racoceanu, D, Lomenie, N, Kulikova, M, Irshad, H, Klossa, J, Capron, F, Genestie, C, Naour, GL, & Gurcan, MN (2013) 'Mitosis detection in breast cancer histological images - an ICPR 2012 contest,' *Journal of Pathology Informatics*, 4:8. doi: 10.4103/2153-3539.112693

Russell, Stuart (2020) *Human Compatible*, London: Penguin

Ryle, Gilbert (1990) *The Concept of Mind*, London: Penguin

Schmidhuber, Jürgen (2007) 'Gödel machines: fully self-referential optimal universal self-improvers,' *Cognitive Technologies*, 8:199–226

Schmidhuber, Jürgen (2015) 'Deep learning in neural networks: an overview,' *Neural Networks*, 61, 85–117

Schulz, Kathryn (2010) *Being Wrong*, London: Granta

Searle, John R (1980) 'Minds, brains, and programs' *The Behavioral and Brain Sciences* 3, 417–457

Searle, John R (1999) 'The Chinese room,' in Wilson RA and Keil F, eds, *The MIT Encyclopedia of the Cognitive Sciences*, Cambridge, MA: MIT Press

Searle, John R (2004) *Mind*, Oxford: OUP

Sermanet, P & LeCun, Y (2011) 'Traffic sign recognition with multi-scale convolutional networks,' *Proceedings of the International Joint Conference on Neural Networks*, 2809–2813. doi: 10.1109/IJCNN.2011.6033589.

Smith, Joshua K (2021) *Robotic Persons*, Bloomington, IN: WestBow Press

Smith, Joshua K (2022) *Robot Theology*, Eugene, OR: Wipf & Stock

Song, Robert 'Robots, AI and human uniqueness,' in Wyatt, John & Williams, Stephen N, eds (2021) *The Robot Will See You Now*, London: SPCK

Soon, C, Brass, M, Heinze, HJ et al (2008) 'Unconscious determinants of free decisions in the human brain,' *Nature Neuroscience* 11, 543–545

Soskice, JM (1985) *Metaphor and Religious Language*, Oxford: Clarendon Press

Spufford, Francis (2012) *Unapologetic*, London: Faber & Faber

Stephenson, Neal (1996) *The Diamond Age*, London: Penguin

Stephenson, Neal (2008) *Anathem*, London: Atlantic

Stephenson, Neal (2012) *Some Remarks*, London: Atlantic Books

Stoppard, Tom (2015) *The Hard Problem*, London: Faber

Stump, E (2003) *Aquinas*, New York: Routledge
Sutton, RS, Barto, AG, & Bach, F (2018) *Reinforcement Learning: An Introduction* – 2nd Edition, Cambridge, MA: MIT Press
Taylor, SE, Klein, LC, Lewis, BP, Gruenewald, TL, Gurung, RAR, & Updegraff, JA (2000) 'Biobehavioral responses to stress in females: tend-and-befriend, not fight-or-flight', *Psychological Review*, 107:3, 411–429
Tegmark, Max (2017) *Life 3.0*, London: Penguin
Tenner, Edward (1997) *Why Things Bite Back*, New York: Vintage Books
Thomson JAK (1965) *Aristotle's Nichomachean Ethics*, London: Penguin
Thomson, JAK (1965) *The Ethics of Aristotle*, London: Penguin
Tinwell, Angela (2014) *The Uncanny Valley in Games and Animation*, Boca Raton, FL: CRC Press
Tolkien, JRR (2009) *Tree and Leaf*, London: HarperCollins
Turing, AM (1950) 'Computing machinery and intelligence,' *Mind* 59, 433–460
Vallor, Shannon (2016) *Technology and the Virtues*, Oxford: OUP
Wallach, Wendell & Allen, Colin (2009) *Moral Machines*, Oxford: OUP
Wallach, Wendell & Asaro, Peter, eds (2017) *Machine Ethics and Robot Ethics*, London: Routledge
Watson, Richard (2016) *Digital VS Human*, London: Scribe
Weng, J, Ahuja, N, & Huang, TS (1992) 'Cresceptron: a self-organizing neural network which grows adaptively,' *International Joint Conference on Neural Networks*, 1, 576–581.
Whitehead, AN (1929) *Process and Reality*, Cambridge: CUP
Williams, Stephen N 'Behind artificial intelligence,' in Wyatt, John & Williams, Stephen N, eds (2021) *The Robot Will See You Now*, London: SPCK
Wittgenstein, Ludwig (1980) *Remarks on the Philosophy of Psychology 1*, trans Anscombe, GEM, Chicago, IL: University of Chicago Press
Wittgenstein, Ludwig (1958) *Philosophical Investigations*, trans Anscombe, GEM, Oxford: Blackwell
Wittgenstein, Ludwig (2016) *Tractatus Logico-Philosophicus*, trans Ogden, CK, Asheville, NC: Chiron Academic Press
Woodhead, LJP (2016) 'The Rise of 'No Religion' in Britain: the emergence of a new cultural majority, *Journal of the British Academy* 4, 245–261
Wyatt, John & Williams, Stephen N, eds (2021) *The Robot Will See You Now*, London: SPCK
Yudkowsky, Eliezer (2004) *Coherent Extrapolated Volition*, San Francisco, CA: Machine Intelligence Research Institute

Index

Note: Page numbers followed by "n" denote endnotes.

ROUTLEDGE LIBRARY EDITIONS:
VICTORIAN THEATRE

Volume 6

ENGLISH THEATRE IN TRANSITION 1881-1914

ENGLISH THEATRE IN TRANSITION 1881-1914

JAMES WOODFIELD

Routledge
Taylor & Francis Group
LONDON AND NEW YORK

First published in 1984

This edition first published in 2016
by Routledge
2 Park Square, Milton Park, Abingdon, Oxon OX14 4RN

and by Routledge
711 Third Avenue, New York, NY 10017

Routledge is an imprint of the Taylor & Francis Group, an informa business

British Library Cataloguing in Publication Data
A catalogue record for this book is available from the British Library

ISBN: 978-1-138-92272-3 (Set)
ISBN: 978-1-315-68102-3 (Set) (ebk)
ISBN: 978-1-138-93437-5 (Volume 6) (hbk)
ISBN: 978-1-138-93465-8 (Volume 6) (pbk)
ISBN: 978-1-315-67785-9 (Volume 6) (ebk)

Publisher's Note
The publisher has gone to great lengths to ensure the quality of this reprint but points out that some imperfections in the original copies may be apparent.

Disclaimer
The publisher has made every effort to trace copyright holders and would welcome correspondence from those they have been unable to trace.

ENGLISH THEATRE IN TRANSITION 1881-1914

JAMES WOODFIELD

CROOM HELM
London & Sydney

BARNES & NOBLE
Totowa, New Jersey

Croom Helm Ltd, Provident House, Burrell Row,
Beckenham, Kent BR3 1AT
Croom Helm Australia Pty Ltd, 28 Kembla St.
Fyshwick, ACT 2609, Australia

British Library Cataloguing in Publication Data

Woodfield, James
English theatre in transition, 1886-1914.
1. Theater-England–History–19th century
2. Theater–England–History–20th century
I. Title
792'.0942 PN2594

ISBN 0-7099-2780-0

First published in the USA 1984 by
Barnes & Noble Books,
31 Adams Drive,
Totowa, New Jersey, 07512

Library of Congress Cataloging in Publication Data

Woodfield, James.
British theatre in transition, 1889-1914.
Bibliography: p.
Includes index.
1. Theater–Great Britain–History–19th century.
2. Theater–Great Britain–History–20th century.
I. Title.
PN2594.W66 1984 792'.0941 84-2840

ISBN 0-389-20483-8

Printed and bound in Great Britain

CONTENTS

PREFACE

Every age is an age of transition: epochs marked by the accession of kings, the fall of empires, the advent of new centuries, are all arbitrary, and at once both useful and limiting. However, a significant event can often crystallize a movement that has been formulating for decades, and provide a point of departure: is there such a data for the beginning of the modern era in English theatre? Some theatre historians would say no, and argue for a steady, evolutionary development throughout the nineteenth century; others might choose the Bancroft-Robertson era of the 1860s, or place the moment later, perhaps in the 1880s with the emergence of H.A. Jones and A.W. Pinero as major 'modern' dramatists; and some would contend that English dramatists had little conception of modern drama until Ibsen became known. Despite the strength of the evolutionary argument, and the undoubted importance of Jones and Pinero in the process, there is no doubt that the advent of Ibsen on the English theatre scene provided both a shock and a stimulus. Therefore, if one tends to the third view, as I do, the question arises as to which is the most significant Ibsen date? Edmund Gosse's first article in 1872? The first performance of an Ibsen play, *The Pillars of Society,* in 1880? The production of *A Doll's House* by Charles Charrington and Janet Achurch in 1889? Or the first performance of *Ghosts* (unlicensed) by J.T. Grein's Independent Theatre in 1891? I have chosen 1889 for the title of my book partly because *A Doll's House* launched a wave of controversy that brought Ibsen to the public attention for the first time; partly because it precipitated a series of Ibsen publications, 1889-90, followed by productions in 1891; and partly because a quarter of century (a convenient epoch) later, the phase of development reached a far from arbitrary conclusion with the outbreak of war in 1914. That year *Ghosts* was licensed and performed publicly--an indication that the years of struggle to effect a transition from the Victorian to the modern theatre had reached a successful conclusion.

This book is written not for the specialist, but for the

student or general reader, and aims to provide accounts of some of the most important events and developments that occurred during this struggle. The transition is largely the story of successive attempts to bring new, realistic and socially relevant drama to the London stage in the face of opposition from the vested interests of theatre entrepreneurs, who were quite happy with the box-office returns yielded by melodrama, farce, and sentimental comedy, and from traditional attitudes, embodied in the censorship, that regarded the stage solely as a medium for entertainment and not as a platform for the discussion or dissemination of serious ideas, whether moral, religious, political or social. Because of these interests and attitudes, there had been a schism--aggravated by the degradation of the conditions of performances in the early nineteenth-century theatres--between the drama and literature, and drama had become an object of contempt for men of intellect. However, throughout the century, serious dramatists and some notable actor-managers sought to repair that schism and to elevate the drama onto a par with literature so that it could take its rightful place amongst the arts as it did in France, Germany and other continental countries. These efforts reached a peak in the 1890s and the pre-1914 years. The era also saw the emergence of a theatrical aesthetic that was anti-realistic: this brought the poet back into the theatre, but more significantly inspired an art of the theatre of which the chief English advocate was Gordon Craig.

Many books have been written on the dramatists themselves and their plays, especially on Shaw, who dominates the period, and the general history is comprehensively surveyed by Allardyce Nicoll, George Rowell, and others; there are also specialist works on certain events or persons. I have not attempted to emulate Nicoll with a play-by-play analysis, nor to repeat the approach of writers who select half-a-dozen or so prominent authors and give them a chapter each, but have chosen to recount the pioneering work of those societies, dramatists, critics, producers and others, who were the chief protagonists in the battle to secure a bridgehead for the modern drama on the London stage. I have also favoured allowing those involved to speak for themselves: this results in a large number of quotations, but has the double advantage of giving the flavour as well as the facts of the events and of providing references which enable the reader to follow up any area of special interest.

I am indebted in general to a large number of writers who have preceded me in this area; to the former Canada Council for financial support; to the University of Southampton for Library and other facilities while researching in England; to the staffs of the British Theatre Association Library and of the Enthoven Collection, Victoria & Albert Museum, for their invaluable assistance; and to the University of New Brunswick for financial and other help.

Chapter One

INTRODUCTION - (A) NINETEENTH-CENTURY BACKGROUND

> The Drama's laws, the Drama's patrons give,
> For we that live to please, must please to live.
>
> Samuel Johnson

> Shame that the Muses should be bought and sold,
> For every peasants Brasse, on each scaffold.
>
> Joseph Hall

In the first half of the nineteenth century, the theatres had been deserted by the middle and upper classes and were forced to play to a predominantly uneducated, lower-class audience who, seeking escape from dehumanising living and working conditions, demanded *vivida vis:* four or more hours of action, emotion, sentiment, spectacle, horseplay and novelty. Moral condemnations of the theatre were not without justification, for prostitutes and their admirers formed a considerable portion of an audience, the fare was vulgar, the physical conditions repellent to persons of gentility, and even violence and riots were not infrequent--notably the 'Old Price' riots that protested John Philip Kemble's attempt to increase prices at Covent Garden in 1809 after he had rebuilt the theatre. A vivid description of a not altogether untypical audience is given by Dickens in an article entitled 'Shakespeare and Newgate' in *Household Words*, 4 October 1851, in which he describes Sadler's Wells at the time Phelps took over in 1844: it 'was in the condition of being entirely delivered over to as ruffianly an audience as London could shake together ... a bear-garden, resounding with foul language, oaths, catcalls, shrieks, yells, blasphemy, obscenity--a truly diabolical clamour. Fights took place anywhere, at any period of the performance'.[1] It is not surprising, therefore, that playwriting, an unhonoured and unrewarded profession, was scorned by the *literati*, who wrote poetry or the much more remunerative novel, and who, like Byron, when they chose the dramatic form, wrote closet dramas never intended for stage performance. Paradoxically, although the myriad forms of theatrical entertainment--which included historical drama, melodrama, burlesque, burletta, farce, pantomime, a wide range of comedy, and a variety of musical and spectacular offerings[2]--bequeathed very little to posterity until after 1890, never has there been an age in English drama when the theatre, as *theatre,* was so vigorous and popular. As many critics and historians such as Michael Booth, Hugh Hunt and George Rowell have been pointing out in recent years, the complaints of contemporary members of the intelligentsia and subsequent literary critics concerning the literary quality of the drama must be put into perspective against the evidence: a true evaluation of the drama of the nineteenth century must focus not on literary criteria, but on theatrical aspects such as acting and staging.

Nevertheless, concern over the quality of offerings, and over the social and physical conditions in which they took place, was not confined to the *literati*. Many within the theatre at the beginning of the century regretted the passing of a more genteel era, the age of Garrick when the audience was predominantly middle-class and relatively well- mannered, and sought to rectify matters. For example, as early as the beginning of Victoria's reign, in an attempt to enhance the social and intellectual status of the theatre and to repair this schism between literature and the stage, William Macready persuaded Browning to write plays, which he produced with only limited success between 1837 and 1844. Macready's higher aims and scholarly aspirations were continued at Sadler's Wells by Samuel Phelps, who was dedicated to raising standards, and at the Princess's by Charles Kean, who combined an antiquarian zeal for accuracy with a flair for spectacular pageantry in his attempts to be both instructive and entertaining. An invaluable impetus towards respectability was given by the Queen herself, who reinstituted theatricals at Windsor, appointed Kean to the revived post of 'Master of the Revels' in 1848, and attended benefits for both Macready and Kean. As the century progressed, the mass audience turned towards the music halls, the middle classes began to patronize the theatre again, and an appropriate drama developed to suit their tastes. Audiences became less demonstrative, but exercised a different kind of pressure: the moral pressure of what Findlater terms 'the perennial Puritanism of English culture'.[3] Hugh Hunt points out that

> the duty of the upper classes ... was to set an example ... If the stage was to qualify as a respectable pastime of organized society it must also set an example. It must not only reflect an idealized picture of social virtues, but must teach a wholesome lesson to fortify the converted and convert the uneducated.[4]

These requirements were enforced partly through the formal pressure of the censorship exercised by the Lord Chamberlain's

Examiner of Plays, whose task, undefined by statute, was to keep from the stage anything that might be offensive to conventional morality or propriety, and partly through the informal but stronger pressure of taste that demanded conformity to the prevailing moral code, the triumph of virtue over vice, and a happy ending regardless of the probabilities of plot or character.

During the century, the moral constraints on the theatre weakened but censorship continued to keep the serious discussion of religion, sex or politics off the stage, while paradoxically allowing immorality--especially sexual licence in the form of conjugal infidelity--full freedom to be treated lightly in farce or stock comedy. It was this duality that added a spice of excitement to theatre-going. St. John Ervine describes how his aunt, who had a passion for the theatre, occasionally fell into a panic 'when she thought of what would be the state of her immortal soul if God should call her home while she was in the theatre'.[5] The Church continued the tradition of Cromwell, observes Mario Borsa, 'lavishing persistent and bigoted condemnation upon the legitimate drama', and even formed an 'Actors' Church Union, the object of which [was] to reclaim actors and actresses who [had] strayed from the right path by the mere fact of having taken that which leads to the stage!'[6] But performers could be as prudish as their audiences, as some experiences of H.A. Jones testify: Evelyn Millard, who had just married, refused to say 'I say to you by my unborn child', because she felt the public would consider the line indelicate, and she lost the part as Jones refused to alter it; throughout rehearsals of the church scene in *Michael and His Lost Angel*, Mrs. Patrick Campbell objected to saying 'I must just titivate a cherub's nose, or hang a garland on an apostle's toe', because she thought the words profane, and she too had to relinquish her part; and Charles Wyndham, who claimed he was 'simply voicing the public instinct', wrote Jones a long letter objecting to the *Case of the Rebellious Susan* because it dealt seriously with a heroine who acted on the principle that 'what is sauce for the goose is sauce for the gander' and attempted to assert that a wife was entitled to the same amount of licence as a husband. As late as 1910, Lady Roberts, who had never been to a music hall before, attended Jones's one-act recruiting play *Fall in Rookies* at the Alhambra with her husband, and as a precaution 'kept her car waiting the whole time in case she wished to leave at any moment'.[7] These instances are symptomatic of a pervading demand for respectability that insisted on the falsification of life on the stage; the late Victorian theatre became more refined, but it still offered only an escape from life, not an examination of it. Paradoxically, it was this same puritan force and suspicion of entertainment that drove intellectual puritans like Shaw to discover in the theatre a pulpit for their own new morality, and to insist that it was the theatre's *duty* to serve the higher good of society: art for life's sake.

The nineteenth century saw many social and economic developments that had important effects on the theatre. A rapidly increasing population enjoyed the benefits of improved education and higher mobility. The former, and higher living standards, created a market for the arts, especially the theatre, while the latter, particularly the railways, gave easy access to the cultural centres. In 1843 the Theatre Regulation Act revoked the patents granted by Charles II in 1660 which limited the performance of the 'legitimate' spoken drama to the two major theatres, Covent Garden and Drury Lane. This Act had forced the minor theatres to resort to a variety of forms which tended, because of the inclusion of song and dance and spectacle (even, to circumvent the law, into Shakespeare's tragedies) to be extremely vigorous and alive with broad entertainment. Thereby, they had flourished, and it should have been no surprise when little immediate change took place in their offerings after 1843. In the second half of the century, however, as the music halls began to draw off the lower-class segment of their audience, the minors began to stage straight plays (for which they were, in fact, more suitable than the capacious majors), attracted a more sophisticated audience, and enjoyed an unprecedented boom in popularity. The changes in taste and various social and economic developments are reflected in the surge of theatre building in those fifty years. In 1851 there were twenty theatres in the London area; by 1901 there were forty-two music halls and thirteen theatres under the Lord Chamberlain, and a further twenty-nine theatres in the suburbs.

The theatre gave employment to a large number of persons--Borsa estimated over 25,000--both on stage and behind the scenes, where a small army of men were required to operate the elaborate machinery even in the smaller theatres, which sought spectacular effects as much as the larger. At the Lyceum, which seated 1,450, when Irving mounted Sardou's *Robespierre* in 1899, over 600 people were employed: 69 speaking parts, 235 supernumeraries, 17 in the ballet and chorus, up to 34 in the orchestra, 236 backstage, and a further 48 in administration and maintenance.[8] Obviously, even at prevailing wage rates, an enormous amount of money was involved, and therein lay perhaps the theatre's greatest handicap--the economic factors that attracted the speculator and imposed an either/or situation: either a play was a great and profitable success, or it failed and came off as quickly as possible to make way for another offering that, with luck, would recoup the losses. In a Preface to William Archer's *Theatrical World of 1894*, Shaw wrote:

> at the London West End theatres ... the minimum expense of running a play is about £400 a week, the maximum anything you please to spend on it. And all but the merest

> fraction may be, and very frequently is, entirely lost. On the other hand, success may mean a fortune of fifty thousand pounds accumulated within a single year. Very few forms of gambling are as hazardous as this ... in the theatre you must play a desperate game for high stakes, or not play at all.[9]

In an article in January 1897, William Archer pointed out that the London theatre was 'not self-supporting at all', but 'bounty-fed' by backers who almost expected to lose money; the entertainment world, he suggested darkly, had 'allurements' which 'attracted capital out of all proportion to any reasonable rate of return'.[10] A more serious aspect was that the economic pressure to cater to a growing mass audience in a fiercely competitive market made 'the long run, with its accompaniments of ostentatious decoration and lavish advertisement ... the one object of managerial effort', and by 1875 'there was not a single theatre in London at which plays, old and new, were not selected and mounted solely with a view to their continuous performance for as many nights as possible, anything short of fifty nights constituting an ignominious and probably ruinous failure'.[11] Archer estimated that in the years 1893-97 out of 235 new 'dramas, comedies and serious prose plays in general', there were 65 successes, 54 doubtful and 116 failures[12]--an indication of the odds against promoters.

The century saw the collapse both in London and in the Provinces of the stock company repertory system, in which companies engaged by a theatre for a season or longer performed a stock of plays that were changed nightly, and its replacement by the long run system. As Granville Barker pointed out in 1908, unless you could get 100,000 people to see a play in London, it was not worth putting on. At the Royal Court Theatre, 1904-07, he and J.E. Vedrenne, his partner and Business Manager, had struggled against the economic imperative of the long run on principle and because they wanted to produce a lot of plays. In an interview in 1908, Barker stated that the long run

> is bad for plays and bad for acting. It also means, what is more serious still, that you are constantly looking for plays that may run, if successful, 200 or 300 nights. You have no right to expect every play to do that; but I do really think that if you are looking for these plays you get this sort of play written.[13]

It was 'bad for acting' because it sapped the vitality and freshness of performers by confining them in single roles for months or even years at a time, often typecasting them for the rest of their careers in a way even more restrictive than the former system with its 'lines of business'. Successful actresses were particularly vulnerable to this 'latter-day slavery', as Elizabeth Robins termed it, finding themselves condemned in bondage to the one type of role. Another unfortunate development was that as soon as a London production established its success, replicas of it were sent on tour with type-cast performers imitating their London counterparts. J.C. Trewin declares that there 'could be as many as 250 [touring companies] on the road' at any one time with 'carbon copied' West End successes or 'routine melodrama'.[14] This practice reduced acting to mere mimicry, and because it drove the last nails into the coffins of the provincial stock companies and circuit troupes--already dying in the face of the ability of the railways to transport whole companies complete with scenery--also destroyed the nurseries for young performers. Acting was no longer studied as a serious art, but, as one contemporary critic put it, was 'picked up, as it were, promiscuously'. In their analysis of the situation at the turn of the century, Archer and Granville Barker pointed out:

> the fact that acting is a trade for which there is no recognised preparation, encourages many men, and still more women, with no special aptitude, to 'go on the stage' for a year or two, and then to drop it as the novelty of the experience has worn off. Thus a 'casual labour' class is created, the existence of which is most prejudicial to the interests of the lower ranks of professional actors, whose sole chance of a decent livelihood lies in continuity of employment.[15]

It is hardly surprising, therefore, that one of the chief concerns of those who cherished the vision of a revitalized theatre should be an endowed National Repertory Theatre and associated acting school.

Immediate success being the condition of survival, it was essential to hedge a dramatic bet by featuring a renowned actor in the leading role. The result was an aggravation of two major abuses of the actor-manager system: the tendency to produce plays especially chosen, written, or re-written to give the actor-manager opportunities to display his special talents, and the practice of insuring against a poor piece by offering expensive palliatives by way of spectacular scenic illusion. For the dramatist, paradoxically, it was 'easier to make a fortune than to earn a livelihood by writing plays'.[16] In his Preface to *Saints and Sinners* (1891), Jones protested against 'the present system in England of manufacturing plays to order and to exploit some leading performer', and contended that this in itself was 'quite sufficient to account for the literary degradation of the modern drama and for the just contempt with which it has been viewed by the intellect of the nation during the last twenty-five years'.[17] Jones had plenty of experience working with actor-managers, collaborating in turn with Wilson

Barrett, E.S. Willard, H. Beerbohm Tree and Charles Wyndham. Barrett, after Jones's success with *The Dancing Girl* (1891), wanted him to write another play for him, but Jones refused because 'it was always Barrett the manager, Barrett the actor, Barrett the author'.[18] E.S. Willard once infuriated Jones by altering the last act of *Wealth* (1889) for his New York production to give it a conventional happy ending--which the critics scorned! Another practice that annoyed dramatists was that of advertising the name of the actor-manager on posters, handbills and programmes in type far larger than that used for the author, which placed the latter very much in a secondary position. Shaw, in the Preface to Archer quoted above, pointed out--as usual both with tongue in cheek and with a sharp eye for reality--that self-advertisement and the demand for a good part were 'not in the least due to the vanity and jealousy of the actor-manager', but were conditions imposed by his popularity, because 'the strongest fascination at a theatre is the fascination of the actor or actress, not the author'.[19] 'Stanley Jones', in a series of articles attacking 'the Noble Art', condemned the actor-manager system as detrimental to the profession and to the drama: the first thing an actor-manager did, he declared, was 'to find a play in which he shall have a good part, and the second to look to it that nobody else shall have so good a part as himself'.[20] Such self-centred practices discouraged young actors, or forced those with ambition and talent to become actor-managers themselves, to the extent that Henry Irving is reported to have complained that he could not produce *Julius Caesar* because all the actors he wished to engage had become managers. The actor-manager of the period, according to Lynton Hudson,

> was giving or doing his best to give the public what it wanted; trying if possible to secure for himself a fortune by an astute flattery of its prejudices and susceptibilities, pandering to its distaste for realism and its naive delight in the romantic and the spectacular, confining his aesthetic enthusiasms to the scenic illustration of his plays and the physical comfort of his audience.[21]

Despite its flaws, the actor-manager system was by no means all bad. Such figureheads gave focus, continuity and style to their theatres, and their commercial interests were often qualified by a high degree of artistry and professional pride. The names speak for themselves: Charles Kean, Marie and Squire Bancroft, Charles Wyndham, George Alexander, Herbert Beerbohm Tree and, above all, Henry Irving, to name only a few. They raised the general level of the acting profession, and, as Archer admitted, did 'for art all that can reasonably be expected of them'; however, they inevitably became 'slaves of their conditions' because of the 'imperative of success'.[22] The constant complaint against the actor-managers is that they always played safe by mounting only plays by proven authors or revivals certain of success, and ignored the work of the aspiring young dramatist. There were occasional exceptions, like Beerbohm Tree whose After Noon matinées, for example, offered experimental fare, but, as Archer complained,

> the actor-managers as a class do not make for progress. They lack insight and initiative. Partly from natural conservatism, partly from dread of the Old Critics, they shrink from every experiment, and will attempt no divergence from the beaten track. The reasons, the excuses for their timidity are plain enough, in the vast pecuniary interests at stake.[23]

Writing in the *Fortnightly Review* in 1902, H. Hamilton Fyfe declared that

> the effect of the frankly commercial theatre has been, then, threefold. It has deprived playgoers of the opportunity of seeing constantly acted the finest plays of the past along with the most interesting of the works of modern authors. It has made the dramatic author merely a component part in a complicated piece of money-getting machinery. It has placed the greatest obstacles in the way of the actor and actress who want to become efficient in their art by means of constant practice in fresh parts ... yet in spite of its effects, the British theatre has in recent years made progress.[24]

To put the era of transition between 1889 and 1914 into its true perspective, it is important to recognize and to trace the lines of 'progress' during the latter half of the century when contemporary critics were most voluble. In 1866, Henry Morley saw the drama as 'an ailing limb of the great body of our literature', and suggested that the revival of neglected Elizabethan and Restoration plays would help restore it to its native health: 'it would be easier as well as wholesomer', he asserted,'to pare the sound old English apple than to scoop and cook and sugar those rotten French windfalls to the English taste'. He hoped that thereby 'good English thought' would be at home again on the English stage and the way would be prepared for a revived drama by contemporary English dramatists.[25] But no such revival was manifest, and thirteen years later we find Matthew Arnold protesting the dearth of native English drama and the poverty of its performers compared with the visiting *Comédie Française*, and Henry James scorning the 'literary nudity' of the English stage, which fed on 'borrowed wares' consisting of

> coarse adaptations of French comedies, with their literary

> savour completely evaporated, and their form and proportions quite sacrificed to the queer obeisances they are obliged to make to that incongruous phantom of a morality which has not wit enough to provide itself with an entertainment conceived in its own image.[26]

Translations and adaptations with French puppets in English clothes dominated the stage because they were both popular and cheap. A mere £50 or so would recompense any translator/adaptor for his pains, whereas a native dramatist could demand £200 or more (still not a very large sum for the time, effort and skill involved). But in the 1860s an important development had occurred with both social and dramatic significance: the actress Marie Wilton, in partnership with the author H.J. Byron, had taken over the Queen's Theatre, commonly known as 'the Dusthole', restored it and reopened it on 21 October 1865 as the plush Prince of Wales's Theatre. This action furthered the return of a fashionable audience to the theatre and provided T.W. Robertson with a venue for his development of the genteel, middle-class, realistic comedy. Subsequently, in conjunction with her husband, Squire Bancroft, one of the first Victorian gentlemen to enter the profession, she took over the Haymarket Theatre and inaugurated some radical and far-reaching changes: the orchestra was hidden; the stage encased in a gilt picture-frame; the pit exiled to the back of the dress circle; the prices raised; and the performers paid handsome salaries.[27] These steps not only enhanced the growing respectability of the theatre, already noted, but also confirmed the general tendency away from stylized and exaggerated acting towards a more realistic mode. Gone were the rant and declamation of the old school, for there was no longer any rowdy pit to shout down, and in its place came a new, intimate, natural style. Although acting became less histrionic and more subdued, it continued to romanticize and idealize characters, and the new mode covered a wide range. At one extreme was the intense character-acting of Irving, at the other the 'cup-and saucer' school who followed the example of the Bancrofts, and included such leading figures as Charles Wyndham, John Hare and George Alexander. On the fringe were bold spirits like Janet Achurch, Charles Charrington and Elizabeth Robins who attempted the psychological realism demanded by Ibsen's roles (for which, as Shaw argued in the 1891 Appendix to *The Quintessence of Ibsenism*, all conventional actors were unsuitably trained). However, there were many who would have agreed with Frank Benson that 'what the cuff and collar brigade, as they were christened in the decade around 1880, gained in formal accuracy they lost in spontaneity, versatility, simplicity and dignity, which were the distinguishing marks of the old school'.[28] Although some exponents of the old school had deteriorated into histrionics, elaborate business and 'theatrical tricks which smacked rather of the circus than of real life', continued

Benson, the school 'at its best had a breadth of treatment, a directness and simplicity' that enabled the portrayal of 'the great ones of humanity, and the tense moments of their life' in a way unattainable by the new school. In 1884, a rhymer in *Truth* proclaimed:

> The tailor-dummy school has had its day;
> What we require is players who can play.
> And 'twould be very silly to rely
> On that which good stage-managers supply;
> Fine scenery and perfect taste, in fact,
> Won't take the place of actors who can't act;
> The public will not pay to see a pack
> Of padded noodles set in *bric-a-brac;*
> Nor pardon actors when they wholly fail,
> Because they sit in chairs by Chippendale.
> No! They will not a feeble piece condone
> Because good taste in mounting it is shown.[29]

Henry James regretted that 'the art of acting as little as possible' had supplanted the 'art of acting as much', and was somewhat puzzled by 'the infatuation of a public which passes from the drawing room to the theatre only to look at an attempt, at best very imperfect, to reproduce the accidents and limitations of the drawing room'.[30]

In an article tracing the shift from an actor's to a playwright's theatre that occurred 1870-90, E.J. West notes the differences between the new 'low-key' actor and his predecessor:

> for the majestic dignity of the latter, he had substituted decorum; for the latter's voice of thunder he had substituted the ripple or chatter or mumble of colloquial conversation; for the knowledge of technique and tradition, he had substituted observation and imitation of contemporary manners; for training and experience he had substituted good looks and fine fashions.[31]

The more respectable content and presentation encouraged other 'gentlemen players' to take up the profession, and they in turn were sought after because they helped to attract a fashionable audience. But the profession had an uphill struggle to establish full social acceptance. The French critic Augustin Filon points out that mid-century, 'the social ostracism under which the stage then suffered was due less to the bad morals of the actresses than to the bad manners of the actors', for actresses had little opportunity to be immoral, having no time between their professional and their social duties, and being constantly on the move.[32] 'The Victorian actor', writes Michael Baker, 'was the object of extraordinary moral and religious disapproval',[33] and actors formed 'a community apart within society' because of this and the special conditions of their profession that required them to spend almost all their time in a theatrical ghetto, rehearsing, performing and travelling together. It is not surprising, therefore, that in an age when respectability was the dominant social virtue, actors sought desperately to improve their public image. Until the advent of the gentlemanly school, actors and actresses tended to come from within the profession--the sons and daughters of performers who inter-married and in several cases created theatrical dynasties such as the Kembles and Terrys. For an outsider to enter the theatre often required a dedication that could withstand--as it had to with Henry Irving--family disapproval and severance from family and friends. In addition to the moral opprobrium, other factors that contributed to the low status of the profession were the wide range of occupation subsumed under the term 'actor' and the precarious nature of employment for the bulk of the profession. Those who made it to the top acquired fortunes--more from being entrepreneurs than from acting itself, despite their personal appeal--but the majority of performers even when employed, were poorly paid, and often had to provide their own clothes, props and even travel costs from their meagre salaries. As the physical conditions of the theatre improved for the patrons, and 'society' returned to the theatre, the general social class of actor improved, as did salaries and conditions of employment. For example, the long run system, although it reduced the number of actors required, did give more stable employment to members of the cast. It also gave them more leisure time, and thereby the chance to project a more genteel image because the need for constant rehearsal for new productions was reduced; and it enabled managers to pay better salaries because they were not committed to the heavy production costs concomitant with a frequently changed multiple bill. Despite these improvements, the stigma on the profession persisted, and as late as 1900 it was still necessary for Irving to write an article vigorously refuting the view that the actor is 'so corrupted by the inherent immorality of his calling, and the vanity fostered in him by excessive adulation, that he is unfitted to hold social intercourse with respectable or intellectual people'.[34]

Irving was one of many leaders of the profession who by their own example, and the prestige built for themselves and their companies, helped to raise its stature in the public esteem. One group of allies for the actors appeared in a most surprising place, the Church, which

> had been intermittantly sniping at mummers throughout the mid-nineteenth century; but in the 'seventies certain members of the clergy, imbued with reverence for the name of Shakespeare, launched a campaign to make the stage an artistic and moral force in the community.[35]

The drive appears to have been started by Bishop Fraser of Manchester, who in 1874 demanded the improvement of theatrical productions, and followed up this call in 1877 by undertaking a church mission to the acting profession, urging actors and actresses to purify the stage. A Dramatic Reform Association was formed later that year, including a number of churchmen in its ranks, and many younger, progressive clergymen began to seek acceptance of the stage as a legitimate and useful adjunct to civil life. Chief among these was the Rev. Stewart Headlam, a Christian Socialist, the founder of the Guild of St. Matthew and later a prominent Fabian. A lecture by Headlam, in which he encouraged attendance at theatres, was published in the *Era*, 18 November 1877, and drew the following letter from the Bishop of London:

> Not for the first time it has caused me to ask pardon of our great Master if I erred, as I fear I did, in admitting you to the Ministry ... I do pray earnestly that you may not have to meet before the Judgment seat those whom your encouragement first led to places where they lost the blush of shame and took the first downward step towards vice and misery.[36]

Headlam was recalcitrant, and lost his post, but undeterred he formed the Church and Stage Guild in 1879 to bring clergymen and actors together. Even by 1877, the Bishop's attitude was beginning to become old-fashioned in face of the toleration brought about by the growing recognition that the theatre had the potential to be an effective force for moral good.

A debate over the respectability of the acting profession and the degree to which it was socially desirable or acceptable went on throughout the 'eighties and into the 'nineties. In 1879 Henry James noted that

> interest in histrionic matters almost reaches the proportions of a mania. It pervades society ... members of the dramatic profession are "received" without restriction. They appear in society, and the people of society appear on the stage; it is as if the great gate which formerly divided the theatre from the world had been lifted off its hinges.[37]

The actors made gradual but inexorable gains, and the gate was irrevocably removed in 1895 when the Queen knighted Henry Irving, an action that, in the words of a contemporary, 'formally recognized the right of the actor to rank socially with other devotees of the liberal arts'.[38] The actor had come a long way from the day when the *Times* had refused to publish a letter from Macready as it could not be expected to notice communications from an actor, and 'Stanley Jones' protested that the Press now gave actors far too much attention: 'it is as if we meant to make up to the actor by over-loading him with favours for the contempt with which his calling has been looked upon in the past'.[39] An indication of the new attitude towards the profession came a few years later when Clement Scott, commenting on stage morality in a *Great Thoughts* interview, 1 January 1898, voiced the out-dated opinion that

> it is nearly impossible for a woman to remain pure who adopts the stage as a profession. Everything is against her ... a woman who endeavours to keep her purity is almost of necessity foredoomed to failure in her career ... her prospects frequently depend on the nature and extent of her compliance ... it is unwise in the last degree to expose a young girl to the inevitable consequences of a theatrical life.[40]

This indiscretion roused the leading West-End managers to protest fiercely, and appears to have precipitated Scott's departure from the *Daily Telegraph*.

It is somewhat ironic that this triumph of the actor should coincide with a shift from an actor's to an author's theatre. The introduction of royalties, successive copyright bills and the publication of plays had made playwriting a lucrative profession for the successful. With increasing respect came increasing influence inside the theatre. St. John Ervine credits Pinero with raising

> the English theatre out of the gutter. The actor was deposed from the chief seat of authority, and the dramatist took his place, and in a comparatively short time, playgoers, who in a previous generation would have said that they were going to see Irving in his new play, were going to see the new Pinero, the new Henry Arthur Jones, the new Shaw, the new Barrie and the new Galsworthy.[41]

This shift had begun in the 'eighties and was well under way by the mid-'nineties. Although Pinero may have been a leader in the author's rebellion against the actor's domination of the theatre, being an actor he did not see himself in that light. Shaw, on the other hand, recognized the conflict and his role, and attacked relentlessly. Irving was his chief target, and as Irving had no time for Shavian ideas on drama, the battle lines were clearly drawn between the arch-romanticist and the arch-rationalist. In the first decade of the twentieth century, Shaw established himself in full control of productions of his own plays, much as Robertson had done in the 'sixties and W.S. Gilbert in the allied world of comic opera, but again an irony is apparent because by proving the effectiveness of off-stage control, such dramatists facilitated the emergence of the all-powerful producer-director. The necessity of such control had arisen with the arrival of realistic drama, and dates back to the ensemble playing pioneered by the Duke of Saxe-Meiningen, himself the first 'producer' in the modern sense. Formerly, when a play revolved around its star performers, no such person was necessary; stage business was relatively routine, and like rehearsals (at which the stars were rarely in attendance) came under the stage-manager, a mere minion. Subordinate actors came and went on cue, and kept themselves subordinate. A production served the stars, whose personality gave whatever artistic direction there might be. The advent of realism, with its emphasis on natural acting and speech and on ensemble playing spelled death to the old hieratic system. Other factors which contributed to the need for overall artistic authority were the control of lighting, and hence atmospheric and scenic effect, and the growing receptivity of the audience, who, cut off in a physical sense from the action by the box stage, could be made more involved by appeals to their sense of imaginative identification. Such manipulations of performers, visual effects and audiences needed subtle integration by one person, ideally with an artistic conscience, who had an overall conception of what he wanted to achieve and the authority to get it. We can go back to the Robertson era to see the beginnings of this development in England, although, as George Rowell points out, 'most of the individual features of Robertson's stage had been introduced by Vestris and Mathews twenty years earlier ... Robertson's particular achievement was to apply the skill and resource widely employed in the staging of spectacular drama to the miniature canvas of drawing-room drama'.[42] Once given the authority by the Bancrofts to control the production, Robertson established the effectiveness of having a non-acting director, and he facilitated the ascendance of the author from the role of lackey to the actor and provider of a vehicle for spectacle, to a position equal to or higher than that of the actor-manager himself. Robertson required the actor to abandon the declamatory style and adopt a more subtle, natural mode that blended with the total presentation, and this shift of emphasis away from the actor to the total production led, via the 'author's theatre' phase, to the modern dominance of the director; in the period under discussion it culminated in the imaginative, cohesive productions of Granville Barker, and reached its *ne plus ultra* in the concepts of Gordon Craig.

Robertson's plays, which now seem sentimental and creaky in design, stand out, in A.E. Wilson's phrase, 'as oases in a wilderness of trash'. As Michael Booth and others have pointed out,[43] this mode did not appear Athena-like from the head of Robertson as some historians and critics suggest, but was part of a general development that was associated with the Victorian predilection for domestic and commercial themes that contained a built-in tendency towards realism. There grew up a new 'intensive art' or 'eavesdropping' mode of realistic, intimate comedy, and although this itself became convention-bound in the 'seventies, and hardly realistic in its far from colloquial dialogue, it did proximate on stage the style of the realistic novel, and helped to direct the drama back towards the literary fold. In 1882, Matthew Arnold discovered the long-awaited fusion of drama and literature in Jones's *The Silver King:* 'the diction and sentiments are natural, they have sobriety and propriety, they are literature. It is an excellent and hopeful sign to find playwrights capable of writing in this style, actors capable of rendering it, a public capable of enjoying it'.[44] The following year the *Saturday Review* welcomed 'a very remarkable improvement in the condition of the English drama': there were 'more good plays', mounting and acting were better, and, the writer announced proudly, 'the British drama is no longer written by Frenchmen'.[45] It had entered the era of Grundy, Jones and Pinero. This recovery still did not satisfy those who aimed at not only a native but also an intellectual drama. Archer, for example, complained that the London theatres still failed to cater for 'the intellectual man', and to illustrate his point, compared the year's offerings in London for 1888 with one Berlin theatre. London saw four plays by Shakespeare, and of the forty others listed only one or two, in his opinion, possessed any literary or artistic merit: the Berlin Schauspielhaus also offered four by Shakespeare, plus two by Lessing, five by Schiller, and one each by Goethe, Kleist and Calderón. Archer goes on to use this comparison and the dearth of English classics--the lesser known plays of Shakespeare and those of his contemporaries--as arguments for a national endowed theatre where such drama could be performed together with modern plays that would not have to be debased by dramatists 'sacrificing artistic considerations to the necessity of conciliating the masses'.[46] Archer may have been over-pessimistic, for Allardyce Nicoll cites ten native plays between 1887 and 1891 that indicated a 'turn of the tide' towards a more vital, serious drama, and the *Saturday Review* in 1888 had boldly announced the 'Renaissance of the Drama' foreseen by H.A. Jones in 1883. This was before 1889, when, according to St. John Ervine,

> Pinero challenged the conventional conception of the theatre with the production of *The Profligate*. It had hitherto been regarded as a place of easy and shallow amusement. The idea that any person could be entertained by a serious theme had not penetrated the mind of the average playgoer who, if he thought about the matter at all, invariably asserted that serious subjects were not suitable for plays, but should be reserved for the pulpit, the press and the study, and, even there, should be discussed with the greatest reticence.[47]

Even Pinero had to bow to the demand for 'wholesome' drama,[48] and re-wrote the end of *The Profligate* to provide a happy conclusion, despite the fact that such a resolution contradicted life's experiences. The popular demand was that the playgoer's digestion must be undisturbed, and his egotistic dreams satisfied; unreflecting optimism must prevail, and any attempts at presenting psychological truth, disturbing complacency, or examining vital social issues were condemned.

Such condemnation greeted the first production of Ibsen's *A Doll's House* in 1889 and *Ghosts* two years later. Paradoxically, the hostility to Ibsen was expressed by theatre critics who by that time were playing, as a group, an important role in stimulating interest in the drama and in giving it encouragement to move with the times. Perhaps contumely was better than the 'judicious silence' on the theatre promised readers of the *World* in 1874, who were assured that they 'need be under no apprehension of [the editors] making a theatrical article a necessary portion of [their] weekly contents'.[49] In the 'eighties the tendency of the newspapers and journals to ignore the theatre, or at most treat it with casual contempt, was reversed, and as early as 1883 H.A. Jones was able to observe an increased amount of space being allocated to the theatre in the press, and to welcome the fact that 'the higher literary criticism has again begun to occupy itself with the drama'[50]--a reference mainly to Arnold, but also to Archer and to Clement Scott, the self-styled 'first modern critic', who, whatever his faults, treated the drama as a serious art and regarded his duties as critic as a precious charge. In the 'nineties critics split into two main groups: the Ancients, who represented conservative, middle-class taste and morality, and the Moderns, who upheld the virtues, both dramatic and moral, of Ibsen, Zola and the dramatists of the naturalist school.[51] Scott headed the group of Ancients, who included J.F. Nisbet, Alfred Watson, Frederick Wedmore and Edward Morton, while Archer, hitherto the lone exponent of 'the new criticism', was joined by such allies as A.B. Walkley, J.H. McCarthy, E.F. Spence, J.T. Grein and G.B. Shaw. The diverging views of these two groups and the vigour with which they expressed themselves attracted an attention that helped to foster interest in the drama and to stimulate a healthy critical attitude towards plays and the art of acting. That hitherto ephemeral dramatic criticism was now taken seriously is indicated by the fact that publishers thought it worthwhile to put out collected editions of critics' columns--nobably those of Archer, Grein, Shaw and Walkley.

By the end of 1891, Archer was enthusing that 'the theatrical world of today is far more truly alive than it was ten, or even five years ago. We are talking, and perhaps even thinking, about the drama with unexampled fervour and pertinacity'. He believed that the native growth of the Pinero-Jones era of the 'eighties had been succeeded by a 'new movement' from Norway and France, and announced:

> the 7th June, 1889, the date of the production of *A Doll's House* at the Novelty Theatre, was unquestionably the birthday of the new movement. But it was on the 13th. March, 1891, when Henrik Ibsen's Gengangere *[Ghosts]* was produced, under artistic conditions devised in Paris by André Antoine, that the two forces coalesced and made their united impact on our theatrical life.[52]

The free theatre movement which brought Ibsen to the English stage did not release a flood of dramatic talent as it had done in France and Germany, but after 1889 the British drama could never be the same. Jones claimed that before the arrival of Ibsen it had begun to reflect the main movements of national thought and character, and

> to deal with the great realities of English life. It was pressing on to be a real force in the spiritual and intellectual life of the nation. It began to attract the attention of Europe. But it became entangled with another movement, got caught in the skirts of the sexual-pessimistic blizzard sweeping over North Europe, was confounded with it, and was execrated and condemned without examination.[53]

But the sad truth was that Ibsen and the new European drama made the old formulas look puerile, and advocates of an intellectual theatre that was relevant and true to life became increasingly dissatisfied. Archer bewailed that in 1895 'a blight [had] fallen on our nascent or renascent drama', and the more intelligent public had been 'left out in the cold'.[54] Despite the efforts of the 'Moderns' to encourage the new drama, and of enterprising groups or individuals to provide it --for example, J.T. Grein and the Independent Theatre, Elizabeth Robins (with productions of Ibsen), and William Archer with the New Century Theatre--the London commercial theatres remained obstinately commercial. The eagerness of some voices to announce a dramatic renaissance in the 'nineties was perhaps the expression of a desire that the drama should not be excluded from the renaissance occurring in other fields--the arts, politics, religion, philosophy--where new ideas, new forms, and new experiences were heralding the oncoming birth of a new century. In this period there were indications of a new drama in the plays of Henry Arthur Jones, Arthur Wing Pinero, Oscar Wilde, R.C. Carton, Haddon Chambers, and a few others who, animated by a distinctly progressive spirit, attempted the serious representation of English social life on the stage, but most dramatists, managers and audiences seemed little touched by the ferment of criticism or by the appeals of those with higher aspirations for the drama.

Some figures for the period 1893 to 1897 drawn from Archer's 'Epilogue Statistical' to *The Theatrical World of 1897* are interesting:

Shakespeare:	97 weeks in 5 years; 20 plays (incl. Elizabethan Stage Society productions).	
Old Plays:	70 weeks (the oldest by Sheridan).	
Modern Plays:	(1) Dramas, Comedies and Serious Prose Plays in General:	740 weeks; 88 plays.
	(2) Poetical Plays:	61 weeks; 7 plays.
	(3) Melodramas:	319 weeks; 23 plays.
	(4) Farces:	657 weeks; 51 plays.
	(5) Burlesques:	33 weeks; 6 plays.
	(6) Musical Farces: (excl. pantomime and comic opera)	858 weeks; 19 plays.
American Plays		196 weeks; 27 plays.
French Plays:		534 weeks; 46 plays.
German Plays:		30 weeks; 8 plays.
Norwegian Plays:	)Ibsen	15 weeks; 8 plays.
	)Other	4 weeks; 1 play.

Obviously, only a small percentage of the offerings rate as serious drama, but a wedge had been formed, and, more importantly, as Holbrook Jackson observed, 'what can be credited to the period is the creation of an atmosphere in which a new drama might flourish at the appointed hour'.[55]

In fact, not 'a new drama' but 'the new drama', as it came to be called by both its proponents and opponents, was waiting in the wings. Put simply, this was the mode that attempted to place real life on stage. It advocated: the portrayal of realistic characters speaking everyday, natural language; realistic plots that developed not by means of artificial devices or highly contrived situations but by the natural behaviour and development of those characters in realistic social situations; and realistic settings that provided an authentic context for the action. Because the focus of its exponents tended to be on social problems, a characteristic of the new drama was a preoccupation with middle and lower-class characters or groups that resulted in it being condemned by its opponents for its obsession with the sordid, seemier side of life. This focus meant that much of the new drama also fitted into the category of 'problem play'; however, this term is too limiting to apply to the drama that was emerging in the latter part of the nineteenth century in reaction to degenerate romanticism, the artifices of the well-made play, and the exaggerations of melodrama. Given its social concerns and concomitant tendency to expose and criticise the established social order, the new drama obviously held a strong appeal for progressives of various hues, particularly those who supported the socialist movement. On the continent, the prevalent political and social unrest provided a far more stimulating and receptive environment for the new drama than the stable, almost complacent social order of England, where the forces of conservatism, together with solid theatrical traditions, provided infertile ground for new growths.

Mario Borsa, the Italian writer who takes an interestingly objective look at *The English Stage of Today* (1908), opens his book by declaring: 'For those who take a serious and absorbing interest in all that pertains to Art, one of the greatest drawbacks to life in London is the lack of good prose drama ... And yet London is overrun with theatres!' He notes a veritable 'histriomania' that extended to innumerable clubs, amateur performances and dramatic recitations, and 'some fifty illustrated theatrical periodicals' as well as theatre columns in the regular press. London critics, he found, blamed this contradiction on the system of actor-managers and the long run; the censorship; public taste; and the lack of state support or interest. Borsa himself places the blame squarely on the 'intellectual apathy' of the British public. A.M. Thompson, writing in the *Clarion* about the same time, confirms this view, but relates it to the economics of the theatre that made success dependent on attracting quality patrons:

> the test of a play's merit is therefore in its power to titillate the epicurean sluggishness of Park Lane and Belgravia. The actor, the author, the British drama itself, hang upon the patronage of Property ... Stalls and boxes come to the theatre, not to be worried but amused, not to digest thought but their dinners.[56]

Borsa complained that the English drama had no connection with the realities of English life, and in fact still offered Anglicized versions of the Scribe-Sardou well-made play formula. Instead of the 'wealth and complexity of London life', the stage presented 'the squabbles of provincial life, conventionalized members of the aristocracy, romantic melodrama, drawing room intrigues ... and a nauseous hash-up of misrepresented history and exaggerated sentimentality, which is as false to art as it is false to life and history'.[57] This falseness reflected the continuing dominant social desire for respectability that required conformity on stage as well as off to orthodox assumptions concerning the inevitability of the triumph of good over evil (the inheritance of melodrama), of social and moral justice (based on hierarchical principles palliated by liberal sentiments), of ultimate happiness for the upright, and, unless redeemed, of misery for the fallen. The Edwardian theatre also pandered to the materialistic tastes of its predominantly middle and upper-class audience not only by staging sumptuous productions and by presenting plays set in a world of opulence, but also by providing an equally sumptuous environment where opulence enveloped the theatregoer with grand, gilded foyers, ornate bars, smoking rooms, lounges and auditoriums, and plush seats and carpets, all creating a cosy, reassuring atmosphere of solid luxury, ideal for relaxation. The theatres had, quite literally, built themselves into a comfortable mode of drama, and were no place for the disturbing, sordid harshness of Ibsen or Zola, Gorki or Tolstoy, Sudermann or Hauptmann: imagine the destruction of the mill-owner's home in *The Weavers* taking place on the stage of His Majesty's--half the audience would reach for their horse-whips!

But at the very time Borsa was writing his book and deploring the absence of good prose drama in London, the long-awaited 'appointed hour' had struck, for one of the most important events in the history of British drama was taking place at the Royal Court theatre: the Vedrenne-Barker seasons which brought the new drama to the London commercial stage, and established Shaw as its leading dramatist. With the advent of a management motivated by both social commitment and artistic ideals, a new British drama emerged alongside and in spite of a theatre that existed to be exploited for the greatest possible profit.

As Samuel Hynes points out in his study of the Edwardian period,

> in the middle of the nineteenth century the established code of values and behaviour did not seem oppressive or arbitrary to most Englishmen, and many artists and thinkers of stature were able to accommodate themselves to it, but by the end of the century code and current thought had parted, and the relation between the established order and the intelligentsia was one of antagonism and suspicion.[58]

Later, Hynes quotes from Edward Carpenter's *My Days and Dreams*, which recalls the last two decades of the nineteenth century as

> a fascinating and enthusiastic period--preparatory, as we now see, to even greater developments in the twentieth century. The Socialist and Anarchist propaganda, the Feminist and Suffragist upheaval, the huge Trade Union growth, the Theosophic movement, the new currents in the Theatrical, Musical and Artistic world, the torrent even of change in the Religious world--all constituted so many streams and headwaters converging, as it were, to a great river.[59]

The new drama, then, flowed out of a wider surge for change

that encompassed movements as disparate as *fin de siécle* decadence and the emergence of the Labour Party as a political force. Dissatisfactions were exacerbated by the frustrations brought about by the Boer War, and the failure of the politicians and army to bring it to a speedy conclusion. The result was an undermining of public confidence in conventional attitudes, established values and orthodox beliefs. R.C.K. Ensor notes the relative absence of any 'solid core of religious belief' in the period 1903-10 compared with the 1870s, and remarks that now 'creed sat lightly on the great majority in the middle and upper classes'.[60] It is not surprising, then, that not even the censor could keep the questioning of traditional moral and social assumptions off the stage. The impulse towards such a new drama, free from commercial restrictions as much as from conventional taboos, was rooted in the desire of serious authors and their supporters to dramatise the problems of their time in a form that presented character and action as true as possible to life, not artificially glossed in stock melodramatic or comic situations. Because of the emphasis on realism during the period, and to provide the background for much of what follows, it is necessary to review the development of Realism as a movement, to recognize its aims and limitations, and to examine its role in shaping modern drama in England.

INTRODUCTION - (B) REALISM AND COUNTER-REALISM

> 'Une piéce est une tranche de la vie mise sur la scéne avec art'.
>
> Jean Jullien

> 'I hate vulgar realism in literature. The man who could call a spade a spade should be compelled to use one. It is the only thing he is fit for'.
>
> Oscar Wilde

The most significant movement in the European drama of the nineteenth century was the development of Realism. Realistic elements had been present in the drama in varying degrees since its origin, but only in the latter part of the century did the term indicate a distinct mode of theatre. Realism as a literary mode developed in parallel with the expansion of science and the scientific method of research, and is closely allied to the Positivist philosophy of Auguste Comte, who 'believed in observable facts and in tentative generalizations formed from these observations'.[61] Fundamentally, Realism is the mimetic representation of life in art. It came as an inevitable reaction against the excesses of Romanticism, which, although not without realistic elements in such aspects as the close observation of nature and the Wordsworthian desire to focus on the common man and on the common incidents of everyday life, rested on a transcendental metaphysic and prophetic mode of expression that invited rejection by minds seeking objective explanations for, and a scientific understanding of human behaviour and the human condition. Just as 'the necessary crisis of Romanticism' (Zola's phrase) was a rebellion against the limitations and conventionalities of Classicism, which confined man and his spirit, so Realism was a revolt against the tendency of Romanticism to lose touch with everyday reality in its release of the imagination and pursuit of the ideal. Through scientific observation and documentation, the realist aimed to slough off exotic unrealities and abstract metaphysics, and to present an objective 'slice of life'. George H. Becker discerns 'three major points of emphasis' in the movement: realism in choice of subject matter, with a particular 'emphasis on the lowest common denominator of human experience'; innovations in techniques, particularly the elimination of the writer's bias in statement or through the manipulation of artificialities of plot and character; and a philosophical basis of determinism which 'was a direct reflection in literature of the prevalent mechanistic science of the age'.[62]

The last of these suggests the extension of Realism known as Naturalism. Although the two terms tend to be interchangeable, particularly in the writings of commentators contemporary with the movement, they should be kept distinct. Stromberg's general division by historical phases--Realism 1848 to 1871, Naturalism 1871 to 1890--is useful, but vulnerable.[63] It is useful in that Naturalism certainly grew out of, or attached itself to Realism, but vulnerable in its arbitrary choice of dates, despite Stromberg's proviso that the modes overlap, because where Naturalism becomes outdated, Realism has proved a persistent mode. 'In essence and origin', declares Becker, 'naturalism is no more than an emphatic and explicit philosophical position taken by some realists'.[64] The chief exponent of Naturalism was Émile Zola, who applied the label *'naturaliste'* to Taine because of Taine's principle that the intellectual world is as subject to laws as the natural, material world; it is therefore essential to find these laws if knowledge of the human spirit is to advance, and the only way of doing so is to follow the scientific method. *'Naturalisme'* was a term already in use in mid-century art criticism, but Zola enlarged it to embrace the scientific method as well as fidelity to reality. As Lawson A. Carter points out, Zola may have utilized the theory as a defence against indecency in his Rougon-Macquart Series (1871-1892), but the theory did inspire the practice.[65] Zola preferred the term 'Naturalism' to 'Realism' because he considered that the latter, already well-used, tended to restrict literary and artistic horizons whereas the former enlarged them. In his essay 'The Experimental Novel' (1880), Zola pleaded for Naturalism, and supported the theories he had been expressing for years by urging the writer to follow the scientific method recommended in Claude Bernard's *Introduction to the Study of Experimental Medicine* (1865) and be both observer and experimenter:

> the observer in him [the novelist] presents data as he has observed them, determines the point of departure, establishes the solid ground in which his characters will stand and his phenomena take place. Then the experimenter appears and institutes the experiment, that is, sets the character of a particular story in motion, in order to show that the series of events therein will be those demanded by the determinism of the phenomena under study.[66]

Thus the naturalist followed a logical extension of the realist method, for if transcendental or supernatural causes are eliminated, all abstractions rejected or ignored, only measureable observables studied, and explanations sought in the twin factors of heredity and environment, then man inevitably emerges as a puppet at the mercy of powers over which he has no control, and an a-moral, pessimistic and materialistic determinism results.

Although Realism characterized the mid-century novels of Balzac, Stendhal, Flaubert and others, it was slow to enter the drama except in the technical advances achieved, mainly in the cause of historical realism, by George, Duke of Saxe-Meiningen, who in 1874 formed a company of players whom he trained in a new ensemble style of acting which eliminated the stars and introduced new concepts of harmonious, integrated production. He adopted the principle of a plastic stage that offered separate acting areas on different levels to serve the actors' movements, and a setting that provided an aesthetic and thematic complement to the action. His influence spread rapidly throughout Europe, notably in his emphasis on realistic acting, his manner of handling stage crowds in which each performer was given a separate identity, his attention to detail, and his substitution of interpretation for stylization. The Duke's practice helped prepare the way for the application of the theories of Zola, who in 1880 was 'waiting for dramatists to place on the stage men of flesh and bone who are taken from reality and analyzed scientifically without lying'.[67] Zola's aims for the drama were an extension of his theories on the novel, and came at a time when the extravagances of Romantic drama had all but disappeared, and in their place stood entrenched the mechanical banalities of the *'pièce bien faite'* --or 'well-made play'--the stage carpentry of Scribe, Sardou and Augier, with its ingenuities of plot, 'flat' upper middle-class characters, bourgeois morality and sentiment, unvarying themes of financial and amatory intrigue, and conventional patterned denoument which resolved all complexities happily. The well-made play succeeded according to the ingenuity of its plot construction; characterization and emotion, if present at all, were supplementary benefits. As a result, writers of sensibility and human understanding were deterred from writing for the stage either because they lacked the necessary degree of devious ingenuity or because they rejected the underlying assumption that what is dramatic is not character in action, but action, or events, in contrived combinations. Despite its artificialities, the well-made play facilitated the advent of Realism because its reflection of bourgeois manners, morals, language and physical setting did represent aspects of real life, and the impingement of circumstance on the fortunes of individuals suggested determinism. What the genre lacked was 'the high morality of truth and the terrible lesson of sincere enquiry'[68] that Zola insisted upon, and its emphasis was a contradiction of his desire that drama should 'analyze the double influence of characters on action and action on character'.[69]

But lacking the expansive scope for detail offered by the form of the novel, how could drama compress and select the essentials of real life, and present them in an entertaining theatrical manner, without distortion? The antithetical demands of Realism and art, the one demanding a replica of life in all its unstructured complexity, the other selection and form, proved a greater problem to the dramatist than to the novelist, and perhaps only Chekhov and Hauptmann ever succeeded in reconciling them satisfactorily. On stage it was Naturalism that emerged rather than Realism, in the dramatized versions of Zola's novels, the social documents of Brieux, the psychological studies of Strindberg, and the grim depictions of squalid peasant or working class life in Tolstoy and Gorki. Head and shoulders above other dramatists stood Ibsen. He was hailed as the master of naturalistic drama, and his combination of realistic setting, characters, speech and action with a devastating depiction of the impingement of heredity and environment on the individual, identifies him as such; but Ibsen went beyond Naturalism because of the metaphysical dimension he achieved through the poetic quality of his work, particularly his use of symbols. His later plays anticipated the shift to symbolism, but the social plays of his middle period, especially *Ghosts*, epitomised the realistic/naturalistic drama, and the play became the flagship of the champions of the new drama. It was chosen to inaugurate both the Berlin *Freie Bühne* (Free Stage) in 1889, and London's Independent Theatre in 1891, which was modelled on Antoine's *Théâtre Libre* in Paris that had produced *Ghosts* in 1890. The violent partisanship that *Ghosts* inspired wherever it was performed is a measure of the struggle the new drama had to endure to establish a beachhead on the European stage.

Nowhere was hostility so marked as in England. English readers had long accepted realism in the novel: Dickens, Thackeray, George Eliot and later Moore and Gissing, were all realists, but their realism was romantically coloured, as in Dickens, or qualified by authorial intrusion, as in George Eliot, and was presented within existing traditions rather than brandished in defiance of tradition. Realistic elements entered the drama in a similar way, first in the details of production of historic and romantic drama, especially Shakespeare, and second, as noted above, in intimate, genteel comedy and in melodrama. The former was authenticity rather than realism, part of the desire to elevate the stage by making it more instructive, but became an end in itself as successive managers sought to outdo each other in spectacular magnificence. The latter was limited to a superficial realism of style and properties, and failed to express any fundamental truths of human life in social or psychological terms. 'All the characters of the plays', wrote Henry Baker, 'lived in the best of all possible worlds in which the troubles of early years were for the happiness of later, tears were always dried up by the sunshine of smiles, and the curtain fell upon love and kisses'.[70] However, the 'teacup-and-saucer-trouser-pocket-school', in bringing a refinement of acting to the stage, and in establishing the box-set, confirmed two important steps towards a more realistic English drama. The era of melodrama capitalized on the vogue for spectacular realistic effects, so that by the 'eighties English audiences had received a partial preparation for a drama that was realistic in content and characterization as well as in superficialities. But the taboos against serious topics, and their enforcement by the censor, meant that although a dramatist might 'see life whole', he could not depict it so until the lumber of prejudice, tradition, convention and sentiment had been cleared away. Neither audiences nor most critics considered 'real life' to have any place on the stage, where the portrayal of the true effects of social or personal evils without idealisation offended moral sensitivities. As Michael Baker observes, it was paradoxical that the stage, which as a profession received moral condemnation, 'enshrined for its audiences a concept of unspoilt purity which contrasted forcibly with the bewildering changes taking place in the real world of industrial expansion and shifting values'.[71] Such attitudes did little to encourage the native playwright who wished to deal with serious issues in a serious manner, but they do account for the strong hostility to 'Zolaism' in general and to *A Doll's House* and *Ghosts* in particular.

Realism was itself an almost obscene word, as Henry Vizetelly discovered when he ran afoul of the National Vigilance Association for publishing Zola's *The Soil: A Realistic Novel*, and was successfully prosecuted in 1888. Although such actions as this were in fact rearguard skirmishes against an inevitable development, much campaigning was necessary before Realism became an accepted mode.

The impetus for a new realistic drama in England came

first from the critics, notably Matthew Arnold, who called for a literary drama, and William Archer, who conducted a twenty-year campaign on behalf of the new drama and championed Ibsen both in his criticism and through his translations. The first dramatists to challenge convention and to begin the transition of Victorian to modern drama were Sydney Grundy, H.A. Jones and A.W. Pinero. After succeeding with light comedies and adaptations of French plays in the 'seventies, Grundy attempted serious themes in such plays as *The Silver Shield* (1885) and *The Late Mr. Castello* (1895), but as Archer complained, 'technically he remained an apprentice of Scribe whereas he ought to have assimilated the lessons of the master and transmuted them into a mastery of his own'.[72] Grundy had the gift of effective, authentic dialogue, and despite his limitations did 'ardently desire to bring the drama into touch with real life', for which Archer was prepared to give him 'an honourable place' in the development of modern drama. A more important role in this development was filled by Jones, whose ambition was to reform the English stage and to reunify literature and the drama. His essential Victorianism lies both in his aim to reform and in the dedicated, missionary manner in which he set about it: writing 'tracts' in essays and prefaces; preaching and exhorting in lectures; utilizing the methods of commerce he learned as a commercial traveller to sell his ideas; bringing a puritanical zeal to his onslaught against English puritanism; and writing plays designed to convert the public through what was familiar to it. However, Jones was no innovator, and tended to be far more progressive in his propaganda than in his plays, for which he adopted the dramatic forms at his disposal--especially the melodrama in both his plot structure and devices and in his high moral stance that idealized conventional virtues. His plays express a compassion for humanity, present complexity of character, emotion and motivation, and above all, without resorting to overt didacticism, which he deplored, criticise the hypocrisies of English middle-class life. Despite obvious affinities with Realism, both in outlook and execution, Jones opposed the movement. He argued that Realism--that is, the naturalistic end of the spectrum--was 'cramping and deadening' in execution, 'parochial' in its aims, and lacking in the essence of great art: 'beauty, mystery, passion, imagination'. He saw its truth as limited, confined to the materialistic side of life. He recognized that modern realistic criticism had played an important role in the assault on 'the great pasteboard strongholds of bunkum and theatricality', but felt it had gone too far in trying 'to seduce us from our smug suburban villas into all sorts of gruesome kitchen-middens'--when what happened there, in Jones's view, did not matter.[73] His own work focused on the occupants of those 'smug suburban villas', and such typical plays as *Saints and Sinners* (1884), *The Middleman* (1889), *Wealth* (1889), and *The Triumph of the Philistines*

(1895), although they do represent attempts to base drama on character in action as distinct from the prevailing focus on action with characters, all suffer from the melodramatic and sentimental tendencies that characterized his first successful serious play, *The Silver King* (1882), and which he never succeeded in overcoming. Amplifying Archer's remark that Jones never could 'penetrate the deep places of the soul', Marjorie Northend observes that his realism was limited, his problems treated superficially, his technique clumsy: 'he had mastered all the ingredients of good drama, but he had never learnt to combine them in an artistic whole, and the effect was to curdle rather than to mix'.[74] Shaw was to take over many of the ideas on the drama preached by Jones, and adopted his technique--as Martin Meisel has amply demonstrated--of utilizing current dramatic forms; even Shaw's enthusiasm for publishing plays had been anticipated by Jones. The essential difference between them is not only that Shaw had the genius Jones lacked, but that the one was an iconoclast, a destroyer of ideals and institutions, while the other was a reformer, an upholder of traditional values whose betrayal he deplored.

Jones's name is invariably coupled with that of Pinero when the 'renaissance' of the English drama is discussed, and quite rightly in that they shared the honours in that period of vital transition which paved the way for the acceptance of the new drama; yet they had different aims, approaches and techniques. Both aspired to a more literary drama, one that was a criticism of life, and both saw society as seriously flawed, but Jones, whose popular and sentimental pieces financed the short runs of his satirical plays, attacked society more directly and boldly than Pinero, a much more cautious man who played safe by ensuring that his unconventional, 'immoral' themes and plots had conventional 'moral' resolutions, such as the suicide of the fallen woman in *The Second Mrs. Tanquery* (1893), and the last minute conversion of the sinner in *The Notorious Mrs. Ebbsmith* (1895). If Jones's roots lay primarily in the melodrama, then Pinero's were in the well-made play. Despite a tendency to write turgid speeches, he had the knack of creating, even in early farces like *The Magistrate* (1885) and *Dandy Dick* (1887), memorable characters, 'so human, so true, so intimately felt', as Borsa put it, and this enabled him to infuse the well-made play formula with a convincing sense of reality when he tackled more serious subjects. The turning point in Pinero's career as a dramatist came in 1889 with *The Profligate*. 'In spirit, if not in technique, it did unmistakably mark a new departure', wrote Archer: 'it was an expression of a strong, and even defiant, artistic will. It was the play Mr. Pinero wanted to write, not the play which he thought the public wanted to see'.[75] Each year thereafter, as Max Beerbohm quipped, Pinero produced 'his latest assortment of Spring Problemings (Scandinavian Gents' own materials made up. West End style and fit guaranteed)'.[76] Where Jones was intent on a theme or thesis, the sin rather than the sinner, as such titles as *The Hypocrites* (1904), *The Masqueraders* (1894) and *The Liars* (1897) suggest, Pinero focused on the development of character within a carefully observed social environment; again, the titles, which define by role or name, are indicative-- *The Squire* (1881), *The Schoolmistress* (1886), *Trelawney of the Wells* (1898) and *The Gay Lord Quex* (1899). As Nicoll remarks, Pinero brought 'conviction, deeper thought and fine sympathy' to his 'problem' plays in which the realism lay in the convincing portrayal of character and social situation rather than in the construction of plot, which, unfortunately, tended to be artificial and romantic and thereby vitiated the impact of his work. Archer, who invariably found Jones inadequate, discovered in Pinero his ideal dramatist: 'in so far as any man can be called the regenerator of the English drama', he declared, 'that man is Arthur Pinero'.[77] Others may have surpassed him later, Archer admitted, but Pinero 'had smoothed the way and set the pace for these other men, some of whom have shown him scant gratitude. He was the brilliant and even daring pioneer of a great movement'. Archer, no doubt, had Shaw in mind when he wrote that, for Shaw as critic poured scorn on inadequate 'Pinerotics', with their graft of spurious realism onto stock society comedy, and never acknowledged that his own success as dramatist might have been impossible had not Pinero helped to gain acceptance for the representation of serious issues on stage.

Shaw's few years of regular dramatic criticism were part of an unremitting crusade to bring the drama into relationship with real life. On the London stage of the mid-nineties he found little to commend; what realism there was appeared to him to be superficial or, worse, spurious. When he turned to write plays himself, his first three 'were what people called realistic', he declared: 'they were dramatic pictures of middle-class society from the point of view of a socialist who regards that society as thoroughly rotten economically and morally ... their purpose was to make people thoroughly uncomfortable whilst entertaining them artistically'.[78] Here we have none of the objectivity of Realism, none of the complex of factors of Naturalism, but an uncompromising admission of didacticism by an advocate of Realism who as practitioner was to redefine it for himself in terms of intellectual truth that persuades by its own reason, or commonsense. Shaw's heroes, or heroines, are realistic in his terms because they are under no romantic illusions concerning life, and consequently behave with a logic devastating to their opponents. In his Preface to *Misalliance* he describes the romantic imagination as 'the power to imagine things as they are not', and the realistic imagination as 'a means of foreseeing and being prepared for realities as yet unexperienced, and of testing the feasibility of serious Utopias'.[79] Here we have the experimental aspect of Zola's method echoed, but, as Nicoll remarks, Shaw was 'too big for realism', because all aspects of his drama were subservient to the didactic purpose (except when his sense of fun appears to run away with him), and his plays embrace a wide range of dramatic modes. If realistic methods will endorse the play's statement, then let a realistic method be employed--to create audience identification and recognition in the domestic situation of *Candida* (1895), for example; if fantasy will complement a world of inverted values, then let it be the Hell of *Man and Superman* (1903); if history can provide object lessons in rationality, then let it be re-written, as in *Caesar and Cleopatra* (1899)--with Britannicus as a Victorian bourgeois for good measure; if symbolism can teach, then let a dramatic metaphor speak, as in *Heartbreak House* (1919), for the ship of state.

Quite obviously, it is not Shaw to whom we look for the flowering of English social realism, but to a group of dramatists who emerged at the time of the Royal Court ventures of the Vedrenne-Barker management, 1905-07: notably to Granville Barker himself, St. John Hankin, and most important of all, John Galsworthy. Of the three, Barker's plays are closest to the realist ideal of comprehensive scope combined with minute, accurate observation, but inevitably, as drama, they lack the force of more traditionally structured plays. *The Voysey Inheritance* (1905), *Waste* (1907) and *The Madras House* (1910), despite their sharp characterization, emotional texture and social relevance, tend to be diffuse, and demonstrate the limitations of Realism even at its best. Galsworthy's narrower focus, structured plotting and greater economy are more successful in creating a compelling sense of actual life under unbiased judicious observation. In *The Silver Box* (1906), *Strife* (1909) and *Justice* (1910) he communicates a sense of compassion and an indictment of social injustice without resort to overt Shavian didacticism; maintains the dramatic interest without descending into melodrama, the downfall of Jones; and constructs logical actions free from the artificialities that weakened Pinero. But the plays have a weakness that no amount of craftsmanship can conceal, for lacking in humour, in the broadest sense, they lack life. Some vital elusive spark is missing. Humour does characterize the plays of St. John Hankin, but his social conscience was not as acute as Galsworthy's. Like Jones, he chose to work within established forms, into which he introduced a satiric edge. His *Return of the Prodigal* (1905), *The Cassilis Engagement* (1907) and *The Last of the De Mullins* (1908) are among the best realistic comedies of the era. The master of the satiric mode was Somerset Maugham, who chose to restrict his dramatic talents to the portrayal of upper middle-class life within a framework unashamedly built on well-made play foundations. A wide range of competent dramatists emerged, or consolidated their positions, at the beginning of the twentieth century, all in one degree or another realistic: J.M. Barrie, Alfred Sutro, Elizabeth Baker,

Arnold Bennett, Harold Brighouse, Hall Caine, Haddon Chambers, H.H. Davies, St. John Ervine, Stanley Houghton, Charles McEvoy, and D.H. Lawrence (who had to wait a long time for recognition in this field). Jones and Pinero continued to write, the former weakening, but the latter producing some of his best work, notably *Iris* (1901) and *Mid-Channel* (1909). Despite continued obstruction by the censor, and thanks to the groundwork carried out in the 'nineties, the barriers against the discussion of serious and controversial topics on stage were collapsing; no longer could the Examiner of Plays claim that by banning such things, or the grimmer aspects of life, he was merely protecting audiences from that which would offend their sensibilities and which they did not wish to see. The new drama required a new audience whose members would come to the theatre not merely as passive spectators to be spoon-fed with entertainment but as participants in a creative process prepared to think about and interpret what they saw on stage--Zola's experiment. Such an intellectual audience was to be developed during the 1890s and 1900s thanks to the popularity of Jones and Pinero, the determined efforts of the champions of Ibsen and of groups like the Independent Theatre and the Stage Society, such ventures as Beerbohm Tree's After Noon matinées and Charles Frohman's Repertory at the Duke of York's, and, above all, the Vedrenne-Barker seasons at the Royal Court.

The burgeoning realistic English drama, with its tendency to social propaganda on squalid themes, sat uneasily on the elegant shoulders of evening-dress Edwardian audiences bent on after-dinner amusement--the 'carriages-at-eleven' theatregoers, so charmingly and nostalgically celebrated by W. Macqueen-Pope, who continued to patronize light comedy, melodrama, spectacle and, most popular of all, musical comedy. Nor did it satisfy those seeking a poetic, transcendental reality, like Arthur Symons, who aspired to '*la verité vrai*', the very essence of truth that was a combination of the truth of appearance to the senses, of the visible world to the eyes that see it (Impressionism), with the truth of spiritual things to the spiritual vision (Symbolism). Since its inception, Realism has been criticized for its inability to penetrate the façade of externals to the inner, or higher truths. In its tendency to see men wholly determined by concrete realities, it ignored, or at best downgraded, those realities of the spirit that defy reason and measurement. In France the desire to reach these realities found expression in the *Symboliste* movement in poetry, and had its counterpart in the drama in the *Théâtre d'Art*, founded by Paul Fort, and in Lugné-Poe's *Théâtre de l'Oeuvre*, where poetic drama flourished in symbolic, suggestive settings. The leading dramatist of this aesthetic mode was the Belgian, Maurice Maeterlinck, who fused reality with a numinous sense of mystery and symbolic forces, but he found few emulators in England, where for two centuries poetic drama had meant either imitations of the Elizabethans or closet drama. Verse dramatists held in contempt the contemporary theatre and its forms, for which poetry was rendered obsolete by the capacity of scenery to create those effects formerly attained through language. Nineteenth-century poets were too sensitive to risk the abuse of unruly audiences, too introspective to be at ease in the dramatic form, too much victims of 'the curse of The Works' (Findlater's phrase) of Shakespeare to discover a contemporary dramatic idiom, too ignorant of the theatre, and too unwilling to learn a difficult craft. Both Browning and Tennyson were persuaded to write for the stage, but lacking in stage experience and out of their natural mode of expression, both failed, despite the support of Macready and Irving respectively. Aside from the unique contribution of Oscar Wilde, poets and aesthetes at the end of the century virtually ignored the theatre, but the revival of poetic drama in Ireland, where Yeats, Synge, Lady Gregory, Edward Martyn and others were inspired by the folk-heritage of their country, set an example to English poets, and helped stimulate an English counter-movement to Realism. Perhaps the success of Stephen Phillips also served as an inspiration, for although such plays as *Herod* (1900), *Ulysses* (1902) and *Paolo and Francesca* (1902) succeeded mainly because of the spectacular treatment of their exotic settings, they did contain both lyrical and poetic elements. Phillips had the distinct advantage of theatrical experience, having served six years in the acting company of his cousin, F.R. Benson, and therefore he had a better sense of stagecraft than his poetic predecessors. He achieved success as a poet before turning to the drama, but repeated the error of so many former would-be poet-dramatists of adopting Shakespeare as his model. Consequently, his idiom is unnatural and pretentious, and the special quality of poetic drama--that its language, through rhythms and images, communicates a sense of universal dimensions to the action--is entirely absent. Other poets who turned to the stage included Lascelles Abercrombie, Lawrence Binyon, Gordon Bottomley, John Davidson, John Drinkwater, Wilfred Gibson, Laurence Housman and John Masefield. Their work, some in verse and some in elevated prose, ranged from the historic fustian of Binyon to the archetypal primitivism of Bottomley; from the industrial present of Gibson to the rural past of Masefield; from the biblical subjects of Housman to the 'tragic farces' of Davidson. Only Masefield, and later Drinkwater, achieved any degree of success on the commercial stage, but most received attention from the growing number of amateur theatre groups throughout the country.

The poetic drama in England never came near to offering an alternative to Realism, and it looked as though Max Beerbohm had been correct in 1900 when he declared: 'regret it as you may, modern realism is the only direction in which our drama can really progress'.[80] Within twenty years of the vituperation that had greeted Ibsen's *Ghosts* on the London stage, Realism had become the accepted mode. Opposition to it continued, but from aesthetes rather than moralists or traditionalists. Notable among the opponents was Gordon Craig, who deplored Realism as 'caricature' where 'Ariel is destroyed and Caliban reigns'; he sought a 'noble artificiality' and a new, comprehensive 'art of the theatre'. His new art was to come not from the poets or artists outside the theatre, but from within. Craig found few supporters in England, where although Realism may have come relatively late, once the trend had been established it permeated the whole of the drama, and became the dominant dramatic mode from Galsworthy to Pinter. However, Craig's impact on the European drama was significant, and many of his ideas had considerable indirect influence on counter-realistic trends in subsequent English drama and theatre production.

In setting the stage for what follows, I have reviewed the development of the Victorian theatre in order to establish the context for the period of accelerated change that occurred between 1889 and 1914. The chapters explore some of the most significant areas of action and development during this era of transition from Victorian to modern, from a conservative theatre relying on well-tried dramatic formulas and operational practices to a forward-looking theatre expressing new artistic and social ideas within a more flexible framework. The emphasis is on the background issues that had to be fought out in order to make a new drama possible, but, inevitably, the focus falls on a few individuals or groups who were in the forefront of the various campaigns to effect a revolution in the English theatre.

NOTES

1. Charles Dickens' *Uncollected Writings from* Household Words *1850-1859*, ed. Harry Stone (Indiana University Press, Bloomington, 1968), vol. 1, p. 344.

2. Allardyce Nicoll, for his Hand-list of Plays, *A History of English Drama 1660-1900* (Cambridge University Press, Cambridge, 1959), vols. 4 and 5, lists over sixty categories.

3. Richard Findlater, *The Unholy Trade* (Gollancz, London, 1952), p. 23.

4. Hugh Hunt, *The Revels History of Drama in English*, general editor T.W. Craik (Methuen, London, 1978), vol. 7, p. 6.

5. St. John Ervine, *The Theatre in My Time* (Rich & Cowan, London, 1933), p. 15.

6. Mario Borsa, *The English Stage of Today* (John Lane, London, 1908), pp. 20-1.

7. Doris Jones, *The Life and Letters of Henry Arthur Jones* (Macmillan, London, 1930), pp. 207, 172-3, 167, 260, respectively.

8. Allan Hughes, 'The Lyceum Staff. A Victorian Theatrical Organization', *Theatre Notebook,* vol. 28, no. 1 (1974), pp. 15-16.

9. G.B. Shaw, Preface to William Archer, *Theatrical World of 1894* (Walter Scott, London, 1895), pp. xiii-xiv.

10. William Archer, 'The Blight on the Drama', *Fortnightly Review,* N.S. vol. 61 (January 1897), p. 32.

11. William Archer, 'Drama', *Encyclopaedia Britannica,* 10th edn., vol. 25, p. 516.

12. William Archer, *The Theatrical World of 1897* (Walter Scott, London, 1898), p. 376.

13. H. Granville Barker, *Pall Mall Gazette,* 14 March 1908, p. 7.

14. J.C. Trewin, *The Edwardian Theatre* (Rowman & Littlefield, Totowa, N.J., 1976), p. 5.

15. William Archer and H. Granville Barker, *A National Theatre. Scheme and Estimates* (Duckworth, London, 1907), p. 101.

16. Leopold Wagner, *Theatre,* N.S. vol. 18 (August 1896), p. 66.

17. H.A. Jones, Preface to *Saints and Sinners,* in *The Renascence of the English Drama* (Macmillan, London, 1895), p. 314.

18. Quoted by Doris Jones, p. 74.

19. *The Theatrical World of 1897,* p. xvi.

20. 'Stanley Jones' (Leonard Merrick), *The Actor and His Art: Some Considerations of the Present Condition of the Stage* (Downey, London, 1899), p. 21. First published as fourteen articles in *Tomorrow,* 'A Monthly Review conducted by J.T. Grein', 1896-98. At first, 'Jones' was thought to be either Grein or Max Beerbohm.

21. Lynton Hudson, *The English Stage 1850-1950* (Harrap, London, 1951), p. 123.

22. William Archer, *The Theatrical World of 1896* (Walter Scott, London, 1897), p. xxv.

23. William Archer, 'The Drama in the Doldrums', *Fortnightly Review,* N.S. vol. 52 (August 1892), pp. 163-4.

24. H. Hamilton Fyfe, 'Organizing the Theatre', *Fortnightly Review,* N.S. vol. 71 (March 1902), pp. 552-3.

25. Henry Morley, *The Journal of a London Playgoer from 1851-1866* (George Routledge, London, 1866), pp. 9, 28, 31.

26. Henry James, 'The London Theatres, 1879', *The Scenic Art. Notes on Acting and the Drama: 1872-1901,* ed. Allan Wade (Rupert Hart-Davis, London, 1949), p. 123.

27. For example, one actor went from £18 to £60 a week, and another from £9 to £50.

28. Frank Benson, *My Memoirs* (Ernest Benn, London, 1930), p. 182.

29. 'A Winter Wealtheries', *Truth,* vol. 16 (Xmas Number 1884), p. 14.

30. Henry James, 'The London Theatre, 1880', *Scenic Art,*

p. 135.

31. E.J. West, 'The London Stage 1870-1890', *University of Colorado Studies*, Series B, ii (1943), p. 73. A shortened version of this essay appeared in *The Quarterly Journal of Speech*, vol. 28 (1942), pp. 430-6.

32. Pierre Marie Augustin Filon, *The English Stage* (John Milne, London, 1897), p. 98.

33. Michael Baker, *The Rise of the Victorian Actor* (Croom Helm, London, 1978), p. 62.

34. Henry Irving, 'The Art and Status of the Actor', *Fortnightly Review*, N.S. vol. 67 (May 1900), p. 746.

35. Drew B. Pallette, 'The English Actor's Fight for Respectability', *Theatre Annual* (New York, 1948-49), p. 27.

36. Quoted in Pallette, p. 30.

37. James, p. 119.

38. Henry Elliott, 'The Stage Under Victoria', *Theatre*, N.S. vol. 28 (November 1896), p. 242.

39. 'Stanley Jones', p. 3.

40. Quoted in 'Stanley Jones', pp. 151-2.

41. Ervine, pp. 105-6.

42. George Rowell, *The Victorian Theatre 1792-1914. A Survey* (Cambridge University Press, Cambridge, 1978), p. 79.

43. See especially, Michael Booth, *Prefaces to English Nineteenth-Century Theatre* (Manchester University Press, Manchester, 1980).

44. Quoted in Doris Jones, p. 63.

45. *Saturday Review*, 3 November 1883, p. 565.

46. William Archer, 'A Plea for an Endowed Theatre', *Fortnightly Review*, N.S. vol. 45 (May 1889), pp. 611-17.

47. Ervine, p. 108.

48. See 'The Wholesome Play', in C.E. Montague, *Dramatic Values* (Methuen, London, 1925), pp. 244-74.

49. *World*, 9 July 1874, p. 7.

50. H.A. Jones, *Renascence*, p. 18.

51. The labels were attached by W.A. Lewis Bettany in 'Criticism and the Renascent Drama', *Theatre*, N.S. vol. 19 (June 1892), p. 277.

52. William Archer, 'The Free Stage and the New Drama', *Fortnightly Review*, N.S. vol. 50 (November 1891), pp. 663, 664.

53. H.A. Jones, *The Foundations of a National Drama* (Chapman Hall, London, 1913), p. 211. From his Introduction to Filon's *The English Stage* (1897).

54. Archer, 'The Blight on the Drama', p. 23.

55. Holbrook Jackson, *The Eighteen Nineties* (Grant Richards, London, 1922), p. 205.

56. Quoted in A.E. Wilson, *Edwardian Theatre* (Arthur Baker, London, 1951), p. 167. The 'digestion' metaphor pervades the criticism of the period.

57. Borsa, pp. 54-5.

58. Samuel Hynes, *The Edwardian Turn of Mind* (Oxford University Press, London, 1968), p. 6.

59. Ibid., p. 135. See Edward Carpenter, *My Days and Dreams* (G. Allen & Unwin, London, 1916), p. 245.
60. R.C.K. Ensor, *England 1870-1914* (Clarendon Press, Oxford, 1936), p. 527.
61. Roland N. Stromberg, *Realism, Naturalism and Symbolism* (Macmillan, London, 1968), p. xi. When capitalized the terms Realism and Naturalism refer to the movements, when not capitalized the terms are used in a general sense.
62. George H. Becker, *Documents of Modern Literary Realism* (Princeton University Press, Princeton, N.J., 1963), pp. 22-35.
63. Stromberg, p. ix.
64. Becker, p. 35.
65. Lawson A. Carter, *Zola and the Theater* (Yale University Press, New Haven, Conn., 1963), p. 72.
66. Zola, in *Documents*, p. 166.
67. Zola, 'Naturalism in the Theatre', in *Documents*, p. 219.
68. Ibid., p. 220.
69. Ibid., p. 225.
70. Henry Baker, *History of the London Stage* (George Routledge, London, 1904), p. 323.
71. Michael Baker, p. 80.
72. William Archer, *The Old Drama and the New* (William Heinemann, London, 1923), p. 283.
73. H.A. Jones, *Renascence*, pp. x-xi.
74. Marjorie Northend, 'Henry Arthur Jones and the Development of Modern English Drama', *Review of English Studies*, vol. 18 (1942), p. 459.
75. Archer, *Theatrical World of 1896*, p. xviii.
76. Max Beerbohm, 9 March 1901, *Around Theatres* (Rupert Hart-Davis, London, 1953), p. 131.
77. Archer, *Old Drama and the New*, p. 86.
78. G.B. Shaw, *Collected Letters 1874-1897*, ed. Dan H. Lawrence (Max Reinhardt, London, 1965), p. 632.
79. G.B. Shaw, *Collected Plays* (Max Reinhardt, London, 1972), vol. 4, pp. 138-9.
80. Max Beerbohm, *Saturday Review*, vol. 90 (July 1900), p. 112.

Chapter Two

IBSEN, J.T. GREIN AND THE INDEPENDENT THEATRE

In days of yore the Drama throve within our
storm-bound coasts;
The Independent Theatre gave performances of Ghosts;
Death and disease, disaster
And darkness were our joy--
Ah, fun flew fast and faster
When Ibsen was our Master
And Grein was a bright Dutch boy, my boys!
(Chorus) And Grein was a bright Dutch boy.

Max Beerbohm

Despite the changes in the latter part of the nineteenth century that brought more serious plays to the stage under conditions that were attractive to middle and upper-class audiences, intellectuals and progressives remained dissatisfied with the state of English drama. H.A. Jones himself saw 'in abundance every element of a great dramatic renascence--except good plays'. He prophesied: 'we are on the threshold not merely of an era of magnificent spectacular and archaeological revivals, but of a living, breathing modern drama--a drama that shall not fear to lay bold and reverent hands on the deepest things of the human life of today and freely expose them'.[1] It was an era of social, intellectual and artistic ferment, and the drama had to rise much higher to meet its challenges.

Perhaps the most important impetus towards the new drama came from Henrik Ibsen, whose work was first introduced into England by Edmund Gosse. While visiting Trondhjem, Norway, in 1870, Gosse discovered Ibsen through a bookseller who showed him *Digte*, a volume of poetry which so impressed him that he reviewed it in the *Spectator*, March 1872. He followed this with an article on *Peer Gynt*, 'a great and powerful work', in the July issue of the same journal, and then dealt more fully with Ibsen's drama in 'Ibsen the Norwegian Satirist', which appeared in the *Fortnightly Review* the following January.[2] This essay dealt with *Love's Comedy*, *Brand* and *Peer Gynt*, which Gosse saw together as 'a great satiric trilogy--perhaps for sustained vigour of expression, for affluence of execution, and for brilliance of dialogue, the greatest of modern times', and he predicted that 'sooner or later they will win for their author the homage of Europe'.[3] He could hardly have foreseen that not these, but the later social dramas were to elicit that homage. About the same time, William Archer also discovered Ibsen while staying at his grandfather's house in Larvick, Norway, but it was March 1878 before he published his first essay on 'Henrik Ibsen's New Drama' in *The Mirror of Literature*.[4] This grew out of his work on a translation of *The Pillars of Society,* and thereafter Archer became the chief translator and advocate of Ibsen in England. The first translation into English of an Ibsen play, *The Emperor and the Galilean,* by Catherine Ray, appeared in 1876, but the first performance of Ibsen in England was not until 15 December 1880 when *Quicksands; or the Pillars of Society,* Archer's adaptation of the play, was given a matinée performance at the Gaiety Theatre--and, in Archer's phrase, 'fell perfectly flat'. Two adaptations of *A Doll's House* appeared: the first, *Nora,* by Mrs. Henrietta Frances Lord, was published in 1882, but not performed until 1885 when it was staged by amateurs at the School of Dramatic Art, London; the second was *Breaking A Butterfly* by H.A. Jones and H. Herman, a mutilation of Ibsen's play (of which Jones was later somewhat ashamed) that opened at the Prince of Wales's on 3 March 1884.[5] The following year, Mrs. Lord serialised a translation of *Ghosts* in *Today,* a socialist periodical, and in 1888 the Camelot Classics brought out a volume of three plays edited by Havelock Ellis: *The Pillars of Society, Ghosts* and *An Enemy of the People*. *Rosmersholm* appeared in 1889 in a translation by L.N. Parker.[6]

By the end of the decade, therefore, Ibsen's name was becoming familiar through Gosse's essays and Archer's persistent promotion, and his work increasingly available in print although sadly absent from the stage. Why was it, then, that the first unadapted production of *A Doll's House,* given by Charles Charrington and his wife Janet Achurch at the Novelty Theatre on 7 June 1889, threw the country into a state of 'moral epilepsy', as Archer put it? Reviewers were almost unanimous in their condemnation of the play, which they treated with disgust or disdain, finding Nora 'unwomanly' and the morality reprehensible. Many conceded it was well acted, and, like Clement Scott, went as far as to admit it had some 'interesting points'. They found Ibsen 'provincial', 'misleading and mischievous in drift': a missionary 'whose mission is to some extent injurious', and even 'an obscene defiler of the purity of the home'. The *Queen* declared:

> Ibsen enforces his extravagant views by means of the most unpleasant set of people it has ever been the lot of playgoers to encounter, and, furthermore, discusses evils

> which we unfortunately know to exist, but which it can serve no good purpose to drag into the light of common day ... We do not go to the theatre to study such social evils as Ibsen delights to discuss in his cynical, uncompromising manner.[7]

Outbursts of this nature are all the more surprising when it is remembered that much groundwork had been done first by critics like Archer himself and Matthew Arnold--who had scorned the British theatre as 'perhaps the most contemptible in Europe', and called for a drama relevant to life--and second by dramatists like Jones and Pinero who had in such plays as *Saints and Sinners* (1884) and *The Profligate* (1889) respectively, attempted serious plays on contemporary themes which had been hailed as 'epoch making' in their realism and social criticism. Audiences had been prepared to a certain extent, but the plays they had seen were put into perspective by Ibsen's social dramas as the conventional pieces that they were. In his essay 'The Coming of Ibsen', Granville Barker points out that Ibsen's plays arrived in England at a time when the theatre had only just become respectable--provided it never treated serious matters too seriously. Puritan attitudes, that identified the theatre with the Gates of Hell, were slow dying, so that a drama which provided moral shocks, disturbed the fundamental relationships between men and women, and openly discussed taboo subjects, could expect hostility. Such a picturing of life as Ibsen's, declared Granville Barker, and 'such drastic judgement upon it, and that hammer-blow method of his which at last compelled you to listen, found our parochial puppet show of a theatre and its sleepier critics very unprepared'.[8] His plays did not deal with the stuff of conventional nineteenth-century drama--sentimental unrealities, melodramatic horrors for their own sake, or mere ingenious contrivances--but with the real issues of everyday living. Critics and audiences found them 'suburban' and their characters 'dowdy', lacking the fashionable charm of the domestic comedies to which they were accustomed, as well as shocking in their assault on conventional morality. Ibsen also perplexed by his method of delayed exposition, an elaboration of the Scribe-Sardou formula, in which the mysteries of the first act are not clarified until the last: 'it was like having to learn a new language', comments Lynton Hudson, 'with a syntax similar to German, in which the verb only makes its appearance at the end of the sentence, and without it the sentence is unintelligible'.[9]

The hostility to Ibsen, therefore, can be accounted for in both moral and dramatic terms, but the very virulence of the attack was productive of an almost equally vehement defence on the part of the 'Ibsenites'. Recalling the reception of *A Doll's House,* Archer in 1901 deplored the 'colossal absurdities' of the hostile Press, and the bias against Ibsen that it generated, but regretted equally 'the facile hero-worship of those who saw in *A Doll's House* a sort of Women's Rights manifesto', and he admitted that Ibsen 'suffered from ignorant enthusiasms as well as from ignorant obloquy'.[10] Shaw, whose *Quintessence of Ibsenism* was first given as a lecture to the Fabian Society on 18 July 1890 at the St. James's Restaurant, also saw both aspects, although he was guilty of overstating the moral and political content at the expense of the poetic and dramatic qualities. His *The Philanderer* (1893) is set 'during the first vogue of Ibsen in London after 1899', and he declares in a Prefatory Note that the Ibsen Club, although then non-existent, represented 'a state of mind ... familiar then to our intelligentsia'[11] which the play satirizes.

In order to produce *A Doll's House,* recounts Shaw, 'the Charringtons had obtained the funds for a week's engagement at the Novelty by signing with Williamson, Garner & Musgrove for a joint engagement to tour the antipodes for two years at £25 a week, and had then mortgaged the salary'.[12] Despite this commitment, and the hostility of the critics, the run was extended to twenty-four days, right up to the eve of their departure, and they lost 'only' seventy pounds. Nevertheless, it was a highly significant production because it established Ibsen as a force to be reckoned with in the theatrical as well as the intellectual life of the times, and led to a demand for more Ibsen that was filled by the publication in five volumes of the *Prose Dramas* edited by Archer 1890-91, and by a burst of Ibsen plays on the London stage in 1891: *A Doll's House,* Terry's, 27 January; *Rosmersholm,* Vaudeville, 23 February; *Ghosts,* Royalty, 13 March; *Hedda Gabler,* Vaudeville, 20 April; *The Lady from the Sea,* Terry's, 11 May; and *A Doll's House* again, Criterion, 2 June. The most significant and notorious of these was *Ghosts,* which launched J.T. Grein's Independent Theatre, and was greeted by an incredible flood of invective.

The Independent Theatre story starts in a most unlikely place: Amsterdam, where Jacob Thomas Grein was born in 1862 of mixed German and Anglo-Dutch parents.[13] Although apprenticed in business in Antwerp and later in an uncle's bank in Amsterdam, he managed to develop a fascination for the theatre into an active involvement in criticism. The collapse of the bank in 1885 rudely interrupted both careers. A job was found for him by his family in the London office of Wellenstein, Krause and Co., a Dutch firm trading with the Dutch East Indies. Grein had only a smattering of English, but less than three months after his arrival he began to contribute articles on London theatre and general topics to Dutch papers and magazines, and within two years he had started to contribute to English periodicals; soon he was also involved in sponsoring and editing several theatrical journals. His general approach to drama is indicated in an editorial in one of these, the short-lived *The Weekly Comedy,* which he edited with C.W.Jarvis:

> To ourselves, the drama is an art; its purpose is to show the tragedy, the comedy, the farce of life; only in the most indirect way can it contribute to the solution of moral or social questions. But it is highly desirable that its area should be widened, its subjects multiplied; whilst its situations and characters should have greater closeness and relevance to life. To the best of our power we shall aim at assisting progress in this direction.[14]

When an article by Ernest J. Andrews in *The Dramatic Review* deplored the fact that plays by 'the great unacted' body of dramatists had no chance of performance, and suggested that here was an opportunity for amateurs to be of great service to the drama through staging such pieces, Grein responded by applauding the idea, but pointed out the drawbacks of amateur performance. He proposed the formation of a 'Proof Stage Association' which would mount one professional performance of a new play attended by members of the Association (which would, he hoped, include many managers) and by members of the Press. There appears to have been no response to Grein's scheme, even when a similar experiment was reported later that year from Paris where Eugene Desroches was promoting new plays at the *Théâtre des Jeunes* by holding competitions--an idea Grein employed abortively in *The Weekly Comedy* in November 1889, with Pinero as judge.

Antoine's *Théâtre Libre* gave its first performance in Paris on 30 May 1887. Exactly six months later *The Weekly Comedy* printed the text of a leaflet previously circulated 'to many literary and dramatic authorities' with the compliments of the editors, Grein and Jarvis, entitled A British 'Theatre Libre' (see Appendix A for full text). It welcomed the new direction towards 'native work' in place of 'foreign fare', but deplored the unwillingness of managers 'to go outside the beaten track' for fear of financial failure. Younger and more ambitious authors, unable to afford 'the doubtful trial of a matinée' themselves, faced a hopeless situation. A solution to their problem was obvious: 'What had been done in France, cannot it be done, too, in England?' The proposal was careful to assure readers that a British *Théâtre Libre* would eschew 'subjects of an immoral, or even unwholesomely realistic nature' but 'would nurture realism ... of a healthy kind'; and 'unlike the French Théâtre Libre ... [it] should banish all that is vulgar, low and cynically immoral'.[15] The proposal suggested that a 'moderate capital (say £2,000)' from contributors and subscribers would be sufficient to initiate the enterprise, and emphasized the importance of the right kind of patronage--from the Press and leading novelists and dramatists such as Meredith, Hardy, Pinero and Jones. Four succeeding articles in *The Weekly Comedy* furthered the idea, and a vigorous discussion ensued through letters to the editor: Pinero declared 'that any scheme for the protection of serious drama has, and always will have, my warm sympathy'; Thomas Hardy felt his opinion would have 'little value', and recommended a return to a more open and less elaborate staging; William Archer supported 'any scheme for stimulating dramatic production and helping the drama' to break conventional chains; and Henry James agreed, 'Oh, yes, by all means. It would be very amusing'. Others were not so encouraging; Jerome K. Jerome, for example, 'did not believe in the scheme', which would create 'a sort of theatrical hothouse for the rearing of dramatic plants, too delicate, or too abnormal to thrive in the natural air of the outer work-a-day world'.[16]

In the final issue of *The Weekly Comedy* (No. 11, 21 December 1889), Grein announced that his suggestion was 'ripening into a more definite scheme', but it was several months before more was heard.

The following summer George Moore, inspired by seeing *Ghosts* (apparently in rehearsal) by the *Théâtre Libre* at *Le Théâtre des Menus* in May 1890, raised the issue in the columns of *The Hawk*, 'A Smart Paper for Smart People' edited by his brother Augustus. 'Why have we not a *Theatre Libre?'* asked Moore:

> Surely there should be no difficulty in finding a thousand persons interested in art and letters willing to subscribe five pounds a year for twelve representations of twelve interesting plays. I think such a number of enthusiasts exists in London. The innumerable articles which appear in the daily, the weekly, and monthly press on the London stage prove the existence of much vague discontent, and that this discontent will take definite shape sooner or later seems more than possible.[17]

In ensuing articles, Moore claimed to have initiated the discussion as far back as 1884, and with even greater arrogance claimed that 'there is nothing in Antoine's past or present programme that was not anticipated in [his] articles' in *Fortnightly* and *The Evening News* in 1887 (a remark omitted when he edited the article for *Impressions and Opinions).* He went on to say that it was now

> within measurable distance of the time when an English *Théâtre Libre* will open its doors to a play written on the new lines, since it has been more than hinted that the man is now among us who will organise the new theatre.[18]

But when 'the man'--J.T. Grein--announced his plans for the opening of London's Independent Theatre, 'Hawkshaw' of *The Hawk* (none other than brother Augustus himself) printed the following:

AXES TO GREIN-D

> I see a paragraph in some of the theatrical papers stating that a Mr. J.T. Grein is about to attempt to found a "Free Theatre" on the lines of Mr. George Moore's articles in this paper, and is in treaty for the Novelty Theatre. I should like it distinctly understood that I do not consider that Mr. J.T. Grein has any of the many qualifications which have led to the success of M. Antoine, that I have in no way been consulted, and that I strongly object to any articles which have appeared in this paper being used to induce anyone to subscribe a shilling to such an enterprise.[19]

The following week the *St. James's Gazette* noted with some surprise that Mr. George Moore, who had been 'advocating with much fervour the establishment of a *théâtre libre* in London ... is very angry, and hastens to disclaim all connection or sympathy with his would-be disciple, Mr. Grein'.[20] George Moore might well have had a grudge against Grein for Grein's co-editor of *The Weekly Comedy,* C.W. Jarvis, had attacked the dramatic criticism of 'The Incompetent Mr. Moore' in the issue of 9 November 1889. However, the very next day the *Gazette* printed a disclaimer from Moore:

> Feeling sure that you do not wish to misrepresent my attitude toward Mr. Grein and his project ... I will ask you to allow me to say, through the medium of your journal, that I am not responsible for anything that appears in THE HAWK except the weekly article which I sign ... and it would indeed be ungracious for me to disclaim sympathy with him.[21]

Augustus also printed the letter in *The Hawk,* but was unrepentant, ignoring, forgetting or not knowing (which is unlikely) Grein's 1889 circular and articles. This skirmish helped to publicize Grein's proposal, but, less fortunately, also caused a lifelong rift between the brothers.

Words there were a-plenty, but action none.

This state of affairs might have gone on indefinitely but for a stroke of fortune arising out of another part of Grein's activities: his promotion of English drama in Europe, especially Holland. He was self-appointed agent for Jones, Pinero, Jerome, and several lesser figures, always ensuring that there was a promise to pay a percentage to the author where a country--like Holland--had no literary convention with England. Orme declares that Grein acted in a 'purely honorary' capacity, receiving no remuneration. However, one tribute was

> the unexpected arrival of a magnificent grandfather clock bearing a brass plate upon which was engraved: "From Arthur W. Pinero and Henry Arthur Jones to J.T. Grein in recognition of his efforts on behalf of the British drama abroad, and especially in remembrance of the performance of *The Profligate* and *The Middleman*",[22]

which had both been produced in Amsterdam 1889/90. A second tribute came from the Managers of the Royal Subsidised Theatre in Amsterdam 'in recognition of the honour of the work done and the happy results'. In Grein's own account in the *Stage Society News*, 25 January 1907, they

> sent me a cheque for £50 to be used in the interest of art in England. At the same time I had received another cheque for £30 for the translation of an English play *[Little Lord Fauntleroy]*. With these gigantic sums, in the wake of Antoine of Paris, I founded the Independent Theatre, the first performance of which elicited no less than five hundred articles, mostly vituperating Ibsen, whose "Ghosts" inaugurated the movement, and obtained for me the honorary, if somewhat unflattering, title of "the best-abused man in London." In parenthesis, I should add here that this distinction clung to me for many years, that some families closed their doors against me because I had produced an immoral play, and that a well-known journalist, since dead [Mr. William Champion of *The Topical Times]*, refused to be present at a banquet if I were invited. It cost me practically ten years of my life to overcome the prejudice created by an undertaking which even the enemy must admit has left its mark upon the history of our stage.

Grein's aim for the Independent Theatre (hereinafter abbreviated to I.T.) was to stimulate the production of new, original English plays independent both of the censor and of commercial, profit-oriented management. To launch the venture Grein needed a powerful draw. Following the production of *A Doll's House* at the Novelty Theatre on 7 June 1889, and the controversy it aroused, interest in Ibsen had grown, which made one of his plays an obvious choice: *Ghosts* recommended itself because it epitomized Ibsen's work (after *Peer Gynt)* and that of the new drama--and it had strong associations with the Free Theatre movement throughout Europe. Furthermore, it was a challenge to the licensing system because when Grein mentioned his intentions to his friend, E.F.S. Pigott, who was the Lord Chamberlain's Examiner of Plays, he exclaimed *'Ghosts!* Never come to me with *Ghosts*. It is a waste of time to ask for a licence'.[23] The problem with an unlicensed play was to find a theatre management willing to take the risk to its theatre licence of allowing such a play on its stage. It was not illegal to do so, provided the performance was not 'public', but the experience of the Grand Theatre, Islington, which had permitted a private performance of *The Cenci* by the Shelley Society on 7 May 1886, acted as a deterrent. No action had been taken, but the Lord Chamberlain's office had issued a warning that the Grand's theatre licence would be in jeopardy if such an evasion of the law was repeated. It is not surprising, therefore, that Grein had difficulty in finding a theatre willing to accept *Ghosts*. After many refusals he opened negotiations with the Novelty, but these broke down, so he settled for the Athenaeum Hall. Orme recounts that there was 'a reading by Dr. Aveling of *Ghosts* at the Playgoers' Club where J.T., in a burst of enthusiasm, convened the whole audience to his opening performance. It was a well-attended meeting and the response to this wholesale invitation was so great that the little Athenaeum Hall could not possibly have encompassed the swelling crowd'.[24] Miss Kate Santley, proprietress of the Royalty, came to the rescue, offering her theatre for Friday 13 March 1891 at a fee of £15. A vehement article in the *Daily Telegraph*, which urged the Lord Chamberlain to prevent the performance, disturbed her sufficiently to make her visit his Controller for reassurance on her legal position: finding that there was no law broken provided it was a strictly private affair not open to the general public, she stood by her offer. The ebullient Grein was undeterred by the obstacles or by the mounting protest (or by the ominous date), and he partially overcame the final hurdle of 3,000 applications for a theatre seating 657 by opening his dress rehearsal to subscribers on the Wednesday evening.

The production of *Ghosts*, in the capable hands of Cecil Raleigh, whose speciality was melodrama, drew enormous attention. The acting was praised, especially that of Mrs. Theodore Wright, a well-known amateur who had been engaged to play Mrs. Alving by Grein himself despite his reservations over amateurs, and in the face of subsequent protests by a group of his literary friends who felt that the importance of the occasion demanded a tried professional. But the performance, as Grein says, brought down a torrent of abuse on Ibsen and on his own head; there was even the threat of a question in Parliament which was never fulfilled, perhaps, as Orme suggests, because 'Downing Street was afraid to make England the laughing-stock of Europe',[25] where for a decade *Ghosts* had been recognized as a masterpiece. As this abuse is well documented in *The Quintessence of Ibsenism*, Egan's *Ibsen. The Critical Heritage* and elsewhere, perhaps two examples will suffice here: 'it was merely dull dirt', writes Hawkshaw, 'and if Mr. Grein hopes for the success of his Independent Theatre, he must make it something but a Dispensary of Dirt';[26] and the *Era* found it 'about as foul and filthy a concoction as has ever been allowed with impunity to fling defiance in the face of a Lord Chamberlain and to disgrace the boards of an English theatre', but gathered some consolation from the thought that 'its inherent dulness supplies an antidote to its own poison'.[27] After the first wave of indignation, more sober evaluations became possible. W. Davenport Adams, writing in the August issue of *The Theatre*, which four months earlier had enjoyed branding *Ghosts* 'loathsome, monstrous and unnatural', is almost apologetic:

> Mr. Grein has been assailed with a bitterness amounting to persecution, but it is certain, all the same, that even those who have attacked him have been glad of the opportunity of seeing "Ghosts" ... I do not believe that Ibsen will secure a permanent position on our stage, but I conceive that his subjects and methods will help to revolutionize our theatre, and that we are already indebted to him for the freshness of topics and treatment noticeable in certain of our recent dramas.[28]

To manage the affairs of the I.T., which refused to oblige its opponents by disintegrating, a committee was formed consisting of Grein, his collaborator, C.W. Jarvis, as secretary, Frank Harris (editor of *The Fortnightly Review)*, Mrs. Julia Frankau (the novelist known as 'Frank Danby'), George Moore, and Cecil Raleigh, who was later replaced after a dispute with Moore by the Dutch-born Herman de Lange. (See Appendix B for list of plays produced.)

For the I.T.'s second production, Grein had intended a triple bill that included Björnson's *The Newly Married Couple*, translated by H.L. Braekstad, but he decided it was too weak a successor to *Ghosts*, and substituted another Braekstad translation, the Swedish play *True Women* by Mrs. Elgren which, appropriately after Ibsen, dealt with the emancipation of women in modern society. The play was put into rehearsal, but unfortunately Grein did not first gain the permission of the translator, who clung to more ambitious plans for the play, so the performance had to be cancelled. Undeterred, but wiser, Grein wrote to Zola for permission to perform *Thérèse Raquin* (first produced in Paris in 1873). It was granted, and the task of translation was undertaken by Alexander Teixeira de Mattos, a subsequent pillar of the I.T. and lifelong friend of Grein's. The I.T. sought a permanent home for its productions, but in vain, and was lucky to secure the Royalty again for the Zola play, this time allaying Miss Santley's fears by obtaining a licence. Orme records that it was a celebrity occasion, including Henry James, Oscar Wilde and Bernard Shaw among its audience, but this did not prevent a 'babble of debate' between supporters and opponents during the intermission to the point that 'two champions of the rival factions nearly resorted to fisticuffs'.[29] The battle continued in the press where again the acting was praised and the play vilified. However, Sydney Herberte-Basing, who played the husband, Camille, secured rights to the play and produced it with the same cast at the Royalty where it ran for a week.

Ghosts was the only unlicensed play produced, but the performances and the affairs of the I.T. continued to provide materials for vehement discussion--and entertaining gossip. For example, William Archer was so angered by the deletions from his translation of Brandes' *The Visit* that he had the excised passages printed and distributed to the audience--to discover a few days later that the cuts had been made not by the Censor, but *before* the play had been submitted for a licence, by George Moore, 'a very diligent and useful member of the Committee, who was inclined to regard the [Independent] theatre as his own child'.[30] This attitude is confirmed by Moore's own record of dining with Yeats at the Cheshire Cheese and treating 'him to an account of the Independent Theatre and of its first performance organized by me'.[31] The problems of the I.T. also persisted. The *Ghosts* handbill had announced that 'ORIGINAL plays have been promised by Messrs. Geo. Moore, W. [C.K.] Wilde, Cecil Raleigh, I. Zangwill, C.W. Jarvis', and had listed translations of ten foreign plays for the repertoire. Of the translations only de Banville's *The Kiss*, a one-act play, had been produced in the first year (only one more of the promised ten, *The Wild Duck*, ever reached production), and the single 'original' British play forthcoming was a one-act adaptation, *The Minister's Call*, by an author not on the list--Arthur Symons. George R. Sims, 'Dagonet' of *The Referee* and writer of several successful melodramas, appealed in his column for a play to fulfill the promise of a new, unconventional British drama:

> Mr. Moore has been to a great many managers with his great strike play. I fancy he even left it in a brown parcel once at the stage door of the despised Adelphi. Why can't we have that at the Independent Theatre? There will be no difficulty about money. If Mr. Moore will allow it to be produced, I will gladly subscribe towards the expenses.[32]

Moore took up the challenge, and Sims agreed to pay £100 to the I.T. for his seat at the first performance. Between 1889 and 1890 Moore had written a play, *The Strike at Arlingford*, which had been rejected in turn by Beerbohm Tree and John Hare. He resuscitated it and proceeded to give it a thorough revision, reducing it from five acts to three, but before the play was produced Bernard Shaw had in fact made the long-awaited breakthrough with *Widowers' Houses, an Original Realistic Play*. The story of its genesis is familiar, and best told in Shaw's own words from the Preface to *Plays Unpleasant:*

> I proposed to Mr. Grein that he should boldly announce a play by me. Being an extraordinary sanguine and enterprising man, he took this step without hesitation. I

> then raked out, from my dustiest pile of discarded and rejected manuscripts, two acts of a play ['Rhinegold'] I had begun in 1885 [1884 in fact], shortly after the close of my novel writing period, in collaboration with my friend William Archer ... Laying violent hands on his thoroughly planned scheme for a sympathetically romantic "well made play" of the Parisian type then in vogue, I perversely distorted it into a grotesquely realistic exposure of slum landlordism [etc] ... Archer, perceiving that I had played the fool both with his plan and my own theme, promptly disowned me.[33]

Archer gave his account of the collaboration in *The World* (14 December 1892), which Shaw incorporated into his Preface to the 1893 edition of *Widowers' Houses* (published as No. 1 in the Independent Theatre Series, edited by Grein, who also wrote a 'sublime' preface). Shaw, according to Archer, had used up his 'scheme of a twaddling cup-and-saucer comedy vaguely suggested by Augier's *Ceinture Dorée*' in 'half the first act'.[34] Archer refused to supply more plot, complaining that what he had given was 'a rounded and perfect whole', and their partnership was stillborn. The Shaw-Grein conversation took place during a nocturnal walk. Grein complained of the I.T.'s desperate need of a new British play, and when Shaw offered to revive 'Rhinegold' Grein undertook to produce it without having read a line. The play was not even finished, and 'when the manuscript was first delivered, the third act arrived in scraps which took days to put together and read'.[35]

An amusing incident concerning the production of this play indicates one of the I.T.'s many problems. Unlike Antoine in Paris, Grein did not have a permanent company or his own theatre, so it was always difficult to find actors willing to donate their services who were free of other engagements on the somewhat uncertain dates of production, and, equally important, who were suitable for the required roles. Such an actor had not been found for the role of Lickcheese; nevertheless, rehearsals proceeded at the Bedford Head, a West-End pub, and the first night drew dangerously close. 'Suddenly, in the midst of rehearsal, a woolly little head popped through the door, and to the little head was attached the quicksilvery body of a little man. "Any actors wanted here?" he exclaimed, and with one voice author, producer, and actors bade him come in'.[36] He was James Welch, then a little-known comedian whose portrayal of Lickcheese established his reputation.

Miscasting of the two leading roles in *The Strike at Arlingford* weakened the play, but did not prevent Sims from honouring his promise, and the I.T. received a very useful boost to its funds. Subsequent British plays included the anonymous *Alan's Wife*, announced as being founded on *Befriad*, a story by Elin Ameen, in which William Archer had recognised the stuff of drama. He had sent a rough scenario to Elizabeth

Robins to pass on to any interested dramatist, and it was not until 1922, at a banquet honouring Grein, that it was revealed by Mrs. Hugh Bell, by then Lady Bell, that she and Elizabeth Robins had been joint authors. The play's morbid theme of infanticide disturbed even some I.T. supporters, and a similar morbidity characterized *A Question of Memory* and *The Black Cat*, both of which ended in suicide. Grein thought it time for a comedy, and Zola's *The Heirs of Rabourdin* appealed to him, with its echoes of *Volpone* and *Le Malade Imaginaire*, but it was a failure. *The Wild Duck* restored the I.T.'s reputation, but exhausted its funds, which had already been subsidised by Grein out of his modest income. Consequently, it was reorganised in 1895 as The Independent Theatre Ltd. with Grein and Mrs. G.C. Ashton Johnson (Dorothy Leighton) as directors, and A. Teixeira de Mattos as secretary. Subsequently, Charles Charrington became Honorary Director and Grein Honorary President. In October 1895, Grein was obliged to resign, as Shaw explained in a letter to Charrington (7 October 1895):

> Grein, who represented, along with a partner, a Dutch firm, has been promoted to the sole representative on the withdrawal of the partner. The Dutch firm, however, exact (very properly) that their representative shall not appear as managing director of such a very shady joint stock company as the I.T. Limited, though they don't mind his amusing himself with it unofficially.[37]

Orme suggests that even Grein felt his new duties incompatible with the burdens of theatre promotion. The *Theatre*, continuing the tradition of its former editor, Clement Scott, treated the event dismissively:

> the retirement of Mr. J.T. Grein from the directorship of the Independent Theatre is not an event that calls for much comment. The institution which he founded a few years ago has never had any real influence upon our stage at all, and of late it has ceased to attract attention even by its eccentricity. Few of the plays performed by it had any value or merit save that of showing how dull and uninteresting pieces that outrage taste and decency generally are ... as Mr. Grein, when he was not trying to make his audience's flesh creep, merely produced rather worse drama than one can get in any provincial theatre, we cannot pretend to regret that he has retired.[38]

A disheartening comment on four years' work, but the phrase 'that outrage taste and decency' gives the game away, for its capacity to disturb was one of the chief justifications of the I.T.'s existence.

Thereafter direction passed into the hands of Dorothy Leighton, Charles Charrington and Janet Achurch. Shaw, although never directly involved in the operation of the I.T., and even scornful towards it when he sensed he had a commercial success to launch in *Candida*, did assist Dorothy Leighton by drafting a 'Short Summary of the Position and Prospects of the Independent Theatre'. He finished 'the cursed thing' on the 28 November 1895,[39] and it was emended and issued in her name in December. The result was negative, because no I.T. productions were given in 1896. Four plays were produced May-June 1897, three Ibsen revivals and Shakespeare's *Antony and Cleopatra*-- 'choice Independent fare', snorted Shaw--and there appears to have been only one further production in 1898, Brieux's *Blanchette*, after which the accounts were closed, with Shaw generously 'fork[ing] out more than £50 to wind up the Independent Theatre solvently'.[40]

The virtual collapse of the I.T. after Grein's resignation suggests that it was very much a one-man affair, yet during its busy years it did not absorb all of Grein's part-time energies. His activities included: writing articles for both the English and the Dutch press; translating plays; acting as Managing-Secretary for an Ibsen series at the *Opéra Comique* in 1893; and helping to arrange the six performances by Lugné-Poe's company given under I.T. auspices, also at the *Opéra Comique*, in March 1895. Concluding his review of these last productions, Shaw expressed 'many thanks to the Independent Theatre for its share in bringing about the visit of the Theatre de l'Oeuvre to this country. Mr. Grein could have rendered no better service to English art'.[41] In turn, Grein declared: 'if the Independent Theatre had done nothing else for the British drama than to give a hearing to George Bernard Shaw, I contend that it justified its existence and fulfilled its mission'.[42] It is possible that without Grein's encouragement, and the staging of *Widowers' Houses* by the I.T., Shaw might never have found his métier as a dramatist.

What else had the I.T. achieved? Certainly not financial success, nor an impressive membership (maximum 175), nor had it created a new school of acting, although its standard of realistic acting and ensemble playing was high. It did not unearth any great native playwright, other than Shaw whose real success was a decade away, despite the fact that half the plays produced were by British authors, nor did it turn up a significant director like its European counterparts. John Stokes suggests that this last failure was because the I.T. gave priority to the literary value of the plays selected rather than to their theatrical qualities. He recognizes that the I.T. 'had to a large extent fulfilled the purposes for which it was founded, if only by offering a viable means of sustaining minority theatre', but paradoxically, such minority theatre, designed to reform, involve, and disturb, preaches to the converted, 'aiming its powers to disrupt only at those already engaged'.[43] But by providing an outlet for new, uncommercial plays, the I.T. stimulated wide interest in and discussion of the drama, its shortcomings and its possibilities, and led to the formation of the New Century Theatre in 1897, and of the Stage Society two years later--which in turn gave birth to the Vedrenne-Barker seasons at the Royal Court from 1904 to 1907. Also, although interest in the Provinces was disappointing, a successful Manchester Independent Theatre Society was formed in 1893 by Charles Hughes, a close friend of Miss A.E.F. Horniman whom he later supported in the Gaiety Theatre repertory venture.[44] Perhaps most significantly,

> the main point about the Independent Theatre ... was not so much the ultimate quality of what it did, as the spirit in which it worked. It kept alive among a great number of people the realisation that drama was not just a commodity for sale, something solely governed by the law of supply and demand, but something worth while for its own sake, a valuable and necessary element in human society.[45]

This assertion echoes the views of contemporaries like Shaw, Granville Barker, H.A. Jones and others who acknowledged the impetus given by the I.T. to the whole movement for a revitalized British drama.

Grein himself had by no means been discouraged by the problems and disappointments of his promotional efforts, and in 1900 was President of a committee and self-styled *'Intendant'* for a German Theatre subscription season of twenty-two plays given by August Junkermann's company at St. George's Hall from January to May.[46] During this season he visited Berlin, and in a report in *The Sunday Special*, for which he had started writing in 1898, he praised the German theatre in terms that indicate his personal criteria: 'there is brilliant acting here, but no star or stars, there is realism, but no brutality; there is passion, but no bathos; there is, last but not least, the atmosphere of daily life undefiled by mannerism and affectation'.[47] London audiences, critics, actors, and producers (notably Granville Barker) were similarly impressed by the Germans, and Grein felt encouraged to follow up with a second season from October 1900 to April 1901, and then six more, ending in 1907. The success of the first two German seasons led Grein to promote a French season along the same lines in 1901, but this venture failed. It also brought Grein under fire from a former ally, William Archer, who argued that the French theatre, unlike the German, was easily accessible in Paris, and he did not want 'third-rate performances in makeshift settings'. He condemned 'the pernicious old habit of looking to France for plays ... By all means let us study the works of modern dramatists, and learn what we can from them; but let us not suffer them to come between us and our one fundamental duty of portraying and interpreting our own life in our own language'.[48] But Grein remained international in his outlook and activities, continuing to promote the interchange of plays and companies between England and Europe, notably the visit of Beerbohm Tree's company to Berlin in 1907 after which the Emperor conferred on both men the Imperial Order of the Red Eagle. That year brought further recognition to Grein in the form of a dinner attended by 400 people at the Criterion restaurant on 1 December to honour his twenty-five years as a dramatic critic.

During these early years of the century Grein was also fully occupied in his business, which frequently took him abroad, and in his duties as Consul-General for the Congo, which he had been appointed in 1897. He was also Honorary Secretary of the Association of Foreign Consuls in London, and became Consul-General for Liberia in 1909. In an article after his death, published in *The Critics' Circular*, S.R. Littlewood, then dramatic critic of *The Morning Post*, recalled Grein's role as a founder member of the Critics' Circle in 1913, and declared that 'the irrepressible and inexhaustible vitality with which [Grein] conducted half-a-dozen social and theatrical campaigns at once, together with his exacting business in Mincing Lane--and his criticism--was bewildering'.[49] Except for the German seasons, and an abortive attempt to launch a French Little Theatre in 1913, Grein's non-business energies in this period went mainly into reviewing, primarily for *The Sunday Special*, its successor *The Sunday Times*, and *The Ladies' Field*, and into organising such groups as The Playgoer's Club, The Dramatic Debaters Society, and its offspring The Sunday Club. He was also active in promoting the idea of an 'English Repertoire Theatre', but did not join in the anti-censorship campaign.

In 1913 Grein launched a theatrical monthly with Herman Klein, a music critic on *The Sunday Times*, entitled *The Independent Theatregoer* (of which only six issues appeared), and then tried unsuccessfully to revive the I.T. The following year he organized a performance of *Ghosts* at the Royal Court on 26 April on behalf of the Constitutional Society for Women's Suffrage, a cause he had long supported, performed by a company he chose and named 'The Independent Players', and directed by Leon M. Lion. This performance received such favourable press notices, in significant contrast to those of 1891, that Grein felt encouraged to give it a repeat with a Professional Matinée on 19 May, at which time he announced a Provisional Repertoire of 'J.T. Grein's Independent Matinées'. Only one of these plays was performed, Maeterlinck's *Monna Vanna*, banned since 1902, for which Grein had obtained a licence. Encouraged by this, and by a private conversation with E.A. Bendall, then Joint Examiner of Plays, who had attended *Ghosts* at the Court in an unofficial capacity, Grein applied for a licence for *Ghosts*. It was granted, and the first public performance of the play was given on 14 July 1914 by the same company at a Commemoration Matinée at the Haymarket Theatre under the patronage of the King and Queen of Norway. Orme declares:

> The wheel had come full circle and brought with it the enfranchisement of the English stage for which J.T. had worked patiently, pertinaciously, and undaunted by many setbacks since the day when he stood on the stage of the Royalty nearly a quarter of a century before the licensing of *Ghosts*, a slim, pale and nervous young man, nailing his flag to the masthead of independence.[50]

NOTES

1. H.A. Jones, *The Renascence of the English Drama* (Macmillan, London, 1895), p. 24.
2. These three articles are included in *Ibsen. The Critical Heritage*, ed. Michael Egan (Routledge & Kegan Paul, London, 1972). This volume contains a wide selection of reviews and articles on Ibsen in English 1872-1906, and a useful introduction.
3. Edmund Gosse, 'Ibsen the Norwegian Satirist', *Fortnightly Review*, vol. 63 (January 1873), p.88. See extract in Egan, p. 50.
4. William Archer, 'Henrik Ibsen's New Drama', *The Mirror of Literature*, 2 March 1878. Egan incorrectly cites Archer's review of Mrs. Lord's *Nora*, *Academy*, 6 January 1883, as his 'first published piece' on Ibsen.
5. Archer's lengthy review, *Theatre*, 1 April 1884, compares the original with this 'mangled and scarified' version. See Egan, pp. 65-72.
6. In 1893, Archer estimated that 'one hundred thousand prose dramas by Ibsen have been bought by the English-speaking public in the course of the past four years'. See Egan, p. 308.
7. *Queen*, 15 June 1889, p. 285. Extract in Egan, p. 106.
8. H. Granville Barker, *The Eighteen Eighties*, ed. Walter de la Mare (Cambridge University Press, Cambridge, 1930), p. 177.
9. Pierre Marie Augustin Filon, *The English Stage* (John Milne, London, 1897), p. 97.
10. William Archer, 'The Real Ibsen', *The International Monthly*, February 1901, pp. 185-6.
11. G.B. Shaw, *Collected Plays* (Max Reinhardt, London, 1970), vol. 1, p. 135.
12. G.B. Shaw, *Collected Letters 1874-1897*, ed. Dan H. Laurence (Max Reinhardt, London, 1965), p. 215.
13. Biography from 'Michael Orme' (Mrs. J.T. Grein), *J.T. Grein. The Story of a Pioneer 1862-1935* (John Murray, London, 1936), and from N.H.G. Schoonderwoerd, *J.T. Grein. Ambassador of the Theatre 1862-1935* (Van Gorcum, Assen, 1963). See also Anna I. Miller, *The Independent Theatre in Europe from 1887 to the Present* (1931; rpt. B. Blom, New York, 1966).

14. *The Weekly Comedy*, 12 October 1889, p. 6.
15. Ibid., 30 November 1889, pp. 6-7.
16. Ibid., Issues, 8, 9, 10.
17. George Moore, *The Hawk*, 17 June 1890, pp. 695-6. See also his *Impressions and Opinions* (D. Nutt, London, 1891), pp. 215-48.
18. Ibid., 24 June 1890, p. 726.
19. Ibid., 15 July 1890, p. 68.
20. *St. James's Gazette*, 18 July 1890, p. 5.
21. Ibid., 19 July 1890, p. 3.
22. Orme, p. 68.
23. Ibid., p. 237.
24. Ibid., p. 79.
25. Ibid., p. 86.
26. *The Hawk*, 17 March 1891, p. 292. Extract in Egan, p. 205.
27. *Era*, vol. 53 (21 March 1891), p. 10.
28. W. Davenport Adams, *Theatre*, N.S. vol. 18 (August 1891), p. 58.
29. Orme, p. 98.
30. Joseph Hone, *The Life of George Moore* (Gollancz, London, 1936), p. 170.
31. George Moore, *Ave*, vol. 1 of *'Hail and Farewell!'* (William Heinemann, London, 1914), p. 50.
32. George R. Sims ('Dagonet'), *The Referee*, 18 October 1891, p. 7.
33. Shaw, *Plays*, vol. 1, pp. 17-18.
34. Ibid., p. 38.
35. Orme, p. 112.
36. Ibid., pp. 114-15.
37. Shaw, *Letters 1874-1897*, p. 562.
38. *Theatre*, N.S. vol. 26 (December 1895), p. 371.
39. Shaw, *Letters 1874-1897*, p. 571.
40. Shaw, Letter to Poel, quoted in Robert Speaight, *William Poel and the Elizabethan Revival* (William Heinemann, London, 1954), p. 126.
41. G.B. Shaw, *Our Theatre in the Nineties* (Constable, London, 1932), vol. 1, p. 79.
42. J.T. Grein, *Stage Society News*, no. 25, p. 100.
43. John Stokes, *Resistible Theatres* (Elek Books, London, 1972), pp. 178-9.
44. The Manchester I.T. programme for *Candida*, 14 March 1898, lists the following productions: Ibsen-- *Rosmersholm*, *An Enemy of the People*, *The Master Builder*, *Hedda Gabler*, *A Doll's House*; Shakespeare-- *Love's Labour's Lost*, *Two Gentlemen of Verona*, *Richard II*; Browning-- *A Blot in the 'Scutcheon*; Moore-- *The Strike at Arlingford*; Goethe-- *Clavigo*.
45. Schoonderwoerd, p. 129.
46. See Orme, pp. 167-86, for a full account of these visits.
47. J.T. Grein, *The Sunday Special*, 1 April 1900, p. 2.

48. William Archer, *Morning Leader*, 4 June 1901, p. 4.

49. S.R. Littlewood, quoted in Orme, p. 232. Grein was second President of the Critics' Circle, 1914-15, after William Archer.

50. Orme, p. 238.

Chapter Three

ELIZABETH ROBINS, THE NEW CENTURY THEATRE AND THE STAGE SOCIETY

> 'Do you know what it is to cast a despairing eye over the whole twenty-three of London's theatres, and to find nothing--positively nothing--that you wish to see?'
>
> P.P. Howe

The production of *Hedda Gabler* in 1891 was as significant for Ibsen and the new drama as that of *Ghosts*, although less controversial, because Elizabeth Robins and Marion Lea, two American actresses in London who had staged the play in conjunction with William Heinemann, the owner of the rights, set about bringing more Ibsen to the commercial stage. Elizabeth Robins had begun her career in America, where she acted with Edwin Booth and in James O'Neill's touring company, and had settled in London almost by accident. After her performance in *Hedda Gabler* she realized that Ibsen not only brought intellectuals back to the theatre, but also 'made reputations' for performers in challenging and satisfying roles;[1] yet she 'shrank and shuddered' when she first read *Ghosts*, and even on second reading found the play 'too dreadful for words--far worse than memory painted. I could never play *Ghosts*'.[2] However, the play fascinated her, and when H.L. Braekstad offered her the role of Mrs. Alving in a production to be put on with the proceeds of a proposed Ibsen Fund, she accepted. Beerbohm Tree (who had appeared in *Breaking a Butterfly* in 1884), agreed to lend the Haymarket on condition that he could play Oswald--a sign of the times as was his triumphant production there of *An Enemy of the People* in 1893--but Miss Robins tried to persuade Fred Terry to take the part. Unwittingly, he in turn sought advice from Tree! Her 'clumsiness' and the failure of Braekstad's fund combined to abort the attempt, but did not discourage her from continuing her efforts to stage Ibsen, and in due course rendering him 'all the pious service of a priestess of the altar', as Henry James put it.[3] One of her services was to involve herself with Archer and Gosse in the task of translating *The Master Builder* as it arrived in instalments in November 1892 from the Norwegian publisher, who sent them one pull each of the text as it was printed. Once the task was finished, she set about getting it performed by first reading the play to Tree, who wanted to play the part of Solness himself, but also demanded unacceptable alterations. Finding no manager prepared to stage the play, she undertook to produce it herself at the Trafalgar Square Theatre, where it ran from 20 February to 3 March 1893 and succeeded in breaking even. Encouraged by this success, she joined J.T. Grein on a committee to organize a series of subscription performances of *Hedda Gabler, Rosmersholm, The Master Builder* and Act IV of *Brand*. After a meeting of interested parties at the home of Mrs. J.R. Green on 13 April 1893, a prospectus was issued dated 15 April inviting one-hundred five-guinea subscriptions, and naming Mrs. J.R. Green and Sir Frederick Pollock as trustees. Sufficient subcriptions were taken up, and the performances took place as planned at the *Opéra Comique* 29 May - 3 June 1893.

Elizabeth Robins had an undoubted charm which stood her in good stead in her efforts to branch out from acting into management. She became a close friend of Archer, a man of few but warm friendships, and they collaborated on several productions. The first of these was *Little Eyolf*, which was given a short series of afternoon performances at the Avenue commencing 23 November 1896, with three of London's ablest actresses in the cast: Elizabeth Robins, Janet Achurch and Mrs. Patrick Campbell. *Little Eyolf* was supported by an anonymous fund, as was her next production, the result of another close friendship--with Henry James, who, attracted by her Southern Lady grace, became her frequent escort on theatrical outings. They collaborated on naturalizing James Graham's literal translation of *Mariana*, by José Echegaray, which was performed at the Royalty 22-26 February 1897--although James's name did not appear on the programme.

The next play in which Elizabeth Robins was involved was Archer's translation of *John Gabriel Borkman*, produced at the Strand 2 May 1897, for five matinées. It 'was ushered in by a newly formed association which had developed out of the Ibsen-Echegaray (Little Eyolf-Mariana) ventures', she wrote, acknowledging that 'the work had been sustained and extended through the unstinted labours of Mr. William Archer'.[4] The association formalized the anonymous fund, and was first called The Minority, but then chose a more resounding and ambitious title: the New Century Theatre (N.C.T.). The programme named a Provisional Committee consisting of William Archer, Elizabeth Robins, H.W. Massingham, and Alfred Sutro, and announced:

> The aim of the Executive of the NEW CENTURY THEATRE is to provide a permanent machinery for the production, from time to time, of plays of intrinsic interest which find no place on the stage in the ordinary way of theatrical

> business. At the same time, they would have it clearly understood that they do not go in search of the esoteric, the eccentric or the mystic; that they are devoted to no special school or tendency; that their productions will not be exclusively "literary," in the narrow sense of the word, and still less "educational" or instructive; that they do not propose, in a word, to present the Undramatic Drama in any of its disguises. They will welcome all *acting plays* of a certain standard of intrinsic merit, which are likely to interest the intelligent public to whom they appeal.
>
> They are actuated by no spirit of antagonism towards the existing theatres. They recognise cordially the artistic spirit displayed by many of the leading Managers, from some of whom they have already received the most ungrudging assistance.

The assistance of 'leading Managers' owed much to the Robins charm. An indication of their help was the appearance of Mr. W.H. Vernon, Mr. Martin Harvey, Mrs. Beerbohm Tree (Maud Holt), and Mr. James Welch 'by kind permission of' Messrs. Geo. Alexander, Sir Henry Irving, Mr. H. Beerbohm Tree, and Mr. Geo. Edwardes respectively. According to Elizabeth Robins, the association aimed 'to pave the way for the permanent institution, artistically administered, which is essential to the development of the drama and of acting':[5] a step towards Archer's dream of an endowed National theatre. The N.C.T. took up where the Independent Theatre left off, and can be regarded as an offshoot of it, but was destined to have a far shorter career. Its second production was *Admiral Guinea* by W.E. Henley and R.L. Stevenson, and a short one-act piece, *Honesty--A Cottage Flower* by Margaret Young, which ran from 29 November to 3 December 1897 at the Avenue. Its 'Third Series of Matinées' presented *Grierson's Way* by H.V. Esmond from 7 to 13 February 1899, at the Haymarket. There appears to have been some difficulty in finding suitable plays, for on 22 January 1900 Archer, searching for a fourth N.C.T. production, wrote to Shaw: 'Why shouldn't it be one of your plays?--either "Candida" or "Captain Brassbound." ... My one condition is that Miss Robins shall have the leading part in whatever we do'.[6] Shaw was very reluctant to become involved with the N.C.T., recognizing in Archer's postscript, 'N.B. NO PHILANDERERS NEED APPLY!' that the prospects of a satisfactory partnership were slim, and nothing came of the suggestion. There appear to have been no other productions until 26 May 1904, when the N.C.T. sponsored Gilbert Murray's translation of Euripides' *Hippolytus* at the Lyric, which was directed by Granville Barker; the play became the first production of the Vedrenne-Barker management at the Royal Court that October. Between the third and fourth productions, Elizabeth Robins, whom Shaw disparaged as 'an

American George Eliot', had returned to America for a while, and had in fact given up acting for a career as a novelist (and dramatist with *Votes for Women*, Royal Court, 9 April 1907). In her memoirs, referring perhaps as much to her efforts with Ibsen as to the N.C.T., she declares:

> our business, as we saw it, was to provide a small side door of escape from the prevailing system and to prove our right to survive by virtue of continuing to be different from what we turned our back on. But this proved far too innocent a reading of the "business."[7]

With an unexplained hint of sour grapes, she goes on to record that the venture aroused heated opposition, and to claim that this arose because not only were the public and the critics unsettled by this new direction, but also the more intelligent and ambitious actors and actresses. 'So far as the N.C.T. existed at all', she continues, 'for the Powers in Possession it was privately an irritant and publicly a reproach'. Nevertheless, Elizabeth Robins made an important contribution towards the ultimate acceptance of Ibsen and the new drama on the London stage.

Despite the failure of the I.T. and the N.C.T., a third attempt was made to form a society for the production of non-commercial drama which had what Archer termed 'intrinsic merit'. On 8 July 1899, one hundred and fifty circulars proposing such a society were sent to persons interested in dramatic art, inviting them to attend a meeting on 19 July at the home of Frederick Whelen, 17, Red Lion Square. (The location was auspicious as it was once occupied by Rossetti, followed by William Morris and Burne-Jones.) Between forty and fifty persons attended, and it was agreed:

> I That this Society shall be called "The Stage Society."
>
> II That the Society shall meet on one Sunday in each month for nine months in the year; that at least six performances shall be given during the year; that the subscription shall be two guineas, and the minimum number of members two hundred, with a maximum of three hundred, and that the tickets issued shall not be transferable...
>
> Managing Committee: Charles Charrington, Laurence Irving, William Sharp, James Welch, Frederick Whelen (Chairman), John H. Watts (Hon. Treasurer), Ernest E.S. Williams (Hon. Secretary).
>
> Reading and Advising Committee: Janet Achurch, Walter Crane, Arnold Dolmetsch, C. Lewis Hind, Henry Holiday, Sydney Olivier, Mrs. Grant Richards, Mrs. G. Bernard Shaw,

Mrs. F.A. Steel, (Plus) E.O. Sachs, Hon. Technical Advisor.[8]

Although the objects of the Society were not set out, the implications were, quite clearly, that here was another expression of the growing desire for an alternative to the standard offerings of the commercial theatre, and that the Society would continue the work of the Independent Theatre and the New Century Theatre in furthering the cause of the new drama, with a distinct bias towards realism and, as the convention-defying Sunday performances indicated, social criticism. One name conspicuous by its absence from the Stage Society list is that of William Archer, who confessed to Shaw that he was 'too old and too busy to take much interest in that sort of thing,' and that the history of the New Century Theatre showed that he was 'a bad hand at coterie-theatre work'.[9] Archer was wary of politically-oriented, 'literary' drama and its advocates, and it would have been uncharacteristic of him to have become involved in a group with such obvious Fabian leanings. However, his New Century Theatre, following in the footsteps of the Independent Theatre, had helped to accustom the intelligent public to the society principle, and when the Stage Society offered such strong committees, a relatively low subscription rate, and the promise of 'at least six performances' a year, it proved a more attractive proposition than its forerunners. It was soon fully subscribed with a complement of 300 ordinary members, 22 Honorary Members and 34 Associates. On an income of £677.6.0 and expenditure of £592.8.3 it held eight 'Meetings' in its First Season and produced eight plays, including one triple bill, by Shaw, Sydney Olivier, Ibsen, 'Fiona MacLeod' (William Sharp), Maeterlinck, and Hauptmann. (See Appendix C for full list of plays.) It achieved this impressive start on a limited budget because stages and private houses had been lent free of charge for rehearsals, no theatre rents had been charged for the performances, the producers had been paid a mere ten pounds fee and the performers 'expenses' of one guinea, and its affairs had been pursued with enthusiasm by a dedicated committee.

The Society knew that it was treading on dangerous ground with its proposed Sunday performances, so wishing to play as safe as possible with its first production, Shaw's *You Never Can Tell*, it sought a hall or picture gallery rather than a theatre, but none large enough could be found. The lessee of the Royalty, Miss Kate Santley, was approached, and she agreed to defy convention. On the evening of the performance, 26 November 1899, as feared, 'representatives of the police arrived to question the legality of even a private performance in a theatre on a Sunday, and were adroitly involved in a long argument by Mr. Whelen and others until the play was safely over'.[10] No legal or other action was taken against the Society or the Royalty. Subsequent productions were accepted by other theatres on Sundays, and appear to have been performed unmolested. To avoid clashes with the Law or Sunday Observance societies, it was agreed that there should be no publicity and no reports in the Press, even by members who were also critics, but this rule was later relaxed 'in the interests of the cast', and the Press was invited officially. The Third Annual Report of the Society points out that

> for so unusual an arrangement as production on Sunday evening, great care had to be taken to secure the consent of all persons concerned, which meant, in certain cases, not only that of the Stage Manager and Lessee, but also of the Refreshment Contractor, the Superior Landlord or landlords and the Lessee's Solicitor.

The most extended struggle to find a theatre occurred when the Society proposed staging *Mrs. Warren's Profession*. The Strand had been engaged for early December 1901, but permission was withdrawn after the issue of notice to Members when the Manager, Mr. Frank Curzon, learnt that the play had been refused a licence.

> Twelve theatres, in addition to those previously approached without success, two Music Halls, three Hotels and two Picture Galleries were then approached in succession ... At last an arrangement was made with the Manager of a Picture Gallery ... Tickets and programmes and a circular to Members were printed and ready within twenty-four hours. Suddenly, just before their issue to Members, the Management of the Gallery vetoed the use of the room on Sunday evenings.
>
> (Third Annual Report)

The Society then booked a hotel banqueting hall, but the Manager soon 'discovered' that he had made an error: the premises had already been booked. Attempts to find a location on a Sunday were then abandoned, a picture gallery engaged for three weekday matinées, and details of tickets and programmes sent off to the printers. 'The next day', continues the Report, 'a leading member of the cast [Madge McIntosh, playing Vivie] wired her inability to perform on the dates arranged, owing to sudden summons for rehearsal elsewhere'. The performance was postponed until finally a small stage was secured at the New Lyric Club, Coventry Street, for two afternoon performances, 5-6 January 1902. The Report pays tribute to the members of the cast, declaring that 'no difficulty could daunt them', and, inevitably, concludes by recommending that Sunday evening performances be abandoned.

The tribute to the cast of *Mrs. Warren's Profession* contains the key to the Society's success. The very first

Annual Report states: 'it has been a genuine "Stage" Society, which owes its first successful year's work, mainly to the co-operation of Members of the stage profession'. The Foreword to the *Souvenir Volume of Fifty Stage Society Programmes 1899-1909* confirms this promising beginning:

> the work of the Stage Society during the past ten years has been a "labour of love" practically to every one who has been connected with its activities. Personal enthusiasm and ungrudging service have laid its present firm foundations ... Throughout its career it has been assisted by much honorary and voluntary work. These honorary activities have not been confined to those few enthusiasts who initiated and directed its fortunes in its earliest years. Hardheaded theatrical managers have given the use of their theatres; prominent actors and actresses whose reputation was already firmly established have willingly given their services. Indeed, throughout the ten years of its existence the Stage Society has been able to rely on practical help and personal service from all branches of the theatrical profession.

In a letter to William Archer, Shaw contended that just as he had been forced to

> fall back on the Stage Society along with Barker & Brieux & all the rest of the author geniuses so it has come to be recognized in the Profession that the serious actor's only chance lies on the same distinguished boards ... the half-amateurs are at the West End theatres walking through the smart plays, whilst the skilled temperamental professionals are playing for the Stage Society, ostensibly for honor & glory alone, but in some cases, I am greatly afraid, because the two guineas "expenses" are not a matter of indifference to them.[11]

Despite Shaw's fears, it is most unlikely that actors were attracted for the sake of the remuneration alone, for, as Lewis Casson explains, even in the Society's 'most prosperous days each production had a Sunday night and matinée on the Monday and Tuesday following, so three guineas was the utmost the actor got for three weeks' rehearsals and three performances'.[12] The actor Aubrey Smith, a convert to the ideals of the Society after he had performed in its production of *The New Idol* by François de Curel (16-17 March 1902), and its Secretary in 1903, declared: 'the fact remains that actors and actresses will sacrifice something for the sake of their success. Their inborn love of acting and artistic sense finds satisfaction in interpreting a play that has real acting value although commercially worthless'.[13] Beerbohm Tree recognized the useful service the Society provided to the profession by 'giving employment to actors and actresses who otherwise would have suffered owing to long runs', and he acknowledged that many players had 'emerged from this Society having won their spurs under its influence and having gained the experience which is so necessary to every artist'.[14] No doubt serious actors also recognized the possibility of bringing about a long overdue revitalization of the art they served through the Society's policy of discovering new playwrights and of producing plays that had 'obvious power and merit' but were unmarketable on the commercial stage or had been censored off it.

Benefiting most from the Society's productions (aside from the Members, who received excellent value for their two guineas), were dramatists of the 'great unacted' variety. Chief among these, although not quite 'unacted', was Shaw, whose career as a dramatist received vital assistance from the Society, and as a later Chairman, Clifford Bax, wrote, 'it is to the lasting credit of the Society's first members that they created a theatre for our most eminent playwright'.[15] Despite the limited number of performances, Shaw valued the Society productions of his work because they received 'the same ceremonies of first-night celebration, press notices, and--what is far more important--the same experience of the stage gained by the author at rehearsals as if they had been built by Mr. Pinero, Mr. Jones or Mr. Cecil Raleigh to run a thousand nights'.[16] Other native dramatists who profited from this experience included Gilbert Murray, St. John Hankin, Somerset Maugham, Charles McEvoy, Arnold Bennett and Granville Barker--who also received his first chance as producer with the Society. Yeats, whose *Where There is Nothing* was produced by the Society in 1904, recognized that his plays would receive 'very considerable advertisement' from production by the Society,[17] which could lead, as it had with Shaw, Gilbert Murray and Somerset Maugham, to a commercial run.

The Society prided itself on being complementary rather than opposed to the commercial theatre, and the first seasons fully justified the hopes and aims of the founders by offering programmes of varied interest chosen mainly on the principle that whether native or foreign, licensed or unlicensed, the plays were unlikely to be risked on the commercial stage. Clifford Bax doubted whether 'the enthusiastic founders' of the Society

> were inspired by a passion for fine drama. I suspect that they were eager to assist at the obsequies of Victorianism; that they wanted socialistic or feministic propaganda quite as much as they wanted beautiful or thoughtful plays; and that they marched forth to a theatre on a Sunday evening with a combative delight in outraging the canons of their age.[18]

There is a good deal of truth in this statement, and part of the hostility of the drama critics can be related to their dislike of the audience of London intelligentsia, who had about them, as the *Weekly Despatch* once put it, 'a suggestion of long hair, willowy, uncorseted females, and supercilious superiority'.[19] Despite this antagonism, the critics accorded the Society's productions full-length reviews, which appeared not only in the London newspapers and journals, but also in a large number of provincial and even overseas outlets, including Birmingham, Brighton, Manchester, Sheffield, Glasgow, Edinburgh, Calcutta, Capetown and New York. Far from damaging the Society, the adverse Press provided invaluable publicity, and ensured the support of all progressives who rebelled against Victorian social, cultural and artistic conventions. The response to *Mrs. Warren's Profession*, doubly damned because it was unlicensed, is illuminating. The *Daily Telegraph*, noting that 'the author himself rightly described the [play] as "unpleasant"', dismissed it in six lines, concluding that 'no further comment is called for'. Other critics were almost unanimous in praising the acting, vilifying the play--'nauseating and unsavoury', 'hopelessly bad', 'dramatically worthless', 'unnecessary and painful'--and condemning the Society, 'a friend of dramatic derelicts' as the *Daily Mail* put it. An extract from the *St. James's Gazette* exemplifies these attitudes:

> Shaw's curtain speech congratulated the cast for their interpretation and overcoming of obstacles. But this was doubtless Mr. Shaw's humour. Had he been serious (and had he not been the author of the play) he might more fitly have condoled with the Society on having found a committee who recklessly sacrificed the convenience of members in order to carry through a performance which was very generally regretted and on having found a cast who were willing to expend really admirable acting on this dingy drama ... The excellent acting secured toleration for the performance, but it is to be hoped that the Stage Society, which has been responsible for several interesting and valuable productions in the two years of its existence, intends to eschew dramatic garbage in future. (7 January 1902)

The play that followed, Granville Barker's *The Marrying of Ann Leete* (26 January), brought a similar reaction from the critics, who found it 'puzzling', 'obscure', 'a barrage of pretentious stupidity', and, most damning of all, 'clever'. On the other hand, the *Daily News* recognized it as 'one of those productions by which the Stage Society justifies its existence'. The *Star* agreed, but the *Topical Times* labelled it 'a dramatic abortion', and warned that if the committee 'desire to kill the society stone dead, they have only to produce a few more pieces after *The Marrying of Ann Leete*'. The two native plays were followed with three imports by Curel, Ibsen and Maeterlinck, all attacked by most of the critics.

This third season was one of crisis for the Society. That its first two years had not been all 'sweetness and light' is indicated by Shaw's correspondence with Charles Charrington (15 and 17 November 1900) concerning problems of casting for *Captain Brassbound's Conversion*, and a subsequent letter to Gilbert Murray (15 March 1901) warning of 'certain wars and rumors of wars at the Stage Society', and indicating a personality clash between Charrington and Frederick Whelen.[20] The third season showed a decline in membership from 459 in 1901 to 412 in 1902, which went some way towards justifying the critics' warnings by suggesting a dissatisfaction among members that was also voiced at the annual meetings at the end of the second and third seasons. The decline was followed by a new threat to the Society's existence when it found itself unable to book a theatre for its fourth season. At the Third Annual Meeting in October 1902, the Chairman, Frederick Whelen, came under attack for lack of economy, but he made a spirited defence, declaring that he had done his best in the face of enormous difficulties. Some of these were later listed in the Fifth Annual Report:

> (1) postponements, (2) changes of theatre, (3) absence of any available theatre, (4) rehearsal anywhere except on the stage finally used, (5) no dress rehearsal, (6) dress rehearsal in one theatre, the first performance in another theatre, (7) the evening performance on one stage, the matinée performance on another (possibly larger or smaller) stage, with the consequent expense in cutting or enlarging the scenery; and other irksome inconveniences.

However, at the height of the crisis between the third and fourth seasons the *Atheneaum* was not alone in declaring that it 'would hear of [the Society's] extinction with regret': an encouraging indication of the position it had achieved in its relatively short life. The immediate problem was resolved when the Imperial was secured for the Fourth Season, which finally opened with Ibsen's *When We Dead Awaken* on 25 January 1903.

There was now a notable shift in the tone of Press criticism. Many critics still condemned individual plays, generally on such grounds as 'inspissated gloom', but they invariably praised the quality of production, especially the acting, and respected the courage, enterprise and usefulness of the Society. For example, although most critics condemned the Ibsen play, there were several who agreed with the *Speaker* that it would be 'difficult to overestimate the excellent work which this society has achieved for the cause of dramatic art in London during its three years of existence' (31 January 1903).

The second production of the season, Maugham's *A Man of Honour* (22 February) collected its share of abuse, and the *Athenaeum* deemed it 'exactly the kind of play to comfort the members of the Stage Society ... It is painful, pessimistic, squalid and, so to speak, morose'. Although many critics agreed, and found Maugham's irony 'sordid and ugly', the play was applauded as 'coherent', in contrast to some of the earlier productions, and 'clever' (again that ambiguous epithet), and the following February the play, slightly revised, launched Maugham's career as a commercial dramatist with a successful run at the Avenue. The critics took kindlier to St. John Hankin, whose *The Two Mr. Wetherbys* (15 March 1903) followed, being pleased to discover that the Society could introduce 'a brilliant light comedy by an English writer, hitherto quite unknown to the stage', although he was known as a writer of 'Mr. Punch's Dramatic Sequels'. With Maugham's play scorned for its 'dismal nature' it is not hard to guess the reaction to Gorki's *The Lower Depths,* which opened the Fifth Season. It was 'not a play' of course, rather a 'four act sketch' made up of 'heterogeneous episodes', and even Max Beerbohm wondered 'why the committee of the Stage Society had anything to do with it?'—but the generally hostile *Daily Telegraph* had to admit that the play had 'a curious exotic interest of its own', and did provide 'some powerful dramatic moments'. Later that season, the Society gained much credit for staging Browning's *A Soul's Tragedy* (13 March 1904), which had lain unacted for sixty years. It was an 'interesting' and 'commendable' effort, but the play failed as drama, being, perhaps, unactable because never really intended for stage performance.

In the middle of the Fifth Season, on 28 April 1904, a Special Meeting of the Society was held to approve Incorporation, which became official on 19 July. The membership limit of 300 had been abandoned after the first season, and except for the small drop in the third year, had risen steadily. By the Sixth Annual Report there was a total membership of 1,194, including the first and only Life Members, Mr. and Mrs. G.B. Shaw (at twenty guineas apiece). The change to Incorporation was necessitated by the growth of the Society and consequent increased complexity of its affairs. Incorporation enhanced its status, increased the size of the Council of Management, and provided an opportunity for redefining its objects as follows:

> to promote and encourage Dramatic Art; to serve as an Experimental Theatre; to provide such an organization as shall be capable of dealing with any opportunities that may present themselves or be created, for the permanent establishment in London of a Repertory Theatre; and to establish and undertake the management and control of such a theatre.
>
> (Clause 3, Memorandum of Association)

The new Council included J.M. Barrie, St. John Hankin, Gilbert Murray and A.E. Drinkwater (Secretary). The need for a 'home' had been recognized earlier, in December 1903, when the Society

> convened a Conference for the purpose of considering whether, by joint action among the many Clubs and Societies in London interested in occasional productions of plays, a sufficient sum could be raised either to lease or build a theatre, Hall or Club, or to combine in some movement for that purpose.
>
> (Third Annual Report)

A committee was formed to investigate the matter, and to approach similar organizations, but it found no suitable building obtainable, and little enthusiasm outside the Stage Society ranks. Nevertheless, the need remained, and the new articles provided for a Capital Fund into which all entrance fees, seasons' profits, and donations or bequests would be placed for the purpose of 'leasing or erection and the equipment of a theatre for the use of the Society'. In 1907 a committee was authorized 'to prepare a scheme for the provision of a small theatre for the use of the Society and kindred bodies', but its efforts came to naught.

After Incorporation, the Society opened its Sixth Season boldly on 19 December 1904 with Tolstoy's *The Power of Darkness*. According to the *Referee*, the Society 'went one worse than ever it had done before', and the *Times* was shocked by the play's 'hideous medley of swinish drunkenness and satyr-like lust and fiendish crime' (21 December 1904). Max Beerbohm put such hysterical criticism in its place by praising the moral and artistic qualities of the play, and declaring:

> we have no excuse for being disgusted with it. If we were disgusted during the course of the play, our sense of art has been imperfectly developed; for no art could be finer than Tolstoi's in the presentment of human character ... The Stage Society need not feel at all ashamed of having produced the play. Not they, but the angry critics, should be blushing.
>
> (*Saturday Review*, 31 December 1904)

Occasional outbursts of condemnation continued to greet the Society's productions, but the shift in tone noted earlier became more marked as critics followed the leaders of their profession, such as Max Beerbohm, William Archer and Desmond MacCarthy, whose cumulative opinion, combined with the growing prestige of the Society, ensured that most productions were evaluated objectively. Most critics would have concurred with Hamilton Fyfe, who opened his review of Brieux's *Maternité*

(8 April 1906) by stating that 'the theatre of ideas has come to stay'. However, the general acceptance of a 'strong dramatic dish' like *Maternité* did not prevent indigestion over the 'intense realism' of Hauptmann's *The Weavers* (9 December 1906), which opened the Eighth Season. The Daily Telegraph found it 'a singularly aimless and inconsequential piece of work', and the *Daily Graphic* considered it 'formless, incoherent, reiterative, undramatic and most unpleasant'. For once, the acting and production were not generally praised, and the Society does appear to have overreached itself in staging a play demanding over forty parts and five different locations. Nevertheless, the tone of respect is apparent: the *Times*, for example, considered that the Society had 'done their duty' in staging a significant play by an established continental dramatist (14 December 1906). It was generally recognized that had the Society not existed, or had it lacked courage, Londoners would have been virtually unaware of the contemporary European drama, and perhaps one of its most important functions was to fulfill the 'duty' in that respect which it had taken upon itself.

The years 1904-07 saw the arrival on the commercial stage of the new drama at the Royal Court Theatre under the Vedrenne-Barker management. Barker himself proudly acknowledged his debt to the Stage Society (see Chapter Four). Prior to the first Court production in 1904, he had acted in several Society productions and had directed six, including his own *The Marrying of Ann Leete*. The Society had also presented five Shaw plays, two of which he had directed, through which he gained invaluable rehearsal experience that for the dramatist, he declared, is 'a part of his apprenticeship that is worth a good deal of solid gold to him'.[21] The Society, therefore, had contributed directly to the success of the Court venture by giving Barker and Shaw crucial preparatory experience. Furthermore, the impact of the Society's productions was far wider than exposure to its membership alone, because they received substantial controversial reviews from the drama critics, who, as Desmond MacCarthy points out, had a 'strong indirect influence' on the taste of the public--particularly on that section which was dissatisfied with the current theatrical fare.[22] And it was that section that provided the bulk of the Court's audience.

But the pioneering work of the Society, although beginning to bear fruit, was by no means finished. Mr. Whelen reported to the Fifth Annual Dinner in March 1907 that in its early years the Society had experienced difficulty in finding suitable plays, but 'we have today more plays which are suitable for production than we can produce, and we feel that this fact is some justification for our existence'. In particular, the Society was becoming increasingly concerned over the censorship question, and took pride

> in the production of plays for which the Censor has

> refused a licence. These include works by Maeterlinck, Brieux, Bernard Shaw, and Granville Barker. The Stage Society, in fact, is an Experimental Theatre unhampered by the crippling influence of the Censor, and in nothing has its work been more justified than by the hearing it has given to these plays of dramatic force and high morality.
>
> ("Foreword" to *Souvenir Volume)*

There was some justification for critics who suspected that the Censor's ban made a play an almost automatic choice for the Society, but it was equally true that the production of a banned piece ensured condemnation by these same critics, regardless of its dramatic qualities. The refusal of a licence for Granville Barker's *Waste,* which he had planned to produce at the Royal Court, gained it considerable notoriety before the Society's production on 24 November 1907 because of the protests that were made. Many critics agreed with the *Times* reviewer (27 November) who found *Waste* 'a work of extraordinary power', but had 'no hesitation in approving the Censor's decision' because he regarded the political subject-matter as 'wholly unfit for performance under ordinary conditions'. A few like Archer in *Tribune* found it 'a great play' and deplored 'the waste of *Waste'*, but more felt it too long, undramatic, 'wearisome and discursive', and, inevitably, 'too clever by half'. Nevertheless, the play received substantial notices (thirty-six column inches in the *Times* and thirty-two in the *Telegraph),* showing up the illogicality of English morality by demonstrating how the Press could freely discuss matters censored off the stage. Another *cause célèbre* arose six months later when the Censor turned down Edward Garnett's *The Breaking Point*. Produced by the Society on 5 April 1908, it turned out to be 'harmless', although 'unpleasant' or 'disagreeable' to many critics, few of whom praised it. This time the futility of the Censor had been demonstrated in his banning of an innocuous piece. In an interview published 24 April 1909 in the *Daily Telegraph* on the occasion of the Society's tenth jubilee, Frederick Whelen referred to the seven unlicensed plays produced by the Society up to that time: 'to have refused these', he observed, 'and passed "The Giddy Goat" and "Spring Chicken" is a curious satire on public taste'. In staging Shaw's deliberate challenge to the Censor, *The Shewing-up of Blanco Posnet,* on 5 December 1909, less than a month after the ineffectual Select Committee Report on Censorship (see Chapter Six), the Society again demonstrated the absurdity of the censorship: very few critics found grounds, other than lack of taste in certain passages, to support the ban, and even the *Daily Telegraph* deemed the play 'agreeable entertainment'. Despite the half-hearted and unimplemented recommendations of the Committee, the Censor did prove more flexible and open-minded in the following years preceding the outbreak of war, and up to its fifteenth season the Society produced only one more unlicensed play, Ludwig Thoma's *Champions of Morality* (22 May 1910).

In introducing the interview quoted above, the *Daily Telegraph* declared: 'unquestionably the Stage Society has done much to foster and advance the interests of the drama. It is also entitled to the full measure of credit belonging to a pioneer in a good cause'. Mr. Whelen noted that the Society had started with *You Never Can Tell* and was giving *What the Public Wants*, by Arnold Bennett, for its jubilee performance: 'the collocation of titles has rather a pretty significance, don't you think?--as though to suggest that, beginning in vagueness, we end in certainty'. *What the Public Wants* (2 May 1909) was not what some critics wanted, and they expressed similar views to the *Evening Standard,* inveterately hostile to the productions of the Society, which found it 'exceedingly clever' but 'not a play'. The majority of critics felt the title justified, and joined the *Times* in welcoming the fact that Mr. Bennett had turned from 'pottering over the Potteries to revealing the secrets of contemporary journalism' (4 May 1909). (This did not prevent the *Staffordshire Sentinel* from devoting forty-eight column inches to quotations from the leading reviews.) The productions for the following five seasons, which Clifford Bax called 'the Halcyon Years' of the Society, show that it continued to offer its members a catholic choice of significant plays, several of whose authors, then unknown in England, are now acknowledged masters of the modern drama. The list includes (in order of production) Yeats and Lady Gregory, John Masefield, Chekhov, Strindberg, Jacinto Benavente, Stanley Houghton, George Moore and Arthur Schnitzler. Adverse criticism continued to appear in the Press, and membership, after reaching a pre-war peak of 1,571 in the Twelfth Season, dropped off slightly, but in only one season, the thirteenth, did the Society show a deficit when the income was £1,694.13.9 and the expenditure £1,779.16.7.

An important result of the success and growing reputation of the Stage Society was the stimulation of other groups with similar aims. These included: the Mermaid Society (1903); the New Stage Club (*ca* 1905); The Pioneers (1905), re-organized as the Pioneer Players in 1911; the English Drama Society (1905); the Literary Theatre Club (1906); the Play Actors Society (1907), for the production of plays 'to benefit the position of the working actor and actress'; the Oncomers Society (1911); the New Players Society (1911); the Drama Society (1911); the Adelphi Play Society (1912); the Religious Drama Society (1913), under the auspices of the West London Ethical Society with William Poel as President and Director; and the People's Theatre Society (1914). These London societies are evidence of what Allardyce Nicoll terms a 'compulsive drive' to establish theatre groups, amateur, professional or semi-professional, all over the country.[23] Examples in the Provinces include: Barry

Jackson's Pilgrim Players (1904), the foundation of the Birmingham Repertory Theatre (1912); the Irish Literary Theatre (1899), which merged into the Irish National Theatre Society (1902), and established itself as the Abbey Theatre Company (1904); the Manchester Playgoer's Society (1906) on which Miss Horniman and Ben Iden Payne built the Manchester Repertory Company at the Gaiety Theatre (1907), drawing much support from the nearby Stockport Garrick Society (1901); the Scottish Playgoers' Company (1909), later called the Scottish Repertory Theatre; and the Liverpool Playgoers' Society which gave birth to the Liverpool Repertory Theatre (1911). Also, 1911-1912 saw the foundation of the Stage Society of New York on the English model.

In the commercial theatre, just as the 1904-07 Vedrenne-Barker seasons at the Court were indebted to the Stage Society, so was Charles Frohman's repertory venture at the Duke of York's. In his announcement in the *Times* (22 April 1909, p. 10), he acknowledged the 'gallant enterprise' at the Court, and recognized that there was now a 'public, who wish to delight in the drama as art, and who would become eager playgoers if they were offered less fitfully the dramatic fare they want'. The audience he aimed to attract, his willingness to consider 'unconventional plays', his promise of 'stars' but no 'starring', and the plays, directors and actors he chose, all indicate that the Society's influence was beginning to permeate the commercial theatre. On the same page of the *Times*, Herbert Trench also announced plans for a semi-repertory theatre in which he proposed two portions: a 'repertory half' offering the 'play of ideas', and a 'long run' half. Trench aimed at a 'wide variety' that would appeal to all tastes, but nothing came of his proposal. Frohman, on the other hand, presented 128 performances of 10 plays in a 17 week season that began on 21 February 1910 with Galsworthy's *Justice*.

Frohman's season failed to turn a profit, and was not repeated, but the repertory principle, so closely allied to the type of drama not being offered by regular theatres committed to the long run, was being kept in the public eye by the Stage Society and its emulators, and was gaining ground. Therefore, on 9 December 1911 the Stage Society took the lead in holding at its office 'a representative Conference of persons actively interested in the Repertory Theatre movement'. It was chaired by Frederick Whelen, who had been impressed by the activities of the American Drama League, and was attended by Miss A.E.F. Horniman, Mr. Alfred Wareing and Mr. Basil Dean, for the Manchester, Glasgow and Liverpool Repertory theatres respectively, and by Janet Achurch, Shaw, Granville Barker, W.S. Kennedy, William Archer and A.E. Drinkwater. Subsequently, a conference was held in Manchester in May 1912, and a British Playgoers' Federation was founded 'as a kind of Dramatic "Clearing House" and organizing centre'; it would hold an Annual Conference and ensure 'co-operation in the encouragement and development of dramatic art'. The impetus continued beyond the war, and although 'the teeming bevy of play producing societies' that Nicoll notes in the first three decades of the century may have owed their origins to individuals and forces remote from the London scene, much credit must go to the Stage Society for the example, initiative and leadership it provided in the first half of that period.

The precise influence of the Stage Society during these formative years of the new century is a matter of speculation. As indicated above, it certainly opened the way for the Vedrenne-Barker seasons at the Court, and it is reasonable to postulate that without the encouragement given to Shaw and Barker by the Society, those seasons might never have come about: in which case, the development of modern drama in England would have been a vastly different story. In accordance with its declared or implicit aims, the Society had introduced London audiences to the work of leading modern continental dramatists; had given an invaluable start or boost to the dramatic careers of many British authors--particularly Shaw--who otherwise might well have found their dramatic talents stifled at birth; had given authors, directors and performers opportunities unavailable on the commercial stage; had provided a testing and training for experimental and innovative work; had gained public attention for, and a degree of acceptance of, the new drama by mounting controversial pieces, both licensed and censored; had contributed both directly and indirectly to the spread of the Repertory Theatre movement; and had assisted (in true Fabian manner) through its close interrelationship with the professional theatre in the evolution of the modern out of the Victorian theatre.

POSTSCRIPT

The Society continued its work during the war, and despite inner frictions and recurrent financial problems (notably in 1922 when it nearly collapsed), it survived intermittantly through the 'twenties and 'thirties, but without any of its earlier impact or influence. It amalgamated with the Three Hundred Club in 1926, but a crisis occurred in 1930 when a motion to wind up the Society was supported by Shaw, C.K. Munroe and other authors: the motion was defeated. By then the Society had perhaps fulfilled its function of providing an outlet for new, experimental and non-commercial or censored drama (although censorship continued until 1968 it was much less inhibiting). By the late 'thirties, dissolution of the Society was inevitable: the commercial theatre had come to accept the (no longer) new drama as staple fare; there were many small theatres prepared to experiment; the days of the censor appeared numbered; and the dawn of a National Theatre was on the horizon. The last production of the Society was Strindberg's *Easter* on 24 February 1940. Formal winding-up took place in 1948, closing a small but highly significant chapter in the history of English theatre.

NOTES

1. Elizabeth Robins, *Theatre and Friendship. Some Henry James Letters* (William Heinemann, London, 1932), p. 30. She also premièred *Hedda Gabler* in New York, 30 March 1898, at the Fifth Avenue Theatre.

2. Elizabeth Robins, *Both Sides of the Curtain* (William Heinemann, London, 1940), p. 258.

3. Henry James, *The Scenic Art. Notes on Acting and the Drama 1872-1901*, ed. Allan Wade (Rupert Hart Davis, London, 1949), p. 289.

4. Robins, *Theatre*, p. 191.

5. Ibid., p. 200.

6. Quoted in *Bernard Shaw Collected Letters 1898-1910*, ed. Dan H. Laurence (Max Reinhardt, London, 1972), p. 136.

7. Robins, *Theatre*, p. 201.

8. Circular and Annual Reports from which information is derived are in the Enthoven Collection, Victoria & Albert Museum. Although it is frequently mentioned by theatre historians, the only account of the Stage Society is a short summary in Anna Miller, *The Independent Theatre in Europe 1887 to the Present* (1931; rpt. B. Blom, New York, 1966), pp. 176-86.

9. Quoted in *Shaw Letters 1898-1910*, p. 140.

10. Allan Wade, 'Shaw and the Stage Society', *Drama*, N.S. vol. 20 (Spring 1951), p. 23.

11. Shaw, *Letters 1898-1910*, p. 364.

12. Lewis Casson, 'G.B.S. and the Court Theatre', *Listener*, 12 July 1951, p. 53.

13. *Tatler*, vol. 97 (6 May 1903), p. 220.

14. Reported in *The Stage*, 14 March 1907.

15. Clifford Bax, 'The Stage Society's Diamond Jubilee', *Drama*, N.S. vol. 54 (Autumn 1959), p. 30.

16. G.B. Shaw, 'How to Make Plays Readable', *Shaw on Theatre*, ed. E.J. West (MacGibbon and Kee, New York, 1958), p. 91.

17. W.B. Yeats, *The Letters of W.B. Yeats*, ed. Allan Wade (Macmillan, London, 1954), p. 383.

18. Clifford Bax, *London Mercury*, November 1929, pp. 40-1.

19. Newspaper quotations extracted from the Stage Society collection of press cuttings obtained through the assistance of the Enthoven staff. Unfortunately, most cuttings are undated, but it can be assumed that they appeared immediately after the performances.

20. Shaw, *Letters 1898-1910*, pp. 199, 200, 220-3.

21. Ibid., p. 455. This remark to H.G. Wells is one of many made by Shaw on the value to the dramatist of practical

experience in the theatre (see also note 11 above).

22. Desmond MacCarthy, *The Court Theatre 1904-1907. A Commentary and a Criticism,* ed. Stanley Weintraub (University of Miami Press, Coral Gables, Florida, 1966), pp. 3-7.

23. Allardyce Nicoll, *English Drama 1900-1930. The Beginnings of the Modern Theatre* (Cambridge University Press, Cambridge, 1973), pp. 48-93.

Chapter Four

HARLEY GRANVILLE BARKER: ASSOCIATIONS AND ACHIEVEMENTS, 1900-1914

'All art constantly aspires to the condition of music.'

Walter Pater

A reference to Shaw, at any stage of his long career, conjures an image of the bearded sage, the quizzically wrinkled Ancient mocking or lambasting the follies of men. With Harley Granville Barker the reverse applies: the picture is of the younger Barker, a clean, scrubbed appearance, with the visionary gleam in his eyes sometimes intense, sometimes dreamily introspective. This is the image that fits him at his greatest, for although he continued to write and lecture on the theatre in later life, and produced his important *Prefaces to Shakespeare* (1927-47), his most vital contribution to the living theatre was made before his thirty-fifth year.

Granville Barker was introduced to the stage at an early age by his mother, Mary Elisabeth Bozzi-Granville, the granddaughter of an Italian physician, who earned a modest living as a reciter and bird mimic, taking her son with her on her tours which were managed by her architect-cum-estate-agent husband, Albert James Barker.[1] Perhaps this ancestry accounts for the duality of Barker, 'an odd compound of cold southern passion and precision and northern principle and drive'.[2] The young Harley began by reciting popular poems and passages from Shakespeare. His first recorded public appearance in a play was at Harrogate, when at the age of thirteen he played Dr. Grimstone in Edward Rose's adaptation of Anstey's *Vice Versa; A Lesson to Fathers*. In 1891 he entered Sarah Thorne's theatrical school at Margate, staying only a few months, but continuing to act on her tours and in those of other companies. His London debut was in the burlesque *The Poet and the Puppets* by Charles Brookfield, ironically to become an object of Barker's scorn when appointed Joint Examiner of Plays in 1911. He continued to play in touring companies, including those of A.B. Tapping and Lewis Waller, and in 1895 joined Ben Greet's Shakespeare and Old English Comedy Company. 1899 was a significant year for him: acting in *Carlyon Sahib* led to a lifelong friendship with the author, Gilbert Murray, and his performance as Richard in William Poel's production of *Richard II* in November not only introduced another important influence into his life but gave him wide recognition as a promising actor. 1899 was also significant in that it saw the production of *The Weather-hen* at Terry's Theatre on 29 June, a comedy he wrote in collaboration with Berte Thomas, a friend from his days at Sarah Thorne's. Their first effort, 'The Family of the Oldroyds', written in 1895-96, has been neither performed nor published; the same fate met their third play, 'Our Visitor to "Work-a-Day"' (1898-99). 1899 also saw the formation of the Stage Society, although Barker did not become a member until after he had played Erik Bratsberg in its production of Ibsen's *The League of Youth* on 25 February 1900. The Society introduced him into a circle of enthusiasts for theatrical reform and gave him his first opportunity as producer when it invited him to direct three short plays for its fourth 'meeting' on 29 April 1900: *The House of Usna,* by Fiona MacLeod (William Sharp), and *Interior* and *Death of Tintagiles* by Maeterlinck. The Society's production of *Candida,* 1 July 1900, in which Barker played Eugene--a role ideally suited to his nature--brought him within the orbit of George Bernard Shaw, and it was the Society that staged *The Marrying of Ann Leete,* 26-27 January 1902, the first play written entirely on his own.

Granville Barker, therefore, is no overnight phenomenon. His early career, although only briefly sketched here, evinces an almost planned, poetic inevitability. Likewise, the historic Vedrenne-Barker management at the Royal Court theatre from 1904 to 1907 emerged out of a set of favourable circumstances, as Barker himself declared at a testimonial dinner to the partners held at the Criterion restaurant on 7 July 1907:

> as far as the artistic part of it goes, we must never forget that we are standing on the shoulders of other men. Our work is but a continuation of that begun by Mr. Grein and the Independent Theatre, and by that body to which I am always inclined to refer as my father and mother called the Stage Society.[3]

The stage had been well set, and as Desmond MacCarthy observed:

> when in 1904 the Court theatre started under new management, the enterprise this time did not wear the truculent, propagandist aspect of the Independent Theatre; Ibsen was no longer a bugbear, though he was far from being a draw; [and] the plays of Mr. Shaw had been widely read, and there was considerable curiosity to see them.[4]

By early 1904, Barker had several productions to his credit, and enjoyed a growing reputation. William Archer recommended him to John H. Leigh, a wealthy amateur actor and proprietor of the Royal Court Theatre, who was in search of a director. The theatre, familiarly known as the Court, lent itself to experiment--and still does---because it is outside the main West-End area, which makes it cheaper to operate, but is easily accessible, being next to the Sloane Square underground station.[5] Leigh invited Barker to assist him and his Manager, J.E. Vedrenne, with a production of *Two Gentlemen of Verona*, one of a series of 'Shakespeare Representations' he had begun with *The Tempest* in October the previous year. Barker agreed, on condition that he could present six matinée performances of *Candida*. The Shakespeare opened on 8 April 1904, with Barker directing and playing Speed, and the Shaw matinées were duly given between 26 April and 10 May. Both productions were well supported and well reviewed, and the £160 Mrs. Shaw had guaranteed to underwrite *Candida*-- unknown, of course, to Shaw--were not needed. Encouraged by the success of their association, Leigh, Vedrenne and Barker decided to mount Gilbert Murray's translation of Euripides' *Hippolytus* after the New Century Theatre had staged it under Barker's direction. With £60 put up by Leigh, and £200 each from Vedrenne, Barker and Murray, six matinées were presented commencing 18 October 1904. In November came a six-matinée run of Shaw's *John Bull's Other Island*, produced by Shaw, with Barker an unwilling and somewhat controversial Keegan. The season's prospects were threatened by severe winter weather, and among the protests to Vedrenne concerning the discomfort in the theatre came one from Shaw, on 26 November: 'four cases of frostbite were treated at the Chelsea infirmary', he claimed; 'the firemen caught one man trying to set fire to the theatre', and Shaw's wife, moved to weep by the play, found 'her tears froze so that it took [Shaw] five minutes to get her eyes open with the warmth of [his] hands, which are now covered with chilblains'.[6] During the three week closure while a new heating system was installed, the opportunity was taken to improve the stage, the dressing rooms, and the lighting and equipment of the public rooms; to provide adequate storage space for frequent changes of programme; and to add a rehearsal room. When it re-opened the matinée series continued with plays by Barker and Housman, Gilbert Murray, Schnitzler, Yeats and Hauptmann, until 1 May 1905 when *John Bull's Other Island* was revived and put in the main bill 'for three weeks only ... Every evening at 8.15 And Wednesday Matinée at 2.30' (Programme). The Vedrenne-Barker management had come of age, and was formalised that day in a partnership agreement, subject to six months notice by either party, drawing capital from each partner in equal shares, and paying each a salary of £20 a week. Barker was to be responsible for the artistic direction, and Vedrenne for the business side.

John Eugene Vedrenne had started in commerce, become a concert agent and then moved on to theatre management for F.R.

Benson, Forbes Robertson and Nat Godwin before joining Leigh. W. Macqueen-Pope describes him as a 'very acute' man: 'he worked to schedules, he was alarmingly punctual. He made appointments at odd times. "Come round and see me at 12.31 sharp to the minute," he would say--and mean it'.[7] He combined a gift for casting with his business talents, and Lewis Casson recalls that he also had a 'flair' for dealing with artists, combining 'firmness with flattery'. His manner was open and confiding, but he invariably managed to engage the artist at the lowest 'summer terms', whatever the season. He had a nose for young talent, and would back his judgement by offering 'a contract for a long term, at a very moderate but slowly rising salary. They then belonged to him. During his day there was a perfect eruption on programmes of plays produced by other managers of players who appeared "By permission of J.E. Vedrenne"'.[8] The partnership of a sober man of business and a dedicated artist had much to commend it in its combination of talents; but there were built-in frictions which did not augur well where their respective responsibilities overlapped, and in the marginal nature of the theatre's finances. The programme was run on a semi-repertory basis of short runs with a fixed number of performances. New plays were tried out in six to nine matinées, then transferred into the evening bill for three weeks if they looked promising. As William Archer remarked, such a system was 'artistically preferable to the long-run system, but economically unsound',[9] and although the theatre needed a 'house' of only £600 a week to pay its way and give a small profit, all Vedrenne's astuteness was required to keep the operation solvent. The status, if not the financial position of the venture was established by *John Bull's Other Island*. Beatrice Webb persuaded the Prime Minister, A.J. Balfour, to see it; in turn he invited the Opposition leaders, Sir Henry Campbell-Bannerman and H.H. Asquith, and King Edward VII commanded an evening performance on 11 March 1905. For this occasion Vedrenne hired special furniture from Maples for the Royal Box, and one can understand his mixed feelings when the King laughed so heartily that he broke one of the rented chairs! Max Beerbohm dated Shaw's popularity from that night, after which his plays became 'a fashionable craze'.

Max Beerbohm was one of the few critics who supported the enterprise from the start. It enjoyed an enviable proportion of press coverage, but most critics, Hesketh Pearson observed, 'received every play as if it had been specially written to annoy or shock them ... their intelligence had become numbed [by artificial stage situations] and they could not respond to anything novel'.[10] In his speech at the complimentary dinner in 1907, Shaw declared that 'the difficulties ... have been labours of love', except for the 'struggle with the London Press which from first to last has done what in it lay to crush the enterprise'.[11] Most first night notices, so important to management, he continued, consisted of 'a chronicle of failure, a sulky protest against this new and troublesome sort of entertainment that calls for knowledge and thought instead of for the usual clichés'. An important supporter among the critics was William Archer, who recognised the significance of the work being done at the Court after the first season, and issued a pamphlet reviewing the record and urging the 'active support of all thoughtful people'. He noted 'one disquieting feature ... the undue predominance of the works of Mr. Bernard Shaw'.[12] This predominance continued throughout the remaining seasons. Out of a total of 988 performances, 701 were of plays by Shaw:[13]

No. of perfs.	*Title*		*Opening Date*
(6)	*(Candida)*		(26 April 1904)
121	*John Bull's Other Island*		1 Nov. 1904
31	*Candida*		29 Nov. 1904
9	*How He Lied to Her Husband*		28 Feb. 1905
149	*You Never Can Tell*		2 May 1905
176	*Man and Superman*		23 May 1905
52	*Major Barbara*		28 Nov. 1905
89	*Captain Brassbound's Conversion*		20 March 1906
50	*The Doctor's Dilemma*		20 Nov. 1906
8	*The Philanderer*		5 Feb. 1907
8	*The Man of Destiny*	(Double)	
8	*Don Juan in Hell*	(Bill)	4 June 1907
701			

With the aid of the Court productions, Shaw confounded the critics and those who 'could not accept [his plays] as plays at all, and repudiated them as pamphlets in dialogue form by a person ignorant of the theatre and hopelessly destitute of dramatic faculty'.[14] Shaw was relatively 'ignorant of the theatre' when he began writing plays, having never acted or been involved in production, but he capitalized on his experience as music and drama critic, and, as he advised H.G. Wells who was eyeing the stage,

> a dramatist wants rehearsal experience, a part of his apprenticeship that is worth a good deal of solid gold to him. By jumping at all my chances I have rehearsed for public performance nine of my plays, with the result that I am as much an expert behind the scenes as Pinero, and am not sent to the stalls to see my work botched by idiots who havnt read it and wouldnt know what it is about if they did. You cant trust anybody to handle your play; and yet it is only by practice that you can make the company accept your direction as a matter of course.[15]

Shaw worked very closely with his cast. As Lillah McCarthy records, he first gave them an operatic reading of the play:

> the parts were then handed to us, and we were allowed to stumble through them. His own conceptions of the characters were withheld. He never harassed us with interruptions in the raw beginning stage. But as he listened to us his pencil was never still; and at the end of each rehearsal we would get plenty to ponder over in the shape of brilliant and brief little personal notes.
>
> He would wait for a week before he came up onto the stage to interfere with our work. Then began a revelation of his knowledge of the theatre and of acting. With complete unselfconsciousness he would show us how to draw the full value out of a line. He could assume any role, any physical attitude, and make any inflection of his voice, whether the part was that of an old man or a young man, a budding girl or an ancient lady. With his amazing hands he would illustrate the mood of the line. We used to watch his hands in wonder. I learned as much from his hands, almost, as from his little notes of correction.[16]

The 'little notes' ranged from a few lines to several pages. Contrasting examples are the long letter to J.L. Shine, who played Larry in *John Bull*, and the shorter notes to Lillan McCarthy and Florence Haydon (*Letters 1898-1910*, pp. 460, 522 and 530). Shaw also took a hand in the design and construction of the sets, and his intense involvement in production did not end until the curtain went up. He rarely attended performances, but when he did, his visit was usually followed by further notes to the cast correcting points of detail. Whenever cast changes were made or revivals undertaken, Shaw appeared to supervise, and all this at a time when he was still involved in the Fabian Society Executive, in Borough affairs at St. Pancras, in negotiations with publishers and overseas agents, in a host of personal and professional commitments and engagements, and, of course, in writing plays and prefaces.

Hesketh Pearson is not alone in believing that the Court seasons in which Shaw made his reputation as a dramatist 'were the most important events in the history of the British stage since Shakespeare and Burbage ran the Globe theatre on Bankside'.[17] But giving Shaw a dramatic outlet was by no means the only achievement of the Vedrenne-Barker partnership. With plays by Galsworthy, St. John Hankin, Elizabeth Robins, and Barker himself, it initiated a 'school' of dramatists motivated by acute social conscience and sympathy who expressed themselves in a realistic mode. Their sombre 'problem' plays formed one end of a spectrum that ranged through the realistic-poetic tones of Ibsen's *Wild Duck*, Maeterlinck's *Aglavaine and Selysette* and Masefield's *The Campden Wonder*, the patchwork of the Pierrot play, *Prunella*, by Laurence Housman and Granville Barker, the sylvan shades of Maurice Hewlett's *Pan and the Young Shepherd*, and the sanguine classical revivals of

Euripides' *Electra*, *Hippolytus*, and *The Trojan Women* made viable for the modern stage and intelligible for its audiences by Gilbert Murray. *The Green Room Book* for 1907 declared:

> The Court has become the Mecca of every serious playgoer. Without starting out to be a *repertoire* theatre, it is fast becoming a theatre with a *repertoire*. It is giving young and previously untried dramatists a chance hitherto denied them, for not only are new plays produced, but they are produced under the most favourable conditions--with admirable casts and stage management equal to the best ever seen in London. And while the Court is encouraging the new or rising dramatist, it is creating a school of acting.[18]

The significant difference between the acting at the Court and elsewhere was the absence of star focus and concomitant emphasis on balanced team-work within a totally conceived framework. 'People often ask', said Max Beerbohm, 'why the acting at the Court seems so infinitely better than in so many other theatres where the same mimes are to be seen'. One reason he gives is that the plays chosen contained characters worth the trouble taken, but the main reason

> is that the mimes at the Court are very carefully stage-managed, every one of them being kept in such relation to his fellows as is demanded by the relation in which the various parts stand to one another--no one mime getting more, or less, of a chance than the playwright has intended him to have.[19]

Lillah McCarthy recalls that 'no one of us was allowed to act away from the rest of the company, nor away from the play as a complete pattern'.[20] The stage-managing for this *gestalt* conception was Granville Barker's. Being an actor, he tended to be actor-oriented, and to place considerable emphasis on the process by which his performers created their own roles from within, for which it was necessary to develop what he later termed a 'histrionic mind' based on the observation and understanding of life, and a deep understanding of the play itself. He regarded 'all acting as interpretation; it can have no absolute value of its own'.[21] The actor's 'creative collaboration' in the artistic process was required to bring the play to life from text to performance: 'the actors must continue what the dramatist has begun by methods as nearly related to his in understanding and intention as the circumstances allow'.[22] Shaw's 'formula' for success was to make 'the audience believe that real things are happening to real people'.[23] Barker obviously shared this aim, and believed that to achieve it, 'something *more* than acting' was required,

> if by acting one only means the accomplishment, the graces, or the sound and fury of the stage ... It is only when they [the externals of acting] are the showing of a body of living thought and of living feeling, and in themselves an interpretation of life itself, when, in fact, they acquire *further* purpose, that they rank as histrionic art.[24]

Barker's work as producer was characterized by the way a pattern of production was built up, 'not merely by variation of tone, change of emphasis, or alteration of pace, but by the interaction of stage movement, so that the action was composed of layer upon layer of movement, speech, and silences held together in the completed form'.[25] He abhorred flamboyant histrionics, but his fondness for understatement and subtle effects did not suit the plays or temperament of Shaw, who demanded operatic treatment and bold effects--not the stylized rhetoric of Victorian melodramatic acting, but a musical diapason. Barker aimed at the same musical harmony as Shaw, having been influenced already in this direction by William Poel. Theodore Stier, musical director for the Court, whose entertaining arrangements kept the audience in their seats and away from the bar during intermissions (much to the chagrin of Vedrenne, and the box-office manager, Mr. Platt), describes Barker conducting rehearsals as he would an orchestra: '"I want a tremendous *crescendo* here," he would cry. "A sudden stop. A *firmata*. Now--down to *pianissimo*"'. And to an actress overplaying her role: '"But my dear child," he would lament, "you deliver your lines as if you were the trombone, whereas you really are the oboe in this ensemble"'.[26]

Barker's style was more intimate than Shaw's--chamber music rather than grand opera or oratorio--and although they shared a common starting point in a reading to the cast, based, of course, on a thorough acquaintance with or study of the play itself, their working methods differed. Barker's reading was unhistrionic, an attempt to impress an overall concept of the play on his performers. Lewis Casson gives a vivid account of Barker at work:

> there was no preliminary exposition and no touch of director's jargon or pretentious analysis. We started rehearsing without even being told more of our characters than the stage directions told us, to see what the actors themselves first made of them. Then he would start moulding us in the direction he wanted, using every device of witty illustration and metaphor to stimulate the actor's own imagination ... With his amazingly sensitive ear for speech and silence, his expressive hands and flexible body he could always help everyone to give clear expression to any ideas the actor or he wanted to convey. He would often demonstrate a rhythm or phrasing or

> emphasis, but seldom give an intonation, and always with the caution that it was given only to convey the thought, and must be made the actor's own before use. Then by detailed criticism he would make it subtler and more musical. This fine polishing went on right up to the last rehearsal, always by notes taken during the run of a scene, not by interrupting the flow. By the time the performance came, the whole piece was moulded into a musical and rhythmic pattern as definite as a symphony, where every word and phrase, every silence, every intonation had been scrutinized and accepted as the best he could achieve with his material.[27]

A Barker production, therefore, was a slow, organic growth, forming to a whole as the individual performers' interpretations of their roles, guided by Barker, developed and were fused into a homogenous totality. The ideal was so to integrate the actor into the dramatic action that he had a sense of freedom: 'we aim, then, through this freedom at an appearance of spontaneity',[28] declared Barker, and paradoxically, through professional competence and discipline, to realize the unity in diversity and diversity in unity, the freedom compatible with order. Barker had a 'completely tidy and disciplined mind that could plan a whole production in detail before starting rehearsals and keep firmly to a schedule',[29] but he was not an authoritarian, as Shaw tended to be, and would accept suggestions from his cast if they reinforced the author's intentions. He got the best out of his actors not by driving them, although he worked them long and hard, but by evoking their enthusiasm and by leading them through his own example. Stier recalls his days at the Court with affection, particularly the spirit of optimism, loyalty and dedication which permeated the theatre, and derived from its director:

> so far as Barker was concerned every soul behind the footlights, from the leading lady to the lowest paid scene-shifter, was automatically bound in a brotherhood of art; that any member of his staff, in any capacity whatever, was not all out for absolute perfection never so much as entered his head. And because he expected so much and put so much of himself into his own work, he succeeded in bringing out the best from everyone else.[30]

There were two weaknesses in Barker's methods, one practical and the other stylistic: the time available for rehearsals was never sufficient for his deliberate approach, and his subtle acting method tended to understatement and consequent loss of impact. Not that he wanted everyday, photographic realism; he was an experienced enough actor to know that realism on stage is an effect, and as Lewis Casson points out, Barker was fortunate in having actors who had been trained in a tradition of clear and significant articulation, and it was a tribute to their skill that the final effect 'gave to so discerning a critic [as Desmond MacCarthy] the illusion of pure naturalism and perfect sincerity'.[31] His refusal to allow or exploit star appeal did not deter competent actors--even stars like Ellen Terry (Lady Cicely in *Captain Brassbound)* and Mrs. Patrick Campbell (Hedda Gabler)--from accepting parts at the Court; nor did the relatively low salaries offered. Serious artists like Lewis Casson, Edmund Gwenn, Louis Calvert, Laurence Irving, Lillah McCarthy, Thyrza Norman (Mrs. John Leigh), Florence Haydon and Dorothy Minto felt the sacrifices worthwhile to work with a producer who drew out their best acting powers and was dedicated to art for its own sake, and not for the sake of what cash profit it might bring. Barker shared Shaw's concern over casting, as is evident from their correspondence, but he had more faith in an actor's flexibility than Shaw, who appears obsessed by the problem: 'get your cast right', he urged Barker,

> and get them interested in themselves and in the occasion, and stage management can be done without, though it does no harm when it does not get into the way of the acting. Get your cast wrong; and you wreck your play just to the extent to which the cast is wrong.[32]

This concern extended to all roles, and it was a feature of the Court productions that even the most minor parts were filled by competent performers and given in-depth treatment: 'any one of us would cheerfully take a small role', claims Lillah McCarthy, 'for we knew that even so we should not have to be subservient, negative and obsequious to the stars for ... there were no stars'.[33] One value of this freedom from what one writer termed 'the incubus of the star' is illustrated by a story Barker recounted at the 1907 dinner:

> I caught influenza and was out of the bill for a night or two. A gentleman descending the pit stairs observed a notice to this effect pinned above the pay box. He asked what it meant, and it was carefully explained that Mr. Barker was not playing that evening. "Who is Mr. Barker?" he asked. The money-taker did not commit himself to a biography, but repeated that Mr. Barker would not play John Tanner. "But I suppose somebody will play it," said the gentleman. "Yes," said the money-taker, "it will be played." "Then," said the gentleman, "take my half-crown, young man, and don't make such a fuss." Now, I think that is the proper spirit in which to go to the theatre.[34]

Barker's dedication to the art of the theatre was founded on a conviction he shared with Shaw of 'art for life's sake', in which the art of the theatre subserved the higher good of society itself: the revitalizing of art was part of a wider ambition to transform social conditions. It is therefore not surprising to find that Barker was a member of the Fabian Society, an activist in the Actor's Association, and a leading advocate in the campaigns for a National Theatre and for the abolition of stage Censorship (see Chapters Five and Six respectively). This social consciousness is reflected in the choice of plays for the Court Theatre, and, as suggested by the title of Margery Morgan's book, *A Drama of Political Man. A Study in the Plays of Harley Granville Barker*, dominated his work as dramatist. It is expressed not in terms of direct social propaganda, but informs the structure of character and plot in the relationship between the individual as politician and as moral being in a social context. The moral development of the protagonist provides the focus of interest in *The Voysey Inheritance*, the only one of his plays to be produced at the Court except for the joint effort, *Prunella*. It was first performed on 7 November 1905, 'a noteworthy date in the history of the modern drama', according to William Archer, who found it 'a great play, a play conceived and composed with original mystery, and presenting on its spacious canvas a greater wealth of observation, character and essential drama than was to be found in any other play of our time'.[35] It was given six matinées, then brought into the evening bill for four weeks the following February, when Barker took over the role of Edward from Thalberg Corbett. The play drew many gestures of respect from the critics, but even supporters of the Court, like Desmond MacCarthy, found it unsatisfactory, more like a novel than a play. A.B. Walkley labelled it '*triple extrait de* Shaw', but conceded: it 'has great merits. It has fresh and true observation, subtle discrimination of character, sub-acid humour, an agreeable irony, and a general air of *reality*. That is the important thing'.[36]

Walkley's comment indicates the question of the extent to which Barker fell under the Shavian shadow in his writing as in his production techniques and in other spheres. When Beatrice Webb met him in 1905 she noted his attractive personality, good looks, and 'medley of talents', but perceived that 'he [had] not yet emancipated himself from G.B.S.'s influence, or found his own soul'.[37] His prime allegiance at that time certainly was to Shaw, but as indicated above, the emerging 'soul' had been forged from a variety of sources. In a perceptive essay on 'The Edwardian Theatre', Gerald Weales confronts this problem and concludes that as a dramatist Barker was essentially independent, influenced perhaps by his association with Shaw in the direction of theme, but not in his dramaturgy.[38] Barker is more of a realist than Shaw because his characters and situations are far more natural; there is a consistent 'slice of life' quality in Barker, only occasionally attained by Shaw, evident in the Chekhovian portrayal of a large number of complex characters and in the absence of formal exposition and well-made conclusions--qualities unfortunately, that militated against box-office success. Margery Morgan contends that Shaw and Barker

> are complementary to each other in their virtues ... Shaw's method is to turn all private experience into a public concern, Barker's is the more introvert way of exploring society: his work has as large a scope as Shaw's, but everything is referred back to the sentient organism, the single human being, whose inner life reflects the buried consciousness of his age.[39]

They are, as Shaw put it, Verdi and Debussy; the declamatory and the suggestive. It is quite evident that although Shaw may have found Barker wanting in some respects, he respected the other man's special genius. For example, in a letter to H.A. Jones he declared that he found the early *Marrying of Ann Leete* 'an exquisite play', and admitted: 'I truckle to G.B. in order to conciliate him when he is forty'.[40]

In his realistic plays Barker may be close to Shaw, but they illustrate only one side of his nature: not shared by Shaw is the other, poetic-romantic side, which gave such deft and imaginative productions to Maeterlinck, and later to Shakespeare, and is revealed in the play he wrote with Laurence Housman, *Prunella or Love in a Dutch Garden*. This was first performed as a Christmas special on 23 December 1904, but disappointed those who expected to see a pantomime. It was given a run of twelve matinées in April-May 1906, and another matinée run the following May, but achieved no success until revived at the Duke of York's in 1910. Housman, recalling the 'happy collaboration' over Prunella and acknowledging Barker's help with *The Chinese Lantern*, declares that 'Barker was a wonderful coach; he knew exactly when to bully me and when to let me alone ... it was mainly through Barker that I had learned my job ... Your story writer relies too much on the printed word, and leaves too little to the actor. Again and again Barker's cuts to my over-valuation of words left me amazed, but they also taught me'.[41] Housman also recalls Barker's share in planning the music for *Prunella* when on a visit to the home of the composer, Joseph Moorat, at Campden, where 'they sat for eight hours a day and hatched music together'.[42]

These glimpses of Barker's dedication to the art of theatre help towards an understanding of the impact on him of the censor's refusal to license *Waste* in 1907. Purdom records that the action 'may be said to have virtually killed the [Vedrenne-Barker] management', because Barker 'had put the best of himself into the play, and the rebuff was severe'.[43] The play was privately performed in full by the Stage Society on 24 November 1907 at the Imperial Theatre, and given its copyright performance 'As licensed by the Lord Chamberlain', i.e. with amendments and omissions, on 28 January 1908 at the Savoy with a cast that included Mr. and Mrs. G.B. Shaw, Mr. and Mrs. H.G. Wells, and William Archer. Ostensibly, the play was banned because of the abortion incident, but Barker was treading on dangerous ground, a virtually taboo subject, when he made his central figure a politician of cabinet rank. As Archer put it, the play was 'strangled at birth by the Censorship', but even if it had not been, it was a difficult play to stage successfully, having fifteen important, well-drawn parts, and is, for an author so much a man of the theatre, surprisingly pedestrian. *The Madras House*, first performed at the Duke of York's on 9 March 1910, posed similar difficulties with twenty significant parts, and, like its two predecessors, was curiously untheatrical (although it adapted well for television), and after only ten performances it was withdrawn in the face of critical hostility and audience indifference.

The banning of *Waste* depressed Barker, and did little to ease developing strains in his relationship with Vedrenne. The two clashed particularly over the repertory principle. Vedrenne's instinct was to keep a good thing running when they had one; Barker insisted on the short run, second-best to the true repertory system as it was, because it did prevent a production from going stale with over-repetition. They also clashed frequently over the choice of play and of performer. Barker's marriage to Lillah McCarthy on 24 April 1906 imposed a strain in this respect, as Vedrenne took seriously a flippant remark of Shaw's that 'now Lillah will have all the best parts', and opposed giving her leading roles thereafter.[44] Nevertheless in 1907, encouraged by the artistic success of their seasons at the Court and by the fact that they had paid their way, including their own salaries, and hoping to reap a financial success, the partners transferred to the Savoy in the West-End, a larger but less comfortable theatre. The Court series closed on 29 June with a Shaw double-bill: the 'Don Juan in Hell' scene from *Man and Superman* (omitted from the first productions of the play), and *The Man of Destiny*. The former was elaborately produced and brilliantly played, but the latter was done rather inadequately. Shaw also opened the Savoy season when *You Never Can Tell* was revived on 16 September. It was followed by special matinées of Galsworthy's *Joy*, which was a box-office disaster, and the Murray-Euripides *Medea*, a modest success. Shaw's *Devil's Disciple* came into the evening bill on 14 October, but Shaw had little to do with the production which, under Barker's direction, lacked fire. He was, in fact, moody and depressed over *Waste*, and his divided mind was matched by Vedrenne's, which was on the chance of managing a new West-End theatre close to completion, the Queen's.

The Savoy venture was an anti-climax to the Court seasons. In the move the partners lost their audience and their spark, and finally their money, for when their tenancy of the theatre expired on 14 March 1908 they were virtually bankrupt. Shaw, too, had lost money. Although he had refused to enter into a proposed conversion of the partnership into a limited company when the transfer to the Savoy had taken place, he did put up the sum of £2,000, to match £1,000 each from Vedrenne and Barker, to launch the Savoy series.[45] When Barker wished to dissolve the partnership at the end of the season Shaw opposed the idea as the name still had value. One company was touring *John Bull's Other Island* under the Vedrenne-Barker banner, and Shaw had *Getting Married* ready to follow their joint production with Frederick Harrison at the Haymarket of Masefield's *The Tragedy of Nan*. In August he wrote: 'Vedrenne and Barker as individuals have created a Frankenstein's Monster (the firm of Vedrenne & Barker with Goodwill for a soul) that they cannot easily slay, however much they may loathe it'.[46] But as Hesketh Pearson points out, they had over-extended themselves:

> Vedrenne wanted to make more money, and Barker's ambition was to reach a wider public by producing plays for which the stage at the Court was too small. Their past achievement seems to have gone to their heads, because they not only took the Savoy, but also the Haymarket for Shaw's new play *Getting Married,* and another theatre for a play by Laurence Housman *[The Chinese Lantern]*. Three west-end theatre rents brought them to the verge of ruin ... "Vedrenne got out with nothing but a reputation," Shaw told me; "Barker had to pawn his clothes, and I disgorged most of my royalties; but the creditors were paid in full."[47]

When the Savoy season closed in March 1908, the *Pall Mall Gazette* was not alone in looking back to 'the indefinable sense of a kind of renaissance at work' during the Court days, and regretting the collapse of a venture that brought out 'brilliant audiences', and created such enthusiasm: and after 'the pleasure and pride and hope of it all, it seems incredible that Londoners should be permitting such an institution to pass from their midst'.[48] But they did. By January of 1909, in a self-drafted interview which appeared in the *Daily Telegraph* the day before the opening of *The Admirable Bashville* at his Majesty's, Shaw was forced to proclaim

> the fact that Vedrenne and Barker is dead, destroyed, ruined; that the passing craze is over; that it is agreed that the Court Theatre plays were not plays at all; that its audiences consisted wholly of unwholesome cranks; that we have all gone back to the daily round ... and that we will see England considerably farther before we again attempt to save her by our private enterprise from the disgrace of having no national theatre. London has nothing more to fear.[49]

The partnership was not officially wound up until March 1911, leaving Shaw the only creditor to the tune of £5,250; he settled for the balance of cash in the bank of £484.3.10 and to the proceeds from the sale of scenery and a few other assets.[50]

The Vedrenne-Barker management, mainly in its three years at the Royal Court, had recorded a remarkable range of achievement, and its effects were significant. It had shown that the repertory idea, slightly modified, could be made to work in London theatre, and that the gap between the commercial and the artistic theatre could be bridged. In doing so, as Lord Lytton claimed, the partners 'have rescued English drama from the chains of a stupid convention by which it has long been bound. They have never tried to run their plays to death'.[51] A wide range of plays had been presented, and new ground had been broken with the introduction of Greek drama in modern translations to regular theatre audiences and with the production in a commercial theatre of drama that dealt with the situations and problems of real life in an unsentimental manner. Desmond MacCarthy declares that the Court theatre

> represented an aesthetic and dramatic movement of remarkably wide sympathies ... If the aesthetic influence of the Court Theatre upon the modern drama were capable of being summed up in a sentence, the truest summary would be that it has expanded enormously the conception of what kind of a story is suitable for the stage; in short that it has enlarged the meaning of the word "dramatic," for that adjective signifies nothing but a quality in actions and persons which would make them impressive on the stage.[52]

Leading this 'dramatic movement' was Shaw, whose plays were so often written off by hostile critics who could not accept them as drama. The Court seasons had established him as a major force in the theatre, and had introduced a new group of realistic, socially concerned dramatists headed by Galsworthy. The new drama had been given an unprecedented chance in stage time, in careful interpretation of the author's intentions, and in the high quality of production, which in turn had both attracted serious, established performers and given other, younger players invaluable experience. Other significant emphases were on the 'natural' style of acting based on ensemble playing, the importance of all roles, the imaginative involvement of the actor, the elimination of the star, and the concept of a harmonious whole. The Royal Court had become a 'temple of high art' for its devotees, and although it may not have drawn many of the general theatre-going public, who still flocked to see Pinero at the St. James's or Tree's spectaculars at His Majesty's, it did provide a stimulus to many developments in the wider theatrical world. Among these was the growth of the Repertory movement in provincial theatres such as the Gaiety, Manchester (1907) and the Scottish Repertory Theatre at the Royal, Glasgow (1909). In London Charles Frohman ran a four-month repertory season at the Duke of York's in 1910, engaging Barker to direct four of the productions including his own *The Madras House* and Galsworthy's *Justice*. Earlier, the Court's example led to Beerbohm Tree's After Noon Theatre matinées at His Majesty's, which began in November 1908. The enterprising management of the Kingsway under Lena Ashwell and of the Little under Gertrude Kingston both drew inspiration from the Court seasons, and the roll of players who spread the invigorating influence of Court acting and production techniques is an honourable one. As Lord Lytton remarked, 'it is necessary, before change can be effected, for some individual to make an experiment and prove its success':[53] the Court experiment had proved the viability of the new drama and of a semi-repertory theatre in London, and had stimulated theatrical development, but it was clear that the most desirable conclusion to the experiment would be the establishment of a National Theatre, which seemed imminent at that time but was in fact still over half a century distant.

Barker was active in the National Theatre cause, serving on the Executive of the Shakespeare Memorial National Theatre Committee, formed in 1908, and he pinned high hopes on its success after the failure of the Vedrenne-Barker promotions in 1909-10. He might well have lapsed into despair had not his wife, Lillah McCarthy, become increasingly drawn towards actor-managership, and it was thanks largely to her encouragement and to her success in fund-raising that he continued as producer. She was attracted to a play by H. Wiers-Jenssen, *Anne Pedersdotter*, sent to her in rough translation by William Archer, who had discovered it while in Norway. After some hesitancy over the probable objections of the censor, John Masefield undertook to adapt the play, renamed *The Witch*. It was first performed in repertory in Glasgow under Barker's direction, then Lillah McCarthy arranged for six matinées at the Court, opening on 31 January 1911. She attracted much attention as the heroine despite the unmitigated horror of the piece. '"The Witch" had made me ambitious', she declared, 'I wanted to have a larger share in chosing *[sic]* and producing plays than I had had hitherto'.[54] After pondering ways and means, she was inspired to approach Lord Howard de Walden and tell him her management dreams: she walked out of his house the same morning with 'a handsome cheque' (£1,000 according to Purdom) in her hands, to which she added contributions by Lily Antrobus and Shaw, who also promised her a new play. The McCarthy-Barker Management was launched when she took the Little Theatre and Barker agreed to direct on condition that he could choose the plays himself. Their season opened with Barker's translation of Schnitzler's *Anatol* on 11 March 1911, in which he played the lead with a strong cast including his wife, followed by Ibsen's *The Master Builder*. Anxious not to place the new management under any stigma of association, and shrewd enough to know the publicity value of a mystery, Shaw insisted that his promised new play should be anonymous. It was billed, therefore, as *Fanny's First Play* by Xxxxxxx xxxx, but 'never was there such a hopelessly unsuccessful attempt to hood-wink the public',[55] wrote Lillah McCarthy, because Shaw's touch was immediately recognized. The play proved no embarrassment to the management, appealing to both audiences and critics, who rejoiced that the wit and style of the Court days had returned (an irony, indeed); Shaw allowed it a long run (624 performances), which brought in the Coronation year crowds and a welcome profit to the promoters.

Barker had no hand in *Fanny's First Play*, but he mounted six new productions that year, and a further five in 1912, the most significant being *The Winter's Tale*, which opened at the Savoy on 21 September. Barker brought to Shakespeare his own unique interpretation--based, of course, on an analysis of the author's purpose--and style (see Chapter Seven) which set off the inevitable controversy among the critics. Although the audiences enjoyed the production, it failed to attract a wide public, lost money, and was withdrawn after six weeks to be replaced by *Twelfth Night*, which began a highly successful run on 15 November. Barker was even more faithful to the text than William Poel, cutting only six lines from *The Winter's Tale* and none from *Twelfth Night*. He followed Poel's example in keeping as close as possible to Elizabethan staging, but allowed his stage designer, Norman Wilkinson, a free hand, with the result that the decor was spectacular not in the pseudo-realistic style of Tree, but in an impressionistic manner, blazing with exotic colour, and tending to the bizarre. The costumes, by Albert Rutherston for the first play and by Norman Wilkinson for the second, matched the decor; and the modern treatment was counterbalanced by Elizabethan airs by Cecil Sharp. Most controversy was aroused by the speech, which was not slow and declamatory but rapid and modulated. Decor, costumes and speech were fused with ensemble playing of the highest order to give the plays a fresh urgency and a new look for the twentieth century.

The following year Barker had four new productions, and the Barker-McCarthy management took the St. James's for a season that opened with Shaw's *Androcles and the Lion* on 1 September 1913, continued with a revival of *The Witch*, and concluded with a three-week repertory of five different bills. In February 1914 Barker completed a Shakespeare triple at the Savoy with *A Midsummer Night's Dream*, remembered by Lillah McCarthy as 'the most beautiful production of [her] career', but by others, unfortunately, more for its golden fairies than for its undoubted poetic qualities. The war interrupted plans to produce *Macbeth* and *Antony and Cleopatra*, and although Barker was now firmly established as London's leading producer, he was discouraged by the constant financial problems and by the ever-receding prospect of establishing a National Theatre where Shakespeare and new, serious drama could be staged on a repertory basis unburdened by the debilitating weight of financial worries.

Barker's life, like that of so many of his generation, was cut in two by the war, which marked the end of his career in the working theatre. The demand for light, escapist entertainment during those grim years set back the development of the serious, new drama of ideas, but the previous decade had seen, thanks in no small measure to the reforming zeal and artistic genius of the youthful Granville Barker, a clear break with Victorian dramatic traditions and the establishment of a distinctly modern era in the English theatre.

NOTES

1. Biography mainly from C.B. Purdom, *Harley Granville Barker. Man of the Theatre, Dramatist and Scholar* (Rockliff, London, 1955). See also Eric Salmon, *Granville Barker: A Secret Life* (Heinemann Educational Books, London, 1983). Barker hyphenated his name after his second marriage in 1918.

2. Bridges-Adams, *The Lost Leader* (Sidgwick & Jackson, London, 1954), p. 4. Also in *Listener*, 30 July 1953, pp. 173-5.

3. Quoted in Desmond MacCarthy, *The Court Theatre 1904-1907. A Commentary and a Criticism*, ed. Stanley Weintraub (University of Miami Press, Coral Gables, Florida, 1966), p. 162.

4. Ibid., p. 6.

5. The theatre had a history that was appropriate for the combination of evangelism and theatricality it would come to represent: originally a dissenting chapel, it had become the New Chelsea Theatre in 1870, was taken over by the actress Marie Litton and renamed the Royal Court in 1871, was demolished in 1887, and finally was transferred across the square to reopen at its present site on 24 September 1888.

6. G.B. Shaw, *Collected Letters 1898-1910*, ed. Dan H. Laurence (Max Reinhardt, London, 1972), p. 468.

7. W. Macqueen-Pope, *Carriages at Eleven* (Robert Hale, London, 1972), p. 194.

8. Ibid., p. 195.

9. William Archer, *Old Drama and the New: An Essay in Re-valuation* (William Heinemann, London, 1923), p. 340.

10. Hesketh Pearson, 'A Great Theatrical Management', *Theatre Arts*, vol. 39 (September 1955), 94-5.

11. *Court Theatre*, Appendix II, p. 172.

12. William Archer, *A Record and a Commentary of the Vedrenne-Barker Season, 1904-1905* (Allen & Sons, London, 1905), p. 10.

13. Compiled from *Court Theatre*, Appendix I, pp. 108-53.

14. Shaw, 'An Aside', Preface to *Myself and My Friends* by Lillah McCarthy (Lady Keeble) (Thornton Butterworth, London, 1933), p. 4. It is a matter of great regret that Granville

Barker, from whom she was divorced, vetoed any mention of his name from this memoir.

15. Shaw, *Letters 1898-1910*, p. 455.

16. L. McCarthy, p. 59. See also: Bernard F. Dukore, *Bernard Shaw, Director* (Allen & Unwin, London, 1971); William A. Armstrong, 'George Bernard Shaw. The Playwright as Producer', *Modern Drama*, vol. 8 (February 1966), pp. 347-61; Raymond Mander and Joe Mitchenson, *Theatrical Companion to Shaw* (Rockliff, London, 1954); Archibald Henderson, *George Bernard Shaw: Man of the Century* (Appleton Century Crofts, New York, 1956).

17. Hesketh Pearson, *The Last Actor-Managers* (Methuen, London, 1950), p. 71.

18. *The Green Room Book* (London, 1907), pp. 397-8.

19. Max Beerbohm, *Around Theatres* (Rupert Hart Davis, London, 1953), pp. 403-4.

20. L. McCarthy, p. 50.

21. Harley Granville Barker, *The Exemplary Theatre* (Chatto & Windus, London, 1921), p. 93.

22. Ibid., p. 226.

23. G.B. Shaw, 'The Art of Rehearsal', in *Directors on Directing. A Source Book of the Modern Theatre*, eds. Toby Cole and Helen Krich Chinoy (Peter Owen & Vision Press, London, 1966), p. 192.

24. Barker, p. 227. See also *Directors*, p. 199.

25. Purdom, p. 164.

26. Theodore Stier, *With Pavlova Round the World* (Hurst & Blackett, London, 1927), p. 259. Stier's last three chapters relate several anecdotes concerning the Vedrenne-Barker days at the Court.

27. Lewis Casson, Foreword to Purdom, p. vii.

28. Barker, p. 238.

29. Lewis Casson, *Listener*, 12 July 1951, p. 54.

30. Stier, pp. 258-9.

31. Casson, *Listener*, p. 54.

32. G.B. Shaw, *Bernard Shaw's Letters to Granville Barker*, ed. C.B. Purdom (Phoenix House, London, 1956), p. 81.

33. L. McCarthy, p. 90.

34. *Court Theatre*, Appendix II, p. 164.

35. Archer, *Old Drama and the New*, p. 357.

36. A.B. Walkley, *Drama and Life* (Methuen, London, 1907), p. 300.

37. Beatrice Webb, *Our Partnership* (Longmann's Green, London, 1948), p. 351.

38. Gerald Weales, 'The Edwardian Theatre', in *Edwardians and Late Victorians*, ed. Richard Ellmann, English Institute Essays, 1959 (Columbia University Press, New York, 1960), pp. 160-87.

39. Margery Morgan, *A Drama of Political Man. A Study in the Plays of Harley Granville Barker* (Sidgwick & Jackson, London, 1961), pp. 3-4.

40. Quoted in Doris Jones, *The Life and Letters of Henry Arthur Jones* (Gollancz, London, 1930), p. 211.
41. Laurence Housman, *The Unexpected Years* (Jonathan Cape, London, 1937), p. 241.
42. Ibid., p. 231.
43. Purdom, pp. 73-4.
44. Ibid., p. 57.
45. Ibid., p. 69.
46. Shaw, *Letters 1898-1910*, p. 809.
47. Pearson, p. 95.
48. *Pall Mall Gazette*, 14 March 1908, p. 2.
49. G.B. Shaw, 'Afternoon Theatre', appended to *The Admirable Bashville*, *Collected Plays* (Max Reinhardt, London, 1971), vol. 2, p. 480.
50. Shaw, *Shaw-Barker Letters*, p. 171.
51. *Court Theatre*, Appendix II, p. 158.
52. Ibid., p. 23.
53. Ibid., Appendix II, p. 160.
54. L. McCarthy, p. 133.
55. Ibid., p. 135.

Chapter Five

TOWARDS A NATIONAL THEATRE

> Our millionaires compete with so much rage
> That all things get endowed except the stage.
>
> John Masefield, Ode on Opening of Liverpool Repertory Theatre

During the latter part of the nineteenth century, it became increasingly evident that any renaissance of the English drama first required the liberation of the English theatre from the bondage of commercialism, with all its inherent evils: long runs, the actor-manager and star system, the general lack of opportunity for both actors and authors, the reliance on well-tried formulas, and the reluctance--enforced, to some degree, by the Censor--to risk controversial subjects or the serious treatment of real life issues on the stage. Consequently, the establishment of a National Theatre came to be perceived as an essential first step in the larger cause of revitalizing the English theatre and bringing it on a par with its continental counterparts.

The question of a National Theatre has been associated inextricably with that of an appropriate memorial to

> The lov'd, revered, immortal name!
> SHAKESPEARE! SHAKESPEARE! SHAKESPEARE!

as David Garrick declaimed in his 'Ode Upon Dedicating the Town Hall and erecting a Statue to Shakespeare' at the first Shakespeare Festival--the Jubilee celebration at Stratford-on-Avon in 1769, for which he was organizer, director and star performer.[1] A 'Shakespeare Club' was formed in London in 1815 by Mr. John Britton, an extraordinarily productive antiquary, topographer, miscellaneous writer and editor. In 1847 a 'Shakespeare Committee' purchased Shakespeare's birthplace for the Nation, and the same year brought the first plea for a National Theatre in a pamphlet *The Stage as it is: by*

Dramaticus. The following year saw further proposals for a National Theatre in two pamphlets written by a London publisher, Effingham William Wilson: *A House for Shakespeare. A proposition for the Consideration of the Nation* and a *Second and Concluding Paper*.

The subject became topical in the 'seventies when the *Echo* printed a letter from Tom Taylor, the dramatist, on 7 June 1871, referring to a meeting of the Society for the Encouragement of the Fine Arts at which the Chairman, F. Godwin, had remarked on 'the want of a national theatre, not wholly controlled by the predominant taste of the public'. Another dramatist, J.R. Planché, had made similar comments in *The Builder*, 29 April that year, but Taylor's letter sparked a leader in the *Echo* on the same day as it appeared, and after two more letters from him led to a discussion in the paper's correspondence columns in which sides were taken by Thomas Purnell, H.J. Byron, George Godwin, and others.[2] That year Taylor also published a pamphlet, *The Theatre in England. Some of Its Shortcomings and Possibilities* dealing with the topic, and Henry Neville gave an address on a National Theatre later published under the title: *The Stage: Its Past and Present in Relation to Fine Art* (1875). 'S. Stringer Bate' (Walter Raleigh) proposed *A Scheme for the Establishment of a National Theatre (ca.* 1875) along the lines of the *Comédie Française*, and in 1877 the then unknown William Archer, in conjunction with R.W. Lowe, published an attack on Henry Irving entitled *The Fashionable Tragedian: a Criticism*, which declared that Irving's faults and the destruction of his 'unquestionable gifts' proved the necessity of a permanent acting school: 'the only remedy lies in a national theatre with good endowment, good traditions, good government'.[3] A year later, on 25 October, George Godwin delivered a paper, published the same year, to the Congress of the Social Science Association meeting at Cheltenham entitled *On the Desirability of Obtaining a National Theatre*, one 'not wholly controlled by prevailing popular taste'. In it he quoted communications in support from Hermann Vezin and Henry Irving who himself endorsed the desirability of a National Theatre, including an acting school, emphasized the need for independence, elasticity and security, but ruled out State aid.[4] The *Times* reported that 'in the discussion which followed the paper a strong feeling was expressed in favour of Mr. Godwin's proposition'.[5] It was also supported by J.R. Planché in his book *Suggestions for Establishing an English Art Theatre* (1879), and between 1878 and 1879 the subject was taken up in the pages of the *Theatre* and other journals.

Added stimulus was derived from the visit of the full company of the *Comédie Française* to the Gaiety from 2 June to 12 July 1879. The opening night brought an article in the *Times* of the following day commending the organisation and acting of 'the highest aristocracy of the theatre' in envious terms, and the visit inspired Matthew Arnold's crucial essay, 'The French Play in London', published in the August issue of *Nineteenth Century*. Arnold deplored the absence of a native modern drama, but saw signs in the burgeoning theatre audiences that the British middle classes were at last escaping from 'the prison of Puritanism' that had estranged them from the theatre: but 'the theatre is irresistible ... I see our community turning to the theatre with eagerness, and finding the English theatre without organization, or purpose, or dignity, and no modern English drama at all except a fantastical one'.[6] The lesson to be learnt from the excellence of the French company was: 'the theatre is irresistible: *organize the theatre*'. The *Comédie Française* gave a model:

> the organization we have before us is simple and rational. We have a society of good actors, with a grant from the State on conditions of their giving with frequency the famous and classic stage plays of their nation, and with a commissioner of the State attached to the society and taking part in council with it. But the Society is to all intents and purposes self-governing. And in connection with the Society is the school of dramatic elocution of the *Conservatoire*. [7]

He then articulates the message implicit in the object lesson of the French performers: 'forget your clap-trap, and believe that the State, the nation in its collective and corporate character, does well to concern itself about an influence so important to national life and manners as the theatre'. What was needed, he concluded, was a state-aided company with a West-End theatre to perform Shakespeare and modern British plays, and an associated 'school of dramatic elocution and declamation'.

While the talk went on in London, there was action at Stratford where, thanks to the efforts of Charles Edward Flower, the mayor of the town, the Shakespeare Memorial Theatre opened with *Much Ado About Nothing* on 23 April 1879. Unfortunately, the acting school that was part of the original scheme in 1874 did not materialize.

Welcome as this event was, it did not go far towards the growing dream--which was also growing complicated:

> the claims were now seen to be threefold: firstly, for a worthy memorial to Shakespeare in the capital of the British Empire; secondly, as Irving had pleaded, for an "exemplary theatre" that would provide a permanent machine or factory for the production of plays on the highest artistic level; and thirdly, as in Matthew Arnold's vision, for a central organization able to spread throughout the country an appreciation of great drama as a major factor in education.[8]

The question appears to have died down during the next decade until 1889 when Archer revived the National Theatre issue in 'A Plea for an Endowed Theatre' in the *Fortnightly Review*, [9] and he became its chief advocate thereafter, frequently pointing out the need for a non-commercial theatre in the course of his articles. Archer defined an endowed theatre as one 'which, apart from the actual sale of its seats, receives a certain yearly income, no matter from what source or sources, on condition that it fulfils, or strives honestly to fulfil, certain artistic functions'. It should be essentially 'a public institution', he declared, 'devoted not to the enrichment (or impoverishment) of individual speculators, but to the service of the English Drama in all its worthier manifestations'.[10] H. Hamilton Fyfe added his voice to Archer's when F.R. Benson's season of Shakespeare at the Lyceum in 1900 prompted him to write an article urging the formation of 'A Permanent Shakespeare Theatre' as a step towards 'a worthy drama of modern English life'.[11] He suggested a small theatre supported by a guarantee fund provided by 1,000 people contributing £10 each. Archer and Granville Barker, who had joined the cause, enlisted Fyfe's support on a committee which also included A.C. Bradley, Gilbert Murray and Spencer Wilkinson (at whose house they met), formed to draw up specific proposals for an endowed theatre. The result came in 1904 in the form of a privately circulated 'Blue Book' written by Archer and Barker which called for the sum of £350,000 to establish a National Theatre. It was published in 1907 under the title of *A National Theatre. Scheme and Estimates*, and was endorsed by a supporting declaration signed by Henry Irving, Squire Bancroft, J.M. Barrie, Helen D'Oyly Carte, John Hare, Henry Arthur Jones and A.W. Pinero. The original proposal, the authors acknowledged, had been the subject of 'many criticisms and suggestions which are embodied in the text as it now stands'.[12] In a Preface in the form of a letter, Barker declares that the intervening years of experience in management had not altered his views at all: 'the need for a repertory theatre remains the same: not less, and it could not well be greater' (p. vii). The one significant amendment he would make would be 'the inclusion in our repertory list of every author whom we so carefully excluded four years ago--Ibsen, Hauptmann, d'Annunzio, Shaw, and the rest' (p. xi), which is a significant comment on the shift in public taste and acceptance brought about by the Vedrenne-Barker seasons at the Royal Court and by the work of the Stage Society.

The proposals are worth summarizing because in attempting to outline a scheme for an ideal National Theatre, the authors reflect not only the specific problems of their era, but also many of the perennial problems of the theatre.

The scheme called for the establishment of a National Repertory Theatre to be located in or near central London, the site, building and initial equipment to be the gift of one or more donors, and the operation, underwritten by a Guarantee Fund created by private contributions, to be managed by a Director responsible to a fifteen-member Board of Trustees. The opening paragraph of the book declares: 'assuming that the theatre-building, with an initial stock of scenery, costumes, furniture, and other requisites, is placed, free of rent, taxes, and insurance premium, at the disposal of the management, our purpose is to ascertain as accurately as may be the probable yearly cost of presenting a worthy repertory in a worthy fashion' (p.1). The authors then proceed to examine in minute detail the actual operation of the theatre, constantly reinforcing the practical proposals with the--by then--familiar arguments for such an institution. The first assumption is that Repertory theatre is far healthier for all concerned--dramatists, actors and audiences--than either the stock or the long run system, yet 'it is impossible worthily to present a worthy repertory at a playhouse held on the onerous terms which now prevail' (p.2).

Five officials would constitute the 'General Staff': Director, Literary Manager (or *Dramaturg)*, Reading Committee Man, Business Manager and Solicitor. The first three would form a Reading Committee to choose the plays to be performed. Two Producers would be engaged, one 'mainly employed upon rhetorical and costume plays, the other upon modern and realistic plays'. The Director 'would have absolute control of everything in and about the Theatre, engagement of actors, casting of parts, &c., &c., excepting only the selection of plays' (p.12).

Much attention is given to the organisation and remuneration of the company, which reflects Granville Barker's constant concern with the actor's well-being in addition to his performance, all of which is expressed in his prefatory letter where he asserts that if the theatre

> is ever to become a part of our civic institutions, its working conditions must be organised as becomes a healthy and stable civil service. And incidentally its servants must be left opportunities to retain that social citizenship which formerly they altogether renounced, and which now the pressure of the prevailing system does not afford them. If they are to depict social life they must be encouraged to enjoy it, not considered and left to become mere emotional acrobats. (p.xiii)

The instability of the acting profession is detrimental to the life of the theatre: even 'actors of great personal popularity will frequently drop out of work for months at a time without any assignable reason. An actor's vogue among the managers (as distinct from the public) is subject to a sort of mysterious periodicity. That is one of the main reasons why so many are eager to "go into management" for themselves' (p.28).

Furthermore, the actor's range is limited, thereby hampering the author because 'the fluidity of the theatrical world, enabling an actor to appear always in parts which he can get through on the strength of his mere personality, leads to the atrophy of whatever talent he may possess' (pp.32-3), and a mechanical hardening into a type ensues which reduces his capability to perform other roles.

A repertory system would go far towards rectifying the prevailing situation, and the proposed scheme gives detailed salaries and fees for thirty actors and eighteen actresses on three-year engagements, reinforced by a pension to become operative after ten years' service. The salaries table given (pp.25-6) is based on the acting demands of a specimen repertory. 'The main principles we had in view in sketching our specimen repertory', declare the authors, 'were that it should be national, representative and popular' (p.37). Accordingly, nine Shakespeare plays account for 124 performances out of a total of 326 of various new and old English plays, plus 37 of foreign plays, to give a grand total of 363 evening and matinée performances. Again, the detail of the scheme is impressive (if highly speculative) in that a complete season's schedule of plays is given (Appendix D), and the full cast of each is itemised using pseudonyms (Messrs. Kingsway, Throgmorton, Ludgate, *et al.)* for real performers. The practical operation of the theatre is not neglected either in front of the house or behind the scenes, and a seat-price schedule is supplemented in Appendix C by a Booking System and a Special Subscription plan, including even a draft 'Application Form for Subscription Seats'. Nor is the playwright forgotten; in addition to receiving a tangible 10% royalty, the authors argue that he would enjoy the immeasurable benefits of writing for a prestige theatre, free of the limitations of the star system and prepared to tackle plays that would stand little chance of performance on the commercial stage. However, the authors were at pains to point out that while seeking 'to break away, completely and unequivocally, from the ideals and traditions of the profit-seeking stage' (p.xviii), 'IT IS NOT AN ADVANCED THEATRE ... but forms part, and an indispensible part, of the main army of progress. It will neither compete with the outpost theatres nor relieve them of their functions' (p.36).

An adjunct to the theatre would be a Dramatic Training School. The lack of organized training for actors had long been deplored, and such a school would be of advantage both to the National Theatre in providing a pool for subordinate roles, and to the theatre as a whole in helping to raise standards, and could in time develop into a fully-fledged Dramatic College.

The scheme raised many contentious issues ranging from fundamental doubts not only over the process of funding but also over the principle of having a theatre that was independent of the public it served--especially if it were to be supported out of public funds--to disputes over the details, which, although intended only as part of a model, tended to work against the proposal. Shaw had been interested in the scheme when it was originally propounded, and wrote to Archer in 1902 indicating his willingness 'to back' the book, but objecting to the inclusion of a Dramatic School and advocating instead a University School of Rhetoric which would prepare students for a wide range of public life, including the stage, by giving instruction in 'platform accomplishments', particularly his hobby-horse, voice production.[13] He now raised further questions, including a concern over the autocratic nature of the Director:

> there is only one condition on which you can establish an autocracy, and that is, by providing such a minute and elaborate constitution and Articles of War that the Director, like the Captain of a battleship, has no more freedom than his subordinates. If you want elasticity and humanity--in other words if you want Art--you must have democracy.[14]

Furthermore, Shaw went on, the scheme 'has two weaknesses in its foundation. In the first place, it madly exaggerates the probable takings ... [and] in the second place the selection of plays is obsolete'. Despite such objections, Shaw continued to support the National Theatre principle and served on later committees (see below). Regardless of its faults, the 'blue book' was a major contribution towards the establishment of a National Theatre (still half a century from realisation) because it stimulated interest in the whole idea and formed a useful working basis for ensuing discussions.

Another persistent and articulate champion of the National Theatre concept was Henry Arthur Jones. In a lecture delivered to the Royal Institute 18 March 1904 entitled 'The Foundations of a National Drama', the title essay of the later book published in 1913, he focused his attention not on the organisation of a National Theatre as Archer and Barker had done, but on the broader concepts of a national English drama, for which it was necessary:

1. To distinguish and separate our drama from popular amusement ...
2. To found a national repertory theatre where high and severe literary and artistic standards may be set ...
3. To insure so far as possible that the dramatist shall be recognized and rewarded when and in so far as he has painted life and character ...
4. To bring our acted drama again into living relation with English literature ...
5. To inform our drama with a broad, sane, and profound morality ...
6. To give our actors and actresses a constant and thorough training ...

7. To break down as far as possible, and at any rate in some theatres, the present system of long runs ... to establish throughout the country repertory theatres and companies ...
8. To distinguish [the true causes of a play's failure]...
9. To bring the drama into relation with the other arts ... [and] to establish it as a fine art.[15]

In the same year Jones published an essay in *The Nineteenth Century Review* on 'The Recognition of the Drama by the State' in which, after considering several possible methods of financing a National Theatre, he concluded that it 'should be built and fostered by the government of England ... the best, the most secure, the most creditable way of founding a National Theatre, and of nurturing a great and popular national drama'.[16]

Meanwhile, other events and developments were bringing the whole issue to a head. The topic of a National Theatre was discussed at a meeting of the O.P. Club, 2 February 1902, and Messrs. Cecil Raleigh (who presided), Carl Hentschel and Charles Warner 'offered to contribute £100 each if 999 other people would promise a like sum'.[17] At almost the same time, a proposal first voiced by William Poel in 1900 was revived: to submit a petition to the London County Council asking for a site on which to build a replica of an Elizabethan theatre.[18] This was the focus of a meeting convened by Mr. T. Fairman Ordish at Cliffords Inn Hall on 23 April 1902 at which a model of Shakespeare's Globe theatre 1599-1613, designed and lent by William Poel, was displayed. It was suggested that the L.C.C. should grant a site between the Strand and Holborn for the erection of a building along the lines of an Elizabethan playhouse, and it was resolved to form a London Shakespeare Commemoration League. Subsequently, the League's aims were stated as follows:

(1) To extend the recognition of the interest which London possesses as the scene of the lifework of William Shakespeare.
(2) To organize an Annual Commemoration of the poet in London.
(3) To focus the movement for a Shakespeare Memorial in London.[19]

The third objective was shared by Mr. Richard Badger, a wealthy brewer, who had attended school at Stratford-on-Avon. He sent a letter to the *Times*, which appeared on 28 May 1903, offering £1,000 towards 'the cost of raising in London and at Stratford-on-Avon a statue worthy of Shakespeare's fame'. Undeterred by the lack of response, he approached the L.C.C. who offered a site, and on 12 August 1904 another letter from

Mr. Badger appeared in the *Times* urging a national statue to Shakespeare, offering '£500 down towards the expenses of the appeal for funds, plus an additional £2,000 in aid of the cost of the statue', and calling for the formation of 'an influential representative committee to make the appeal for funds'.[20] This time the response was enthusiastic, and the London Shakespeare Commemoration League led the way in the formation of a Shakespeare Memorial Committee, which in turn called a public meeting at the Mansion House on 28 February 1905. Committees and sub-committees proliferated, as did the suggestions for alternative memorials and sites, but a basic division was developing between the advocates of a living theatre commemorating Shakespeare, incorporating a National Theatre as put forward by Archer and Barker, and the supporters of a more limited, but more specific statue, as supported by Mr. Badger, or a grander edifice along the lines of the Albert Memorial. Some enthusiasts, like Walter Stephens, supported both a National Theatre and a statue of Shakespeare. He published a pamphlet early in 1905, *A Plea for a National Repertory Theatre,* in which he made 'a public offer of £5,000 towards the permanent establishment of a National Repertory Theatre in the West-End of London, if the public first subscribed £20,000 to such an object'.[21] He then expanded this proposal in May the same year, presumably as a result of the various committee meetings, in a second pamphlet with the full title: *The Proposed World's Tribute to Shakespeare: A Plea for the Erection of a Memorial Statue and National Theatre*. Stephens regarded the theatre as 'a handmaid of religion itself', and saw it as 'a shame and a national disgrace' that England possessed no 'Temple of the Drama' such as the *Comédie Française* or the *Deutsches Theatre*. He even suggested that every theatre in London and the Provinces hold a special matinée, the proceeds of which to be sent to a National Theatre fund. A suggestion in a lighter vein came from St. John Hankin in an article entitled 'How to Run an Art Theatre in London': he observed 'that as the expense of an evening at the theatre was a major obstacle, and as that expense was primarily to the benefit of cab owners and restaurateurs (and the modiste who dressed the ladies), then the restaurant keepers should subsidize the theatre by offering seats as bonuses to meals'.[22] National Theatre supporters received encouragement from a speech given by Winston Churchill (then Secretary of State for the Colonies) at a banquet in honour of Ellen Terry at the Hotel Cecil, 17 June 1906, in which he praised the efforts of individuals like Ellen Terry, Henry Irving and Beerbohm Tree to present Shakespeare on stage, and went on to regret the absence of a National Theatre. 'Think with what excitement and interest this nation witnessed the construction, or launching, of a Dread-nought', he exclaimed: 'what a pity it was that some measure of that interest could not be turned in the direction of the launching of, should he say, a national theatre?' Furthermore, he 'held that it was the duty of the State to be the generous but discriminating patron of the arts and the sciences'.[23] Unfortunately, this declaration was the closest any scheme came at that time to receiving any official government commitment.

Publication of the Mansion House Report on 5 March 1908, recommending 'an architectural Monument including a statue' in Portland Place, and announcing competitions for the designs, launched a wave of pamphlets, articles and letters to editors (notably that of Sir John Hare in the *Times*, 10 March 1908), and led to the formation of a rival committee in support of a National Theatre as a Shakespeare Memorial. This group called a meeting at the Lyceum on 19 May 1908, under the chairmanship of Lord Lytton, at which 'demonstration' the vote was overwhelmingly in support of motions 'in favour of the establishment of a national theatre as a memorial to Shakespeare', to set up the necessary action committee, and to co-operate with the Shakespeare Memorial Committee, who in a letter to Lord Lytton had anticipated friction by proposing a joint meeting.[24] After a preliminary meeting of representatives at the House of Lords on 28 May, both general committees met at the Mansion House on 23 July when they agreed to amalgamate as the "Shakespeare Memorial National Theatre General Committee" (S.M.N.T.), and formed a joint twenty-three member Executive Committee that included Sir John Hare, William Archer, Granville Barker, Edmund Gosse, Hon. Mrs. Alfred Lyttelton, A.W. Pinero, Bernard Shaw, Beerbohm Tree and Professor Israel Gollancz. The target date was 23 April 1916, the tercentenary of Shakespeare's death. The immediate concern was to secure at least one substantial contribution on which to base an appeal for funds. Apprehensions on this account dissolved in March 1909 when Mrs. Lyttelton announced the anonymous donation of £70,000. (The benefactor was later identified as Mr. Carl Meyer, who thereby ensured the knighthood which he received the following year.) A trust fund was formed and a general appeal for £500,000 was launched in 1909 by the publication of *An Illustrated Handbook* which formulated the aims of the S.M.N.T. as follows:

(1) to keep the plays of Shakespeare in its repertory;
(2) to revive whatever else is vital in English classical drama;
(3) to prevent recent plays of great merit from falling into oblivion;
(4) to produce new plays and to further the development of the modern drama;
(5) to produce translations of representative works of foreign drama, ancient and modern;
(6) to stimulate the art of acting through the varied opportunities which it will offer to the members of the company.[25]

Further publicity was obtained by Shaw's *The Dark Lady of the Sonnets*, first performed at the Haymarket on 24 November 1910, and various fund-raising activities were undertaken including 'The Masque of Shakespeare' in Regent's Park on 30 July 1910, a 'Shakespeare Ball' at the Albert Hall on 20 July 1911, and a Shakespeare Exhibition at Earl's Court the same year, featuring a replica of the Globe theatre.

Despite all these efforts, funds were not forthcoming, and an attempt was made in a Private Member's Bill (debated on 23 April 1913!) to obtain State assistance. The *Times* commented that the House was no place to debate artistic matters, being comprised of practical men who 'regard the drama as a digestive recreation rather than a serious art',[26] but the vote went 96 to 32 in favour of the motion. However, this was ruled an insufficient majority by the Speaker (a Private Bill required 100 votes), so much to the relief of many S.M.N.T. supporters, who were apprehensive of State aid, or 'control' with its socialistic overtones, the matter ended there. Nevertheless, some State support remained a virtual necessity in the face of the economic realities, and many of those hostile to full government financing would agree with H.A. Jones, no socialist, that because the public could be 'led to take an interest and delight in the drama as an intellectual entertainment', if given time a National Theatre would be able to pay its own way and give a lead to other theatres in London and the Provinces; therefore, it should be subsidized until it was self-sufficient, but not perpetually for then it would become inevitably 'a national mausoleum for the preservation of defunct specimens of dramatic art'.[27] Even after the S.M.N.T. failure to secure state support, Jones remained 'persuaded that it is the business of the government ... to supplement the funds for the establishment of a National Theatre, as a wise and economical expenditure of public money'.[28]

Supporters of a National Theatre received a set-back with the failure of the American equivalent. On 8 November 1909 the 2,300-seat New Theatre, in Central Park, New York, which had been erected by a group of millionaires to elevate the drama in America, opened its doors with a sumptuous production of *Antony and Cleopatra*. The theatre offered a true repertory, but many plays chosen were inconsistent with its size, and its variegated programme lacked any overall artistic direction or guiding policy. It was abandoned after two seasons, failing to discover any National American Drama and sustaining enormous losses. This collapse strengthened the hand of those urging caution in England. H.A. Jones suggested an interim solution whereby the S.M.N.T. should take over the Academy of Dramatic Art, founded in 1904 under Kenneth Barnes, and finance it out of the interest on monies gathered as 'a school of acting in public' with ultimate incorporation into the fully-fledged National Theatre when the time was ripe for it.[29] But the only action that was taken in this phase was the acquisition of a Bloomsbury site (over an acre freehold for £50,000) in 1913, after which the S.M.N.T. was forced to suspend activities by the outbreak of war.

One significant event in theatre history at the close of this period must not go unnoticed--the opening of the Old Vic in 1914 as the London home of Shakespeare. The history of the theatre was not encouraging for such a venture. It started life in 1818 as the Coburg and was renamed the Royal Victoria in 1833. It offered melodrama and gin to its Lambeth audiences, but closed in 1871 after attempts to transform it into a music hall. It became the New Victoria Palace, closed again in early 1880, then was reopened later that year by Miss Emma Cons as the Royal Victoria Coffee Music Hall, offering song, dance and temperance beverages to its customers. Her niece, Lilian Bayliss, took over in 1898, staging variety shows, ballad and symphony concerts, 'animated pictures', and opera in English. Finally, thanks to a gift from the musical comedy writer and manager, Sir George Dance, and against the advice of theatre experts, Lilian Bayliss launched the first of many Shakespeare seasons in October 1914 with *The Taming of the Shrew, Hamlet* and *The Merchant of Venice*-- all produced by Mr. and Mrs. Matheson Lang.

Shakespeare may have found a London home, but it was a precarious one, and the fulfilment of the National Theatre dream seemed as far off as ever. Although a detailed narration of what occurred subsequently is beyond the scope of this book, given the impetus provided during the period under discussion, it is appropriate to conclude the account. Briefly, events moved as follows. At the end of the war, the Drama League was founded, and included the establishment of a National Theatre in its aims. The New Shakespeare Company under Bridges-Adams was formed in 1919, financed by S.M.N.T. funds, which received a boost three years later from the sale of the Bloomsbury site. Proposals followed to support or amalgamate with the Old Vic or with Sadler's Wells, and to acquire various London sites, but they all met with objections from the Charity Commissioners or other obstacles. William Archer took up the cudgels again in the 1920s, and Granville Barker updated the 1907 scheme in *The National Theatre* (1930) in which he proposed two theatres under one roof. All appeared ready for launching in 1939 with the acquisition of a one-third acre site in the Cromwell Road for £75,000, which left £75,000 in the bank, but the war forced another postponement. In 1945 the S.M.N.T. amalgamated with the Old Vic, and in 1948 the years of effort bore fruit in the National Theatre Act, which provided for up to £1,000,000 towards the building and equipment of a theatre, but left the date of implementation to the discretion of the Chancellor of the Exchequer. A foundation stone was laid by the Queen Mother on 13 July 1951 on a site adjacent to the Royal Festival Hall, but the following year it was agreed to move to a better location adjoining County Hall. Finally, in 1969, work was commenced on yet another site, Princess Meadow, below Waterloo Bridge, and the doors of the National Theatre opened in March 1976.[30] Six years later, Shakespeare, too, obtained a true London home--the Barbican, where the Royal Shakespeare Company, after twenty-one years at the Aldwych, now has its own specially designed theatre and operates in association with the Guildhall School of Music and Drama. The inter-war and more recent post-war years had proved as demanding as those before 1914, but the problems were more with ways and means of implementing a general agreement to establish a National Theatre than with obtaining consensus between groups with competing proposals. The significance of the earlier phase of the campaign can be missed if measured only by immediate results, which, as in other areas discussed in this study, were nil or short-lived or many more years in coming to fruition. Those first efforts to establish a National Theatre and to commemorate or find a national home for Shakespeare, epitomize the idealism and energy of people like Arnold, Jones, Archer and Granville Barker, who were committed to the vision of a revitalized British theatre freed from the restrictive practices and narrow thinking that had come to be characteristic of the bulk of commercial theatre at the end of the Victorian age, and who campaigned on many fronts to achieve their goals.

However, now that those goals have been reached, one question still remains: to what extent will the new ventures, despite subsidies, in turn be victims of the evils of commercialism in one form or another? The causes may not be quite the same as at the turn of the century--inadequate budgets or inflation-driven costs instead of hard-nosed entrepreneurs--but the result is no different: to exist, theatre must pay its way, which means, ultimately, that it must attract patrons. One essential difference between the period discussed above and the present day is that the education of the audience, which was so important to the revitalization of the Victorian/Edwardian theatre, has succeeded beyond anything those pioneers of modernism could have foreseen or hoped, and audiences expect--indeed, demand--an enormous range and variety of theatrical experiences. The challenge now is not to persuade audiences to attend new forms of theatre, but to maintain a vigorous classical repertoire while at the same time creating dynamic new forms and modes of presentation that will attract the substantial numbers that are necessary to keep the enterprise solvent: a new face for an age-old problem.

NOTES

1. Geoffrey Whitworth, *The Making of a National Theatre* (Faber & Faber, London, 1951), p. 24. Throughout this chapter I am indebted to the comprehensive and detailed account this book

provides.

2. Letters from Taylor, *Echo,* 13 and 19 June 1871 and others 20-26 June.

3. William Archer and R.W. Lowe, *The Fashionable Tragedian: A Criticism* (n.p., London, 1877), p. 24.

4. See Whitworth, pp. 31-3, who quotes Irving in full.

5. *Times,* 26 October 1878, p. 6.

6. Matthew Arnold, 'The French Play in London', *English Literature and Irish Politics, Works,* ed. R.H. Super (Ann Arbor, 1973), vol. 9, p. 81.

7. Ibid., p. 83.

8. Whitworth, p. 37.

9. William Archer, *Fortnightly Review,* N.S. vol. 45 (May 1889), pp. 610-26.

10. William Archer, *Theatrical World of 1896* (Walter Scott, London, 1897), pp. xi-xii.

11. H. Hamilton Fyfe, *Fortnightly Review,* N.S. vol. 67 (May 1900), pp. 807-14.

12. William Archer and H. Granville Barker, *A National Theatre. Scheme and Estimates* (Duckworth, London, 1907), p. vi. Subsequent page references in parentheses.

13. G.B. Shaw, *Collected Letters 1898-1910,* ed. Dan H. Laurence (Max Reinhardt, London, 1972), pp. 264-7 and 268-9.

14. G.B. Shaw, *Bernard Shaw's Letters to Granville Barker,* ed. C.B. Purdom (Phoenix House, London, 1956), p. 144.

15. H.A. Jones, *The Foundations of a National Drama* (Chapman Hall, London, 1913), pp. 17-18.

16. Ibid., p. 115.

17. *Times,* 3 February 1902, p. 9, and 4 February 1902, p. 8.

18. Poel's account is given in 'The Memorial Scheme', *Shakespeare in the Theatre* (Sidgwick & Jackson, London, 1913), pp. 227-40: a reprint of his article in *The New Age,* June 1911.

19. Quoted in Whitworth, p. 40.

20. *Times,* 12 August 1904, p. 3.

21. Walter Stephens, *A Plea for a National Repertory Theatre* (n.p., London, 1905), p. 3.

22. St. John Hankin, *Fortnightly Review,* N.S. vol. 82 (November 1907), pp. 814-18.

23. *Times,* 18 June 1906, p. 10.

24. See Whitworth, pp. 74-9.

25. Quoted in Whitworth, p. 83.

26. *Times,* 24 April 1913, p. 12.

27. Jones, p. 83.

28. Ibid., Note, p. 120.

29. Ibid., p. 133.

30. For details after 1914, see Alfred Emmet, 'The Long Prehistory of the National Theatre', *Theatre Quarterly,* vol. 6, no. 21 (Spring 1976), pp. 55-62.

Chapter Six

THE CENSORSHIP SAGA

> 'I haven't written plays for a number of reasons, but one of the chief of these was the persuasion that my work might in the end be made abortive by the incalculable whim of the Censor'.
>
> H.G. Wells

Hand in hand with the campaign for a National Theatre, and sharing much the same objective of liberating the English drama, was the campaign to abolish the Censor, who was judge and warder of the 'prison of Puritanism' (Arnold's phrase), and ensured that no play--or even scene or line--which might offend the moral, religious or political sensitivities of audiences should escape his vigilance and spread its corruption. Asked what happened to a play that was refused a licence, the Hon. Spencer Brabazon Ponsonby, Comptroller of the Lord Chamberlain's Department in 1866, replied: '[it] is merely banished, and there is an end of it'. But his Department was to discover in the following decades that it was far from 'the end of it'.

The history of dramatic censorship in England dates back to 1543, when Henry VIII, concerned with the protection of Church and State, proclaimed 'an Act for the advancement of true religion and for the abolishment of the contrary'. There was great fear that the stage would be used as a pulpit for political and religious heresy, so the Act gave approval to plays 'for the rebuking and reproaching of vices and the setting forth of virtue', but forbade anything which challenged the new orthodoxy. Edward VI repealed this Act, but things began to get out of hand; therefore, in 1551 a Royal Proclamation declared that all plays or interludes required a Royal licence before being performed, and subsequently it was ruled that a licence to print plays was also required.[1]

Problems arose as to who was to read and censor the plays. During Elizabeth's reign this lucrative task became the prerogative of the Master of Revels, under the jurisdiction of the Lord Chamberlain. In 1737 Walpole brought in the Licensing Act aimed primarily -- and successfully -- at silencing Fielding's satiric onslaught against his regime. It transferred the censorship from the Master of Revels to full-time 'Licensers of the Stage', still under the wing of the Lord Chamberlain. In a speech opposing the bill, Lord Chesterfield, echoing Milton's *Areopagitica,* declaimed:

> If Poets and Players are to be restrained, let them be restrained as other Subjects are, by the known Laws of their Country; if they offend, let them be tried as every *Englishman* ought to be, by God and their Country. Do not let us subject them to the arbitrary Will and Pleasure of any one Man. A Power lodged in the hands of one single Man, to judge and determine, without any Limitation, without any Controul or Appeal, is a sort of Power unknown to our Laws, inconsistent with our Constitution. It is a higher, a more absolute Power than we trust even to the King himself; and therefore I must think, we ought not to vest any such Power in His Majesty's Lord Chamberlain.[2]

Following the work of a Committee of Enquiry established in 1832, in which the dramatist Edward Bulwer-Lytton (later Lord Lytton) played a leading part, a Theatre Act was passed in 1843. This Act abolished the monopoly of the 'patent' theatres, Covent Garden and Drury Lane, granted in 1660 by Charles II to stage 'legitimate' drama; restricted the Lord Chamberlain's powers to license theatres to those in London; and, rather than abolish the censorship of plays, as Bulwer had hoped, strengthened the Lord Chamberlain's powers in this respect by requiring submission to his office of every new play or addition to an old play, and, when an unlicensed or banned piece was staged, by empowering him to fine the offending theatre, or worse, deprive it of its licence. The statute of 1737 had conferred upon the Lord Chamberlain an unfettered power of veto, with no indication of the grounds upon which he was to act: the Act of 1843 vaguely restricted his powers of prohibition to cases in which 'he shall be of opinion that it is fitting for the preservation of good manners, decorum or of the public peace so to do'.

The Examiner of Plays became a semi-permanent official; during Victoria's reign there were eighteen Lords Chamberlain, but only five Examiners.[3] In 1855 the Examiner was obliged to add the task of Inspector of Theatres to that of reading 200 or more plays a year, and was required to inspect annually every London theatre licensed by the Lord Chamberlain for such things as structural soundness and safety precautions. William Bodham Donne (a descendant of John Donne related to William Cowper), former librarian and Examiner from 1857 to 1874, complained:

> I am fallen on evil times ... I am paid no more, indeed rather less, than my predecessors in the Examinership, but I am set to do as much work as the whole series, since there was a censor, ever performed: I mount upon such pinnacles as Satan stands on in *Paradise Regained:* I inhale evil smells: I cross dangerous places: 'sometimes I fall into the water and sometimes into the fire', and all for £500 a year, besides injuring my mind by reading nonsense and perilling my soul by reading wickedness.[4]

Fortunately for Donne's successors, the Examiner was relieved of this extra task in 1878, because the number of submissions increased steadily, more than doubling by 1900.

The Examiner was required both to act as a watchdog to defend Society and, to the extent that he had to gauge what the public would or would not tolerate, to function as an interpreter of public opinion. Like a good politician, he would, ideally, follow and lead at the same time. His alertness was required on three fronts: religious, political and moral.[5] For most of the nineteenth century, in the interest of maintaining religious decorum, the Examiner insisted on a complete ban on biblical incident and quotation of passages or phrases from scripture, and on the elimination of most religious references, even to the extent of excising, or substantially reducing, such common phrases as 'thank Heaven'. Curiously, opera was given far greater latitude than drama--presumably because music dignified the presentation. There is little doubt that for most of the century, particularly the middle years when the evangelical movement was at its zenith, the Examiner interpreted public religious sensitivity correctly. However, by the end of the century, although the public view had shifted, the Examiner remained conservative. In 1884 he did licence Jones' *Saints and Sinners,* which had religion as its theme and quoted scripture, but this was a minor breach, soon sealed.

For the most part, dramatists were self-censoring regarding religious material, but in the political field the Examiner was required to maintain constant vigilance. This was particularly necessary early in the century when audiences were volatile, and the fear of them being aroused was not unfounded, but as audiences became more genteel, this justification no longer applied--yet the prohibitions on political content continued. Political and personal satire was the object of great suspicion, and was effectively prevented by the ban on the portrayal of or allusion to notable personages--especially politicians and members of the Royal Family--and on references to current events. (The Music Halls, not being subject to censorship, suffered no such restriction.) The fear of sedition also lay behind the strong opposition to 'Newgate Drama' mid-century, particularly plays based on the notorious highwayman Jack Sheppard, because even though the conclusion might teach a terrible moral lesson, sensationalising crime and romanticising the criminal might encourage the younger elements in particular to vice and incite violence (c.f. the current debate on t.v. violence). The popularity of this genre declined in the last quarter of the century, and the censor's moral opprobrium focussed on matters such as irregular liaisons that lay outside the accepted code of respectability. From 1880 onwards, English dramatists, taking their cues from the French, and responding to the interests of the 'society' theatre audience, began to explore social issues and sexual relationships, becoming almost obsessed with the woman-with-a-past theme. The Examiner responded in a curious way, tolerating the comic or flippant treatment of such themes, but, as the dramatists and critics like Archer and Shaw complained, preventing any serious discussion of them. Again, the Examiner accurately reflected the prevalent public view that the chief, and perhaps only, function of the drama was to entertain, and the majority of critics, led by Clement Scott, loudly upheld this view; but a growing number of dramatists inspired (or tainted, according to your viewpoint) by Ibsen and Zola and their continental emulators, aspired to do more--to examine, analyse and question prevailing personal, social and political beliefs, practices and problems with the same freedom available to their fellow authors in the novel and to contributors to periodicals--to everyone, in effect, except dramatists. And, as indicated in earlier chapters, a new audience was being created for the new drama, despite the difficulties of getting it staged.

During the century, successive Parliamentary committees of enquiry were appointed in 1853, 1866 and 1892, each of which endorsed the system, despite some incredible absurdities on the part of the Examiner. One example was the refusal of a licence for a stage version of Disraeli's *Coningsby* because of its 'quasi-political' content. Another was the banning of Augier's tragedy *Les Lionnes Pauvres* which the Examiner recognized as 'profoundly moral in its ultimate purpose', but vetoed because he considered that 'if presented to a mixed English audience it would give much offence', while at the same time he gave his stamp of approval to *The Man with Three Hats*, a farce that William Archer condemned as 'stupidly gross'.[6] Objections were made to innocuous detail, like the refusal to allow a waiter in *Twins* to appear as brother to a bishop (approved when changed to a professor!). H.A. Jones' *Welcome Little Stranger* was refused a licence mainly because of a preliminary sequence which showed a nurse cross the stage, a servant open the door to let in a doctor carrying his bag, some agitated passing to and fro', and finally the nurse's return to announce: 'It is a fine boy'.[7] Statistically there could be little complaint: of 19,304 plays submitted between 1852 and 1912, only 103 were refused a licence. Of these, 30 were banned between 1895 and 1909 out of a total of 7,000, which indicates the substantial increase in volume in these years. Other plays, of course, had obtained licences only after modifications had been made to ensure that anything the Examiner considered prejudicial to public morals or religious sensibilities had been expunged.

Opposition to the censorship increased steadily in the latter part of the nineteenth century not only as a result of the actual plays banned, but also, as Charles Kingsley put it in 1873, because 'few highly educated men now think it worth while to go to see any play ... and still fewer highly educated men think it worth while to write plays, finding that since the grosser excitements of the imagination have become forbidden themes, there is really very little to write about'.[8] But significant shifts were occurring in society, notably an increasing middle-class interest in the theatre, which was, as noted in the first chapter, becoming more 'respectable' and attracting growing audiences, many of whom would not be at all averse to attending serious drama, as the success of Robertson, Jones, Grundy and Pinero was to prove. The rising young critic William Archer led the opposition with such articles as 'The Censorship of the Stage', inspired by the 1866 Enquiry, in which he gives an account of the history of stage censorship, citing its countless absurdities and concluding that the censorship, largely by the confession of the conscientious but naive Bodham Donne, was 'alternately tyrannical and futile, odious and ridiculous ... inconsistent ... anomalous ... unjust ... [and] destructive'.[9] Other voices began to be heard. For example, writing in December 1889 in the last issue of the conservative *Theatre* to be edited by Clement Scott, W.H. Hudson asked:

> whether the time has not come for the dramatic Censorship to take its place in the Limbo of outworn institutions ... the drama labours under disadvantages which no longer beset any of the sister arts ... England is the country of free speech and a free Press; why is it not the country of a free drama also?[10]

And he called for the Censorship 'to be replaced by the truer Censorship of public opinion and a free Press'.

In March 1892 a Select Committee was appointed 'to inquire into the operation of Acts of Parliament relating to the Licensing and Regulation of THEATRES and PLACES of PUBLIC ENTERTAINMENT, and to consider and report any alterations in the law which may appear desirable'. The terms of reference included an appraisal of the operation of the Censorship. Archer seized the opportunity to present the case for abolition, but he was unsupported, and his moderate and careful evidence was more than outweighed by the pro-censorship managers, who felt secure from prosecution when in possession of a licence, and by the statements of the incumbent Examiner, E.F. Smythe Pigott, whose self-justification can now be recognized as self-indictment of the first order:

> [5178] ... what is sometimes invidiously called a "censorship" is nothing in effect but the friendly and perfectly disinterested action of an advisor who has the permanent interests of the stage at heart ... With the widest freedom of abstract political opinion and sentiment in stage plays, I have never deemed it my right or duty to interfere, but I have taken the liberty to ask intelligent managers to consider for themselves whether, in a country and community so saturated with politics as our own, the public would care to have places of amusement turned into political arenas; and I have cautioned them against allowing the stage to be converted, by dull and impudent buffoons, at a loss for real wit and humour, into pillories for public men.

> [5227] I have studied Ibsen's plays pretty carefully, and all the characters in Ibsen's plays appear to me morally deranged. All the heroines are dissatisfied spinsters who look on marriage as a monopoly, or dissatisfied married women in a chronic state of rebellion against not only the conditions which nature has imposed on their sex, but against all the duties and obligations of mothers and wives; and as for the men they are all rascals or imbeciles.

Examples of Mr. Pigott's 'disinterested action' became the subject of attacks by Shaw, who from 1895 onwards joined the assault on 'that insane institution for the taxation of authors, the Censorship of the Lord Chamberlain'. Shaw berated Mr. Pigott--a 'despised and incapable old official'--for refusing to license three plays in particular: *A Freedom in Fetters,* by Sydney Olivier, which embodied 'his observations of human nature as developed in the British colonies by a tropical climate', because it criticized public life; *The First Step,* by William Heinemann (who, ironically, had refused to publish *A Freedom in Fetters)* because 'the hero and heroine are living together without being legally married'; and *A Leader of Men,* by Charles E.D. Ward, which was based on the actual events of the Gladstone-Parnell-Mrs. O'Shea affair. In order to be licensed, Ward's play had to undergo a process of adaptation to Mr. Pigott's ethical code that 'consisted in taking a real episode which made a profound moral impression on the nation, and ruthlessly demoralizing it'. The death of Mr. Pigott in 1895 brought a tirade from Shaw entitled 'The Late Censor' in which he condemned Mr. Pigott as 'a walking compendium of vulgar insular prejudice', and went on to attack the ultra-conservative attitudes of mind he represented, especially as upheld in the *Daily Telegraph* obituary, which Shaw assumed to have been written by Clement Scott. Shaw apologized when he discovered it had been written by Lionel Monckton, who had not only imitated Scott's style, but had also reiterated Scott's ideas, so Shaw's argument was not completely invalidated. Shaw's article also asserted that the censorship, an 'abomination', was largely to blame for the 'relative poverty and inferiority' of British drama since 1737, and challenged: 'Would Shakespear *[sic]*, or the great Greek dramatists have stood a chance with Mr. Pigott?'[11] H.A. Jones made much the same point some fourteen years later when he declared that 'no modern serious English dramatist has claimed nearly so great a freedom as is found in almost every book in the Bible, and in every play of Shakespeare'.[12]

The opportunity given by Mr. Pigott's death to abolish the office was not taken, and the appointment went to Mr. George Alexander Redford, former bank manager, whose single qualification appears to have been the friendship of his predecessor, for whom he had deputised on occasion during periods of illness. The appointment of un unknown came as a surprise, considering that the seventy original candidates included such notables as Clement Scott, Edmund Gosse and Joseph Knight, and the final choice lay between Redford and Ernest Bendall, editor of *The Observer* (who eventually succeeded Redford in 1911--see below).

A matter closely related to the censorship was the licensing of theatre buildings, a complex affair. Under the 1843 Act, the Lord Chamberlain's jurisdiction extended over the cities of London and Westminster, the boroughs of Finsbury, Marylebone, Tower Hamlets, Lambeth and Southwark, Windsor, and other places of Royal residence. Outside these areas most licences were issued by local councils. In Dublin theatres were under the control of the Lord Lieutenant, and those at Oxford and Cambridge were the responsibility of the two universities. Within jurisdictions there were different types of licence. The London County Council, for example, offered five options: (1) for plays, but no drink; (2) for plays and drink; (3) for plays and drink and smoking; (4) for variety entertainments, and smoking without drinks, and without plays of any kind; and (5) for variety entertainments and drinking and smoking. In a lecture, 'The Licensing Chaos in Theatres and Music Halls', given on 27 February 1910 to the National Sunday League, H.A. Jones catalogues some of the 'endless and futile absurdities' that arose out of such a 'bewildering and mischievous chaos of stupid restrictions'. One of his many examples concerns the L.C.C. licensed Camden Theatre, which

> was opened as a theatre, and like most theatres in these bad days it didn't pay. So it was sold to a Music Hall Syndicate. They opened it with a variety performance. A common informer sought the parish constable ... and the theatre closed. It was reopened with a cinematograph and an electric piano. Down came the common informer again and

> said "You are not licensed for music." The manager said an electric piano was not music; but this unanswerable plea did not serve. He was fined forty shillings, and was told he ought to be fined four hundred pounds, for providing harmless amusement for his fellow citizens. And again the theatre was closed. Is that common sense? Is that fair play?[13]

The genesis of many such problems lay in the different historical origins of theatres and music halls: the former had a long record of regulation, as indicated above, but the latter did not come under any legal supervision until the Disorderly Houses Act, 1751, under which Music Halls in London and Westminster and districts within twenty miles were issued music and dancing licences, and were not licensed to perform stage plays. Their fare was recognized as being of 'low' character for the entertainment of the 'lower orders'. However, by the turn of the century music halls had begun to improve their offerings by including, illicitly, sketches and short plays. There were some prosecutions, but the sheer volume--Jones reports 'estimates of four to six hundred of these plays .. enacted nightly in Great Britain'[14]--rendered court action impossible in all but a very few flagrant cases. Jones, and many others, concluded that there was only one way to settle the matter with any degree 'of common-sense and fair play all round', and that was to permit every theatre and music hall 'to give and perform whatever entertainment the manager may choose and the audiences may wish to see; the only restriction being that such entertainment shall not be indecent, or dangerous, or harmful to the general public'. As this statement implies, the licensing of theatres was associated with censorship by more than their legal connection with the Lord Chamberlain's office. 'Thousands of uncensored plays' were performed a year, and 'without ... a single prosecution or even a single complaint on the score of immorality or indecency'.[15] This fact alone, Jones claims, proves that English audiences 'do not need a censor to protect them from their dramatists'.

It is therefore not surprising that one of the main arguments of the supporters of the abolition of stage censorship was that the serious dramatist was being discriminated against. Not only were the music-halls free from the Examiner's veto, but also the novelist, poet and artist suffered no such control, and even dramatists could publish their plays subject only to the normal laws of libel and decency. William Archer, in *The Old Drama and the New,* records the shifting status of drama as literature:

> throughout the eighteenth century, and even down to the days of Knowles and Bulwer Lytton, the drama was still recognised as a branch of literature. Plays were not only printed, but bought and read ... [But by the middle of the

> nineteenth century] the divorce between the stage and literature was so complete that people entirely lost the habit of reading plays.[16]

Piracy and plagiarism also deterred dramatists from publishing until the Dramatic Copyright Act, 1883, the International Copyright Act, 1887, and the American Copyright Bill, 1891, gave them protection. This last act gave an added incentive to publication because to secure copyright in America, two copies of the play had to be delivered to the Librarian of Congress not later than the day of publication. 1891 saw the issue of collected editions of plays by both Pinero and Jones. In his preface to *The Times* (1891), Pinero declared: 'I have long hoped that the time would arrive when an English dramatist might find himself free to put into the hands of the public the text of his play simultaneously with its representation on stage'.[17] Jones, too, in his 1891 preface to *Saints and Sinners* recognised the 1891 Act as being 'of the highest import to English playwrights and the future of English drama'.[18]

Commenting on the American Copyright Bill, the *Era* urged authors 'to prepare their plays for press in a readable form', and warned that 'we are never likely to have a native drama of much literary merit without the practice of publication to emphasise conscientious finish and rebuke slovenly writing'.[19] It was not only the authors who needed to ensure a 'conscientious finish', but also the publishers, because the sixpenny pamphlet, paper-back prompt copy or 'acting editions', which had been the standard form for sixty years, gave little encouragement to the general reader. Despite the success of Pinero and Jones with their published editions, and of William Archer with his published translations of Ibsen, publishers and authors were slow to exploit their opportunity, and it was Shaw who was first to capitalize fully on the market for printed plays. Ironically, it was the Examiner's prohibition, which immediately enhanced a play's sales potential, as much as the unwillingness of commercial managers to stage his plays, that drove Shaw to publishing in 1897--and brought him initial fame and fortune as a dramatist. St. John Ervine claims, not without hyperbole, that 'the whole traffic of play production in book form was revolutionised by G.B.S., and the fact that publishers' lists now commonly include plays is entirely due to him'.[20]

With Shaw entering the field, and others following his example, the volume of published plays increased rapidly, and their evident popularity made a nonsense of the licensing procedure, especially as the 1883 Act implied that a dramatist lost his rights if a play was published before it had been staged. This led to the practice of giving one 'copyright performance', often with the author's friends in the cast, and an audience of one, as soon as the Lord Chamberlain issued his licence. If a licence was refused, the author would then excise all offensive material and re-submit. A licence would be duly issued, and a 'copyright performance' of the emasculated version staged, after which the author was free to publish the original, unexpurgated text. This procedure fooled nobody, but it protected the author's interest in his work, and satisfied the Lord Chamberlain, who knew that the unlicensed version could not be staged.

A significant result of publication was that opposition to the censorship was able to cohere around specific plays whose full texts were known to the literate public, and it became increasingly apparent that it was not the smutty, indecent play that was being suppressed, but the serious attempt to put controversial social issues onto the stage: i.e., the new drama.

The first organised attempt to circumvent the licensing laws was made by the Shelley Society, founded by Dr. F.J. Furnivall in 1886 primarily to stage *The Cenci* (1819), which no manager had been able to license because of its theme of a father's incestuous passion for his daughter. The Society staged a 'private' performance, open to its members only, at the Grand Theatre, Islington, on 7 May 1886. The general public was not admitted, and no money was taken at the door. Although no action was taken against the theatre, when the manager applied for renewal of his licence he was warned against further complicity in such evasions of the law, and the theatre owners inserted a clause in the lease to the effect that no unlicensed play was to be performed in their theatre. This did not deter the Society from attempting to celebrate the Shelley centenary in 1892 by staging the play again. Early in that year Shaw, who had handled press relations for the first performance, negotiated with Beerbohm Tree for use of the Haymarket Theatre on behalf of the Shelley Society and the Independent Theatre. By August he had to concede defeat. Writing to Mrs. Forman (Alma Murray), he complained:

> It is impossible to get the Cenci licensed. We tried our best; but Pigott is evidently determined not to take the responsibility. It was said that he was quite ready to wink at an invitation performance; but when Beerbohm Tree was on the point of lending us the Haymarket, an interview which he had with Pigott completely changed his tone: he remained sympathetic, and offered to lend us the scenery &c; but it was quite evident that he had been effectually bound over by the censorship.[21]

This rebuff occurred after the Independent Theatre had followed the lead given by the Shelley Society and staged *Ghosts* unlicensed at the Royalty Theatre, 13 March 1891, to an audience of 'invited' members and guests. No prosecutions followed, but the Independent Theatre discovered that all theatre managers were 'bound over' like Tree, and *Ghosts* was the only unlicensed production given by that body. However, a chink in the Censor's armour had been discovered, and in due course a wedge was driven in by the Stage Society (see Chapter Three) and similar groups like the London Maeterlinck Society, formed to give performances of the censored *Monna Vanna* by Lugné-Poe and his *Théâtre de l'Oeuvre* at the Victoria Hall, Bayswater, on 19 June 1902. The result of the Censor's action was typical, comments H.A. Jones: *Monna Vanna*

> was played six or eight times, that is, it was probably seen by four times the number of people who would have seen it if the Censor had licensed it. Therefore, moral or immoral, the net result of the Censor's action was that a scandal was caused, the Censor was defeated, and the play was performed to increased audiences.[22]

Such evasions had little direct value in the anti-censorship campaign, which went on intermittently throughout the 1890s and early years of this century, except to draw attention to the question and to provide a focus for further diatribes from the 'Ancients' led by Clement Scott on the one side, condemning the plays and upholding the censorship, and from the 'Moderns' led by William Archer on the other, condemning the censorship and extolling the plays.

The new Examiner of Plays, George Alexander Redford, was not long in perpetrating his own absurdities in the Donne-Pigott tradition, and insulting the intelligence of both dramatists and their public. His explanations, when given, were examples of *obscurum per obscurius*, serving only to perplex and incense: *Bethlehem*, by Laurence Housman, was banned because of its subject, but *Everyman* was permitted because written before 1737, and *Eager Heart*, by Florence Buckton, was licensed because it was 'a very simple little imitation of a miracle play ... done at Christmas'; *Monna Vanna* was forbidden because of 'immorality of plot', yet *The Devil*, with a very similar situation, was passed, being merely 'a flamboyant piece of stage business' rather than a serious literary work; and the Strauss Opera *Salome*, based on Wilde's banned text, was refused a licence until 'all biblical allusions were removed', John the Baptist renamed 'The Prophet', and his head on the platter 'replaced by a bloodstained disk covered with a cloth'--subterfuges that could have deceived not a single member of any audience.[23]

Censors had been asked repeatedly for statements of principle for the guidance of authors. Bodham Donne had 'explained that he deleted from the English drama anything in the shape of an oath, anything which turns religion into ridicule, and any political joke'.[24] H.A. Jones observed how the office subsumed the man:

> Mr. Pigott, who in private life was so broad and liberal and easy-going, became a different creature in his official garb. He once told me that managers were mainly licentious in their tastes and aims; that dramatic authors were mainly licentious in their tastes and aims; and that they were naturally so because licentiousness paid in the theatre.[25]

We have seen that Mr. Pigott felt it his duty to protect 'public men' from being pilloried on the stage, but writers and artists, no doubt because they were kin to dramatic authors in 'licentiousness in their tastes and aims', were fair game, as Oscar Wilde discovered when soon after *Salome* had been refused a licence one was granted to *The Poet and the Puppets*, by J.M. Glover and Charles Brookfield, a burlesque of *Lady Windermere's Fan* which featured an actor imitating Wilde in dress, voice and manner. This was not the first time Wilde had been caricatured, having been the butt of Gilbert's satire in *Patience* (1881). The prohibition of plays with religious subjects, and censoring of all references to God or Biblical figures or events, became increasingly difficult to understand or justify, except on the grounds that it was 'law' by virtue of being the established practice of the Examiner. A Scriptural play depicting the life of Joseph was presented at the Coliseum, a theatre not licensed for stage plays. It would have been forbidden at a regular theatre, but avoided censorship or prosecution by being given in dumbshow! Mr. Pigott told the 1892 Committee that he was proud to have prevented

> (5183) ... the proposed representation of the Ober Ammergau Passion Play at a London theatre; [and] the placarding of the town with a title of a sensational drama *[God and the Man* by Robert Buchanan] offensive to the religious feelings of the public.

How could such an attitude be maintained after 1901 when William Poel's production of *Everyman* launched a wave of pageants and revivals of miracle plays? *Everyman* itself was revived annually and attended by what one writer termed 'Phalanxes of Clergymen', but when Laurence Housman's *Bethlehem* was refused a licence in 1902 he had to form a 'Bethlehem Society' to stage it privately. After considerable difficulty, he succeeded in finding a suitable stage available to him at the Great Hall of the Imperial Institute, part of the University of London. His troubles were not over (he had many with this play, mainly related to the demands of his producer, Gordon Craig): at the last minute the fire department objected to a pile of stuffed sacks representing sheep, and even when this was overcome, Housman had to turn away 'an *agent provocateur*, sent presumably by the Censor to offer gate-money and so bring us within the reach of the law'. The play was subsequently licensed on condition that the Virgin not speak and the Holy Child not be seen. Many years later, Housman declared:

> among my thirty-two plays that have been censored, two up to date have received a free pardon. And I have no doubt that when I can no longer have the benefit of them, the rest will follow, and find grace with a department which has the unique power in this country of destroying property at the fiat of a single official, whose opinion in matters of taste has the weight of law.[26]

Officially, the subject matter and the play's content determined the censor's verdict, but there is little doubt that the author's name and reputation swayed his decisions. W.S. Gilbert, having established as early as 1872 that on three separate occasions he had 'systematically declined to take the slightest notice of [the Examiner's] instructions',[27] testified at the 1909 enquiry that he had experienced no interference from the Examiner. However, back in 1873 there had been a confrontation with the Lord Chamberlain over *The Happy Land*, written in collaboration with Gilbert À. Beckett, because of changes in performance to the original licensed text and the making up of actors to represent three politicians: Gladstone, Lowe and Ayrton. Also, as recently as 1907, on the occasion of the visit of the Japanese Crown Prince and Fleet in 1907, the Lord Chamberlain himself had banned *The Mikado* for a year for fear of giving offence to 'our allies'.[28] But neither of these incidents constituted interference in what Gilbert had written; he had quite freely let his satire range widely over the political and social spectrum, and he obviously held in contempt an official who dared not provoke a National Institution with a strong temper and a sharp tongue:

> ZARA: This is a Lord High Chamberlain
> Of purity the gauge--
> He'll cleanse our Court from moral stain
> And purify our Stage.
>
> LORD BRAMALEIGH: Yes--Yes--Yes
> Court reputations I revise,
> And presentations scrutinize,
> New plays I read with jealous eyes
> And purify the Stage.

(*Utopia Limited*, 1893)

His reputation established, Pinero too was able to trespass where others feared to tread--or were blue-pencilled back over the line of decorum if they did trespass--and was allowed to treat the woman-with-a-past theme seriously in *The Second Mrs.*

Tanqueray, for example, without incurring the displeasure of the Examiner over a single line. However, a play by Robert Buchanan with a similar theme and treatment, *The New Don Quixote* (1895), was refused a licence (Buchanan was incensed and protested vehemently to no avail), and in order to get permission for the copyright performance of *Mrs. Warren's Profession* in 1898, Shaw had to produce a bowdlerised version.

When asked at the 1909 Enquiry on what principles he proceeded in licensing a play placed before him, Mr. Redford replied:

> [194] ... Simply bringing to bear an official point of view and keeping up a standard. It is really impossible to define what the principle may be. There are no principles that can be defined. I follow precedent. I was under Mr. Pigott for a great many years--that is to say as a personal friend--and I obtained an insight into the duties then.

The humour of such declarations was no doubt lost on the unfortunate dramatist when, as Shaw said, his 'livelihood, his reputation, and his inspiration and mission are at the personal mercy of the Censor'.[29]

Matters came to a head in 1907 when Edward Garnett's *The Breaking Point* and Granville Barker's *Waste* fell under the Examiner's axe. Frederick Harrison, manager of the Haymarket, had accepted Garnett's play in December 1906 because, as quoted in Garnett's Preface to the published edition, he wanted to introduce it 'to that section of the public which is alive to what the theatre might be'. Mr. Redford privately advised Harrison not to apply for a licence, but Garnett insisted on doing so. When a licence was refused, Garnett asked for an explanation, and Mr. Redford's reply so infuriated him that he wrote back, roundly condemning the Examiner and all he stood for. This letter was included in the Preface, and incorporated Mr. Redford's reply, which ran:

> I trust you will absolve me from any discourtesy if I point out that my official relations are only concerned with the Managers of Theatres. It is always painful for me to decline to recommend a licence, and in this case I hoped to avoid any possible appearance of censure on anyone by suggesting privately to Mr. Harrison the desirability of withdrawing this piece. I cannot suppose that he has any doubt as to the reason.[30]

'If reputation alone was in question', Garnett snarled, 'who would not rather incur your frown, along with Sophocles and Shelley, than share the smiles which you lavish on prurient frivolity' (pp.xxiv-xxv). In Barker's case, the Examiner's refusal to license *Waste* was a bitter blow, although it could not have been unexpected. He refused to make the changes required by Mr. Redford, who, as Barker told the subsequent 1909 Enquiry, wanted him 'to moderate and modify the extremely outspoken references to sexual relations'. The hero of *Waste*, Henry Trebell, a professional politician, seduces a married woman, who becomes pregnant and seeks an abortion. All references to this 'criminal operation' had to be eliminated. As Barker pointed out, he had recently produced under licence 'a play *[Votes for Women]* by Elizabeth Robins, the plot of which partly turns upon a criminal operation which was quite openly referred to on stage'.[31] The Examiner made no complaint against the exposé of politics (behind the scenes machinations, a disestablishment bill, and an election), but the theme was undoubtedly anathema to him.

In an Appendix to *The Breaking Point*, Garnett proposed 'A Society for the Defence of Intellectual Drama' which would 'challenge authoritatively the Censor's vexatious and unintelligent verdicts' (p.xix). No such society was ever formed, but Garnett suggested to Galsworthy that a league of literary men should be formed to protest against the censorship. The matter was discussed, but nothing definite was done until the banning of *Waste* in early October 1907. At Galsworthy's suggestion, Gilbert Murray

> induced J.M. Barrie to join in the agitation; the three formed themselves into a provisional Committee for the prosecution of the movement, working with the help of William Archer and Granville-Barker, while Sir W.S. Gilbert and Sir A.W. Pinero lent a measure of support. Meanwhile, Galsworthy had drafted a circular letter which was later signed by no less than seventy-one authors.[32]

A letter incorporating the circular appeared in the *Times* on Tuesday, 29 October 1907 protesting 'the power lodged in the hands of a single official', asking that the dramatist's 'art be placed on the same footing as every other art', and claiming 'that the licensing of plays shall be abolished' (see Appendix F for full text and signatories). An accompanying article, 'The Censorship of Plays', from an obviously sympathetic 'Correspondent', summarized the origins and controversies of censorship. Expanding the argument of the letter, it pointed out that while upholders of censorship maintain that it does 'keep our stage free from the grosser forms of offence, the attackers, on the contrary, declare that its effects are the precise opposite of this--that it tends to degrade English drama; that it keeps the better form of play and the more ambitious and capable form of dramatist from the theatre, while admitting and encouraging the foolish and even the pernicious'--for example, *Education du Prince*, which 'should have been refused a licence if the censorship is to justify its existence as a moral engine'. It goes on to assert the impossibility of censoring a play from its written text alone, and then puts the Licenser of Plays in his place: he is

> merely a subordinate in the Lord Chamberlain's office, paid out of the Civil List and is in an impregnable position. You cannot ask a question about his decisions in the House ... You cannot even abolish him until a new Civil List comes up for sanction with a new reign. This, in a country enjoying Parliamentary Government, is, to say the least of it, anomalous.

The deputation of dramatists, headed by J.M. Barrie, was not seen by the Prime Minister, Sir Henry Campbell-Bannerman, on the appointed day because he was ill, but was received four days later on 25 February 1908 by the Home Secretary, Herbert Gladstone. As a result of this deputation, strongly reinforced by the urging of the author Robert Harcourt, recently elected M.P. for the Montrose Burghs, who was allowed 'his hereditary right to a parliamentary canter of some sort',[33] a Joint Select Committee of the Lords and Commons was appointed in July, consisting of Herbert Samuel (Chairman), the Earl of Plymouth, Lord Willoughby de Broke, Lord Newton, Lord Ribblesdale, Lord Gorell, Robert Harcourt, A.E.W. Mason, Col. M. Lockwood and Hugh Law. The Committee was charged:

> to enquire into the Censorship of Stage Plays as constituted by The Theatres Act, 1843, and into the operation of the Acts of Parliament relating to the licensing and regulation of theatres and places of public entertainment, and to report any alterations of the law or practice which may appear desirable.[34]

The first of twelve sittings was held on 29 July 1909, and forty-nine witnesses were heard.

Although Barrie had been put forward as spokesman of the deputation, the driving force came from Shaw:

> he was determined to be the star witness, and to this end he set to work on a written statement which would eclipse anything submitted as evidence in 1892, particularly the published evidence of Henry Irving. He printed 250 copies at his own expense for distribution to committee members, colleagues, and the press. Being chief actor and author was not sufficient, however. Shaw also appointed himself director, stage manager, puppet master, and fencing instructor! He conferred endlessly with Herbert Samuel, who had been appointed to chair the committee. He drafted letters to fellow dramatists, which he had multigraphed and distributed through the Society of Authors. He sent appeals to his translators to gather and send all

> available information on censorship in their own countries.[35]

However, when Shaw appeared before the Committee on 30 July, it refused to accept his printed statement as evidence. Shaw cited precedent from the 1892 Enquiry at which written statements had been read out and accepted from Henry Irving, John Hare and Clement Scott (all three, as Shaw was quick to point out, in favour of retaining censorship), but to no avail. Shaw turned the manoeuvre to his own advantage by sending a letter to the Times, 'the last refuge of the oppressed', in which he protested against the treatment he had received, complaining that after clearing the room and holding a 'secret conclave', the Chairman had 'informed [him] without explanation that [his] statement could not be received and placed on the notes'.[36] Shaw enclosed his fifty-five page 'Statement of the Evidence in Chief of George Bernard Shaw before the Joint Committee on Stage Plays (Censorship and Licensing)' and the *Times* obligingly reprinted the nine-point summary. Shaw appeared again on 5 August to be told that the Committee had no further questions to put to him, and to be further snubbed by the return of his pamphlet. This served as another occasion for a letter to the *Times* protesting 'a very pointed and deliberate rebuff'.[37] Ironically, the Committee's action produced 'a lively demand for copies', and Shaw incorporated 'the terrible statement' into the Preface to *The Shewing-Up of Blanco Posnet* (1910). It is, in fact, a very long-winded piece of work, a typical exercise in Shavian polemics, undoubtedly designed to goad Lord Newton and 'the establishment'.

Much of what Shaw says was repeated at the Enquiry, which resolved into a contest between the dramatists on one side and the managers and actors on the other, as the following extracts indicate:

> J.M. Barrie: (1750) ... in favour of the abolition of the Censor.

> Mr. Whelen: (2362-4) ... I think that in no way can it [censorship] be defended. It seems to me that it simply acts as a retarding influence on the theatre and upon the drama ... and is pernicious in its influence on the English stage ... any form of censorship is an outrage.

> L. Housman: (2529) ... I submit, therefore, that refusing even to consider my play *[Bethlehem]* on account of its Scriptural character, and in subsequently licensing "Eager Heart," "Hannele," and "Samson and Delilah," the Examiner of Plays had done me a grave injustice; and that is the more gratuitous in that it is based,

not upon any Act of Parliament, but upon departmental traditions.

Mr. Bram Stoker: (2800) Do you consider that the censorship has hindered the growth of the great British drama? --Absolutely not.

Mr. Gilbert Murray: (3870) ... it seems to me that on principle it [censorship] is totally indefensible, and even, I might almost say, absurd.

Mr. George Alexander: (4145) ... in my opinion, a censorship of plays is of great use and value, and I should deprecate its abolition.

Mr. George Edwardes: (4367) ... I am perfectly satisfied with the Censor as he is--as he is constituted by Law.

The Committee heard no spokesman for the mythical 'man in the street', (although G.K. Chesterton, of all people, claimed to be such), and the views of the Right Hon. The Speaker were accepted as representative of public opinion. He declared: '(4187) ... personally I am in favour of retaining the censorship. If I have cause to quarrel with it at all, and if the public has cause to quarrel with it at all, I think the censorship has been too lax, and it wants tightening up'. One of the most impressive witnesses was Granville Barker, whose triple role of actor, manager and dramatist placed him in a unique category. He argued:

> (1224) ... A dramatist in sending in his play for a licence, or in having his play sent in for a licence, is running a great risk of having his property destroyed, and therefore the one thing that he does not want to do is to make the Censor think about his play, and he naturally is inclined to send in a play which contains only such subjects, and such a treatment of subjects, as have grown so familiar to the Licenser of Plays that he no longer thinks about them at all. For instance, I think it may be said, without offence to the authorities, that the Censor no longer stops to think about a certain treatment of the subject of adultery on the stage. If that treatment comes within certain dramatised limits--I mean limits practised by dramatists--he passes it practically without question. But the moment that any original point of view, or unusual point of view, on any subject is put before the Censor he naturally stops to think about it, and the process of his thinking very often interferes with the licensing of the play. That is my particular point. The result of that has been to narrow the field which drama covers in England, and I regard the extreme narrowness of the field in

> English drama as being distinctly influenced and brought about by the operation of the censorship.

Quite clearly, compared with serious dramatists, managers had very little to lose from the refusal of a licence, but their support of censorship received its motivation from the fact that the inevitable alternatives to it were control by local licensing authorities or through prosecutions, either of which would make their position intolerable. As Shaw pointed out: 'the censorship, then, provides the manager, at the negligible premium of two guineas per play, with an effective insurance against the author getting him into trouble, and a complete relief from all conscientious responsibility for the character of the entertainment at his theatre'.[38] Basically, the managers (and actors) wanted the legal--and consequent economic--security that a licence provided, and the dramatists wanted the freedom of expression granted to literature and the other arts so that serious work would not be stillborn, or worse, never conceived.

The 375 page *Report* was published 11 November 1909. It recommended that it should be optional to submit a play for licence, and legal to perform an unlicensed play, whether submitted or not, but provisions were made for the prosecution of improper or offensive plays. It suggested guidelines for the Lord Chamberlain, who should:

> licence any play submitted to him unless he considers that it may reasonably be held--
>
> (a) To be indecent;
> (b) To contain offensive personalities;
> (c) To represent on the stage in an invidious manner a living person, or any person recently dead;
> (d) To do violence to the sentiment of religious reverence;
> (e) To be calculated to conduce to crime or vice;
> (f) To be calculated to impair friendly relations with any foreign power; or
> (g) To be calculated to cause a breach of the peace. (p.ix)

Other recommendations included the bringing of the Censor under some Parliamentary control, the abolition of the practice of banning Scriptural characters, and the granting of a single class of licence to both theatres and music halls. The *Times* of 12 November printed the Committee's recommendations in full, and commented:

> we venture to think that the proposals which it [the *Report*] offers will not be generally approved; and that they will be classed with those compromises which solve no

> questions and please nobody ... it is probable that they will do neither good nor harm, for the simple reason that no government is likely to take legislative action upon them.

As predicted, the *Report* was duly 'filed' in Whitehall, its recommendations unheeded; ruffled feathers lay down for a while, and the *status quo* was restored.

After a normal year in 1910, when only two plays were banned, the censor refused six in 1911 and six more in 1912. One that incurred disfavour in 1911 was Housman's historical play *Pains and Penalties: The Defence of Queen Caroline*. The refusal to license was not, as first rumoured, because of unfavourable comments on George IV, but, as Housman explains in his Preface in which he quotes a letter from the Examiner,

> because it dealt with "a sad historical episode [of comparatively recent date] in the life of an unhappy lady." The "unhappy lady," as I at once pointed out, had been dead for ninety years, and during the whole of that period her memory had rested under a cloud which the main trend of my play was calculated to remove.[39]

A 'Caroline Society' was specially formed to hold a private performance of the play under the auspices of the Pioneer Players at the Savoy, 26 November 1911. It served as an occasion for Elizabeth Robins to bring Granville Barker onto the stage at the end of the first act to address the audience on the subject of censorship. He proposed a Resolution, which passed with only two dissenting voices, censuring the Lord Chamberlain's 'despotic control' and protesting the appointment of a new Joint Examiner of Plays--none other than Charles Hallam Elton Brookfield, author of some forty plays including the afore-mentioned burlesque of Oscar Wilde (whom he also helped defeat in the Queensberry suit of 1896), and of the smuttily indecent *Dear Old Charlie*. (He added insult to injury when this play was revived in 1912 by inserting satirical references to 'Sewage' by a 'Mr. Bleater'--i.e., Barker's *Waste)*. 'With singularly infelicitous timing', as Findlater puts it, an article by Brookfield, 'On Plays and Playwriting', appeared the month of his appointment in the *National Review* in which he upheld the 'Golden Age' of 1870-90, and declared that English drama had begun to decline with the introduction of Ibsen: a 'misguided dramatic aspirant ... a pygmy type' had arisen,

> the earnest young writer who, far from understanding the importance of the drama, pays it the highest compliment he can imagine by regarding it as the heaven-sent trumpet through which he is to bray his views on social problems of his own projection ... His only equipment for his

> self-imposed task is a morbid imagination--an ingenuity for conceiving horrors in the way of unusual sins, abnormal unions, inherited taints. And this is the kind of young man who inveighs against the discretionary powers of the Lord Chamberlain and cries out against the merry humours of Labiche.[40]

Redford resigned in December 1911 (to become Chairman of the British Board of Film Censors the following year), and Ernest Bendall, a respected critic, took his place as Joint Examiner with Brookfield. Major obstructions and petty irritations continued to plague dramatists and producers--including the banning of Reinhardt's production *A Venetian Night* in 1912. Reinhardt challenged the Lord Chamberlain to come and see a rehearsal for himself, thereby setting a precedent all the more significant in that after seeing it, the Chamberlain granted the play a licence once some token modifications had been agreed. A protest on a large scale followed the banning of Eden Phillpott's dramatization of his novel *The Secret Woman*, which had enjoyed an unchallenged place on the circulating library shelves since 1905. This veto provoked questions in Parliament and another letter to the *Times* signed by twenty-four leading authors protesting the ban and proclaiming that 'the dramatist's indeed is the only calling on British soil that is not free', and announcing six matinées of *The Secret Woman* without charge so that 'we can have the public verdict in this case'.[41] A list of distinguished persons attending the performances, including Peers of the Realm, was published daily, and the general 'public verdict' in favour was endorsed by Lord Ribblesdale, who wrote to the *Times* saying that as a member of the 1909 Stage Censorship Committee, he had come 'with some misgiving, to the half-hearted conclusion that no sufficiently strong case had been made out for the abolition of this authority'.[42] Having seen *The Secret Woman*, he now felt 'most uneasy' at the way the reconstructed censorship operated; 'I confess I do not like the look of things ... We must look out'. This recantation must have encouraged the dramatists and their friends because in June the Stage Society sponsored a petition to the new King, George V, which was signed by sixty dramatists and supported by a large number of prominent people in the theatre, the arts, and even in Parliament. This petition was anticipated in April by the Society of West-End Theatre Managers, supported by some leading actors and actresses, who petitioned the King in support of the censorship. 'A Memorial in Favour of the Censorship' was also forwarded to the King by the Touring Managers' Association. Consequently, the dramatists' petition was nullified, and nothing happened: rather, the censorship seemed more deeply entrenched than ever.

In 1913 the death of Brookfield, who was replaced by G.S. Street, ushered in a more enlightened regime, and the following year the censorship participated in what Samuel Hynes describes as a 'curious last-minute plunge toward the twentieth century that marked so strikingly that last peace-time summer',[43] by licensing *Damaged Goods*, *Monna Vanna* and *Ghosts*. The Theatre Censorship Saga was far from over, but the right to discuss serious social issues on the stage had been irrevocably established, and the abolition of the most controversial of all public appointments, the existence of which had hamstrung all aspirants to the new drama, became largely a question of time. In fact, the office of Examiner of Plays was not finally laid to rest until 26 September 1968.

Resistance to the abolition of the censorship can best be understood in the context of an established order fighting a last-ditch stand against the incursions of a marauding enemy. Had control of the censorship been in the hands of Parliament, there is little doubt that changes would have been made after the 1909 Enquiry, but the Examiner of Plays was a minion of the Lord Chamberlain, whose direct Royal connection made him a bulwark against the heresies of socialism, the chaos of anarchism, the spectre of moral (especially sexual) disintegration, and the vacuum of atheism. Logic and a great deal of persuasive and emotive power were on the side of the abolitionists, but against them they had the traditional conservatism of the ruling classes and a deep-rooted suspicion of all that was new, un-English and, worst of all, intellectual. The censorship of plays provided a focus of contention whose significance was not merely a matter of the rights and freedoms of dramatists and the new drama, but was symptomatic of the surge for political and social freedom that found vigorous expression in the Suffragette movement, the Fabian Society, the growing Trade Union movement, and the foundation of the Labour Party itself. Perhaps Lord Ribblesdale was aware of this when he warned: 'we must look out'.

NOTES

1. The history of stage censorship is summarized in the preamble to the 1909 *Report of the Joint Select Committee of the Lords and Commons*, which also appears in an edited version in John Palmer's *The Censor and the Theatre* (Fisher & Unwin, London, 1912). See also Richard Findlater, *Banned! A Review of Theatrical Censorship in Britain* (MacGibbon & Kee, London, 1967) and John Russell Stephens, *The Censorship of English Drama 1824-1901* (Cambridge University Press, Cambridge, 1980).

2. Quoted by Frank Fowell and Frank Palmer, *Censorship in England* (Frank Palmer, London, 1913), p. 363: this gives the full speech pp. 357-68.

3. The Examiners were: Charles Kemble, 1836-40; John M. Kemble, 1840-57; William Bodham Donne, 1857-74; E.F. Smythe Pigott, 1874-95; and George Alexander Redford, 1895-1911.

4. Quoted by Findlater, p. 63.

5. For an extended discussion of these areas, see Stephens.

6. William Archer, *About the Theatre* (T. Fisher Unwin, London, 1886), pp. 141-4.

7. Doris Jones, *The Life and Letters of Henry Arthur Jones* (Gollancz, London, 1930), p. 58.

8. Charles Kingsley, *Plays and Puritans and Other Historical Essays* (Macmillan, London, 1889), pp. 73-4.

9. Archer, *About the Theatre,* pp. 156-7.

10. W.H. Hudson, 'Censorship of Plays', *Theatre,* N.S. vol. 14 (1 December 1889), p. 282.

11. G.B. Shaw, *Our Theatre in the Nineties* (Constable, London, 1932), vol. 1, pp. 22, 23, 38, and 48-55.

12. H.A. Jones, 'The Censorship Muddle', *The Foundations of a National Drama* (Chapman Hall, London, 1913), p. 285.

13. Ibid., pp. 272-3.

14. Ibid., p. 283. Appendix 15 to the 1892 *Report* tabulates 45,000 persons nightly attending 35 London Music Halls; 270,000 weekly; 14,000,000 yearly.

15. H.A. Jones, *Foundations,* p. 284.

16. William Archer, *The Old Drama and the New: An Essay in Revaluation* (William Heinemann, London, 1923), p. 252.

17. Quoted by Archer, ibid., p. 309.

18. H.A. Jones, *The Renascence of the English Drama* (Macmillan, London, 1895), p. 309.

19. 'The American Copyright Bill', *Era,* vol. 53 (10 January 1891), p. 15.

20. St. John Ervine, *George Bernard Shaw. His Life, Work and Friends* (Constable, London, 1956), p. 329.

21. G.B. Shaw, *Collected Letters 1874-1897,* ed. Dan H. Laurence (Max Reinhardt, London, 1965), p. 361.

22. H.A. Jones, *Foundations,* p. 289. The *Times,* 20 June 1902, p. 7, commented on Maeterlinck's 'ethical innocuousness'.

23. Information and quotations gleaned from the 1909 *Report* and L.C. Records.

24. Quoted by Findlater, p. 66.

25. H.A. Jones, *Foundations,* pp. 294-5.

26. Laurence Housman, *The Unexpected Years* (Jonathan Cape, London, 1937), pp. 191, 194.

27. Letter to the *Era,* 14 January 1872, quoted by Stephens, p. 118.

28. It was also forbidden for Naval and Marine bands to play music from the opera--a prohibition broken only by the band of the Japanese warship Tsukuba, which welcomed visitors aboard at Chatham with *Mikado* selections!

29. G.B. Shaw, Preface, *The Shewing-Up of Blanco Posnet, Collected Plays* (Max Reinhardt, London, 1971), vol. 3, p. 406.

30. Edward Garnett, *The Breaking Point* (Duckworth & Co., London, 1907), pp. xxii-xxiii.

31. Quotations from Granville Barker's evidence in 1909 *Report,* para. 1232.

32. H.V. Marrot, *The Life and Letters of John Galsworthy* (William Heinemann, London, 1935), pp. 216-17.

33. Shaw, Preface to *Blanco Posnet*, p. 404.

34. 1909 *Report*, p. iii.

35. Dan H. Laurence, ed. Shaw, *Collected Letters 1898-1910* (Max Reinhardt, London, 1972), pp. 748-9.

36. *Times*, 2 August 1909, p. 6. Shaw's 'Statement' was reprinted in Shavian Tract No. 3, 1955, by the Shaw Society.

37. *Times*, 6 August 1909, p. 7.

38. Preface to *Blanco Posnet*, p. 403. The fees set in 1837 of two pounds for plays of three acts or more, one pound for one or two acts, and five shillings for a 'Song, Address, Prologue or Epilogue' remained unchanged until censorship terminated in 1968.

39. Laurence Housman, *Pains and Penalties: The Defence of Queen Caroline* (Sidgwick & Jackson, London, 1911), p. vi. Parenthesis from L.C. Records. Housman wrote no more for the commercial theatre.

40. Charles Brookfield, 'On Plays and Playwriting', *National Review*, vol. 58 (November 1911), pp. 420-1.

41. *Times*, 14 February 1912, p. 10.

42. *Times*, 28 February 1912, p. 6.

43. Samuel Hynes, *The Edwardian Turn of Mind* (Oxford University Press, London, 1968), p. 273. The social aspects of censorship are treated more fully in his chapter on 'The Theatre and the Lord Chamberlain', pp. 212-53.

Chapter Seven

SPECTACLE, AUSTERITY AND NEW DIMENSIONS: THE STAGING OF SHAKESPEARE FROM VICTORIAN TO MODERN

How many ages hence
Shall this our lofty scene be acted over,
In states unborn, and accents yet unknown?

Julius Caesar III. i.

Paradoxically, nowhere was the schism in the nineteenth century between the theatre and literature so evident as in the staging of Shakespeare, and an important achievement of the quarter-century under review was a resurgence of the popularity of his plays and, more significantly perhaps, the reintroduction into the theatre of the plays *as written* rather than as adapted. As early as 1844, J.R. Planché, following suggestions first made by Ludwig Tieck a decade earlier,[1] persuaded Benjamin Webster, manager of the Haymarket, to allow him to 'superintend' a production of *The Taming of the Shrew* 'from the original text as acted divers times at the Globe and Blackfriars Playhouse, 1606'. This was the first performance for two centuries of a Shakespeare play in the Elizabethan style using the full text, unadulterated, and anticipated the productions of William Poel and the Elizabethan Stage Society by fifty years. Unfortunately, the experiment was not followed up for it had long been the prerogative of actors and managers to manipulate Shakespeare's texts to suit their own tastes, and current acting editions, such as Bell's of 1773, Harrison's of 1777-80 and Kemble's of 1788-1817, bore the inheritance of Colley Cibber and others, offering a variety of corrupted versions. By mid-century, the manner of presentation had begun to shift from the conventional stock sets of the eighteenth century towards a combination of historical accuracy and noble spectacle. John Philip Kemble and his brother Charles had introduced specially designed scenery for their Shakespeare productions, and they were emulated by William Macready, who also followed the lead of Robert W. Elliston, manager of Drury Lane 1819-26, and Edmund Kean in attempting to restore Shakespeare's own text to the plays. For Macready to mount

Shakespeare at all was an indication of his dedication to the highest in dramatic art because he could make far greater profits with romantic dramas like Bulwer Lytton's *Lady of Lyons* (1838) and *Richelieu* (1839). That most managers preferred the more popular and profitable types of entertainment was confirmed when the Theatre Regulation Act was passed in 1843, ending the monopoly of the 'legitimate' drama by the 'major' theatres, Drury Lane and Covent Garden, because the 'minors', instead of giving Shakespeare the expected new lease of life, neglected him. There were two notable exceptions: the actor-managers Benjamin Webster and Samuel Phelps. Webster's productions of Shakespeare were fairly faithful to the text and not over-elaborately staged, but the path of fidelity was pursued with greater consistency by Phelps who mounted all but four of the plays at Sadler's Wells, which 'probably did more to popularise Shakespeare in the course of eighteen years (1844-62) than did any other theatre in the whole domain of English theatrical history'.[2] Despite Phelps' policy of restoring the original texts and eradicating 'the compilements of Colley Cibber', he was as guilty as his contemporaries with respect to substantial cuts, scene transpositions, and encrustations of time-consuming stage business. He also became increasingly tempted, within the limitations of his small stage, to indulge in scenic display. An example is his *Pericles* in 1854, here described by Henry Morley:

> When Pericles is shown on board ship in the storm during the birth of *Marina*, the ship tosses vigorously. When he sails at last to the temple of Diana of the Ephesians, rowers take their places on their banks, the vessel seems to glide along the coast, an admirably-painted panorama slides before the eye, and the whole theatre seems to be in the course of actual transportation to the temple at Ephesus, which is the crowning scenic glory of the play.[3]

Phelps never allowed scenery and effects to draw attention away from the play and its poetry, but such was not the case with Charles Kean, dubbed by *Punch* 'The Great Upholsterer', whose decade at the Princess's from 1850-59 was reactionary with respect to the text and revolutionary in the direction of absolute accuracy and realism regarding architecture, scenery, costume, accessories, and even botanical detail, all of which were combined to create spectacular and beautiful effects. Kean 'was as proud of being an F.S.A. [Antiquaries] as of being a distinguished producer', Nicoll declares, and his playbills became 'miniature essays in which his own learning was set forth and ample indication given of the scholarly assistance which his enthusiasm had invoked'.[4] When it came to a problem, like the age of Theseus, 1200 B.C., Kean made it the occasion of a spectacle regardless of the historical probabilities: Athens appeared in its era of architectural magnificence. Kean claimed to have employed as many as 500 persons in his spectacular revivals, but the scenic display necessitated many manipulations to avoid scene changes, and such substantial cuts (because of the time factor) that Macready described the productions as 'scenes annotated by the texts'. Nicoll is somewhat dismissive: all Kean's 'research and historical endeavour was designed, not simply to depict the past accurately, but to choose from the past that which made a goodly show ... the antiquarian "correctness" was a sop to public taste and to his own vanity'.[5]

Kean's mantle eventually fell on Henry Irving, who took over the Lyceum in 1878 and utilized its advanced machinery to the fullest advantage. Irving had already made his name as a Shakespearian actor, notably with his 'revolutionary' Hamlet in 1874 that rejected the declamatory style of acting Shakespeare and introduced character interpretation and projection. Despite the widely-held view that 'Shakespeare spells ruin', Irving chose to open his management by playing Hamlet again, but under his own direction. From then until 1902, the Lyceum was the London home of Shakespeare, even when Irving was away on his frequent tours, and it became virtually a 'national' theatre. Irving firmly believed that 'to succeed as an art the theatre must succeed as a business', and he made Shakespeare pay through beautiful staging, splendid costumes, and impressive theatrical effects. A measure of his success is the financial statement given by Austin Brereton in his biography, which cites Irving's total receipts between 1878 and 1905 (including tours and his unprofitable years of decline) as £2,261,637.10.1, and his expenses as £2,168,290.6.1, to show a profit of £93,347.4.0, or £3,457.6.1 a year.[6] Irving's reputation for scenic effects must not be allowed to overshadow his abilities as an actor, eccentric though they may have been, especially, as Joseph Knight complained, his 'indescribable elongation of syllables', nor his ability to attract and inspire excellent fellow artists, notably Ellen Terry, Jessie Millward, Winifred Emery, Forbes Robertson, William Terriss, George Alexander, Martin Harvey, and many others whose names are still familiar. In the prologue to his biography of Irving, Gordon Craig declared that he had 'never known of, or seen, or heard a greater actor than was Irving'.[7] It was as much Irving's magnetic acting as the spectacular staging, therefore, that drew the crowds to the Lyceum to see Shakespeare.

By Irving's time it was accepted that Shakespeare's own text would be used, but the amount and its sequence was at the manager's discretion: the plays were therefore subject to the requirements of the theatre, the whims, personalities, and abilities of the actors, and the manager's assessment of the taste and expectations of his audience. For example, 'Irving's view of Hamlet was obviously Hamlet with as much as possible left out except Hamlet; consequently, when Hamlet was dead, nothing else mattered. While he lived, though, he was allowed to speak all his soliloquies, practically uncut'.[8] One wag suggested that as Irving's *Hamlet* at Stratford was so cut, it should be retitled 'Incomplete Scenes and Detached Quotations from the Tragedy of *Hamlet*'. Irving stated his own principles in his advertisement for *Macbeth:*

> to meet the requirements of the stage, without sacrificing the purpose or the poetry of the author should be the aim of those who produce the plays of Shakespeare; and I trust that any change which I have ventured to introduce on this occasion in the ordinary scenic arrangements has been made in the spirit of true reverence for the works of our greatest dramatist.[9]

Irving aimed at an integrated artistic whole, only subordinating the play to spectacle once, in 1892, when he indulged in pageantry for its own sake in *Henry VIII* --and lost several thousand pounds. Irving believed that embellishment should never hamper the natural action, but was justified if it functioned as a commentary on the action and contributed to the total artistic effect. However, the degree to which he was faithful to his principles, or perhaps self-deceived, is debatable. For example, Laurence Irving observes that when his grandfather staged *Twelfth Night* in 1884, not only did he puzzle his audience by his tragi-comic portrayal of Malvolio, but also 'perhaps ... he erred in overloading delicate comedy with stage effects'.[10] Odell's description of the opening scene of *Macbeth*, where Irving embellishes tradition, although written in admiration, raises similar doubts:

> the first appearance of the demoniac beings flying through the air was startling, but the chief spectacle was that of the great host of singing witches holding revel by misty moonlight "over woods, high rocks and mountains" ... they seemed literally to thicken the air as they dimly appeared and disappeared in that weird light of which Irving alone seemed to be master.[11]

As indicated, such spectacles posed considerable problems not only technically but also with respect to the elapsed time of presentation and to the flow of rapid scene changes demanded by Shakespeare. Obviously, not every scene could be given the full treatment without inordinate delays. A compromise solution, much used by Irving, was to have one or two full sets and to play the rest of the scenes before a series of painted drop curtains which concealed the process of scene changing. Ben Greet's composite arrangement for *The Merchant of Venice* at the Olympic in 1897 followed Irving's lead, but brought down scorn from Archer:

> the first two acts must be remodelled so that almost their whole action may pass in one "set," a roughly effective but topographically absurd representation of the Piazzetto and a corner of the Riva, with the Doge's Palace in the background. To this end all the Belmont episodes are crowded together in the third act, in which Portia makes her first appearance; while the precious scene for which so much is sacrificed becomes as conventional as the "street" of a classic comedy, and it finally appears that Shylock is the Doge's next-door neighbour.[12]

Such things are 'topographically absurd' only when pretensions to authenticity invite 'academic' criticism. The far more serious and fundamental offence was the butchery of the plays by the transposition of scenes to minimize set changes. In F.R. Benson's *Merchant of Venice* all the early scenes in Venice were also given together, followed by those in Belmont, which in turn were played consecutively, and in Daly's *Twelfth Night* in 1894 the play opened with the sea-coast scenes, I.ii. and II.i., followed by I.i. and I.iv. (the Duke's Palace), I.iii. and II.ii (Olivia's house and street). In the same production, Daly was also guilty of another common corruption, the interpolation of songs from outside the play. He introduced 'Come unto these yellow sands' from *The Tempest*, and 'Who is Sylvia?' from *The Two Gentlemen of Verona*, changing the first line to 'Fair Olivia. Who is she?' Daly's treatment of Shakespeare sparked protests from the *Theatre* in 1895, and other critics joined in the condemnation, with the notable exception of Clement Scott, drama critic of the *Daily Telegraph*, who championed Daly's practice: 'he knew, as all our actor-managers know', wrote Scott, 'that Shakespeare must be reverently edited for the stage; and that the text, the whole text, and nothing but the text is impossible'.[13] In the same vein--which followed the arguments of Lamb, Hazlitt and many nineteenth-century scholars--another critic wrote:

> we would rather not have Shakespeare's plays on the stage at all than have them in the form in which they are familiar only to the student. For the plays of Shakspere belong to literature, not to the stage, and I do not believe that they could, on their merits alone, draw any larger audiences to the Lyceum than the burlesques of Aristophanes would attract to the Gaiety.[14]

There were, however, a growing number of enthusiasts who demanded Shakespeare unadulterated on the stage, and to them perhaps the chief offender in degrading the dramatist into an accessory of the scenic artist was the last in line and most extravagant mounter of spectacular revivals, Herbert Beerbohm Tree. Gordon Crosse recalls that when Tree 'opened Her Majesty's ... in 1897, and found himself master of a large theatre with every modern appliance of lighting and staging to play with, his love of magnificence went to his head, and a succession of spectacles each more splendid than the last became a burden rather than a delight'.[15] Tree's first Shakespeare production at Her Majesty's was *Julius Caesar* in 1898. He rearranged the traditional five acts into three--a practice applied to all his revivals--following the Aristotelian principle of a unified beginning, middle and end, but also to save some time without, one suspects, over-sacrificing interval refreshment receipts. In the case of *Julius Caesar*, the arrangement gave the curtain tableau in each act to Antony, played, of course, by Tree, an arresting performer at all times. (Irving, never too proud to learn, adopted the three-act arrangement for his *Coriolanus* in 1901). Tree's style is well summarized in Shaw's account of *Much Ado About Nothing:* the production offered

> fair ladies, Sicilian seascapes, Italian gardens, summer nights and dawns (compressed into five minutes), Renascential splendours, dancing, singing, masquerading, architecture, orchestration tastefully culled from Wagner, Bizet, and German, and endless larks in the way of stage business devised by Mr. Tree and carried out with much innocent enjoyment.[16]

This production contained a typical modification: 'an elaborate representation of daybreak, the stage growing gradually lighter amid the twitterings of mechanical birds', which necessitated the omission of Don Pedro's lines on the dawn.[17] Tree's *Macbeth* included an elaborate procession for Duncan's retirement to bed, complete with harpist and hymn, after which the witches entered the stage for a quick cackle. Similarly, in *King John* he included a spectacle of the signing of Magna Carta and in *Antony and Cleopatra* he could not resist the temptation to include an elaborate tableau of Cleopatra as the goddess Isis in procession through the streets of Alexandria to greet Antony on his return, complete with crowds, priests, dancing maidens, marching soldiers and music--voluptuous for Cleopatra and martial for Antony. The play, incidentally, opened in Caesar's house in Rome (I.4), then moved to Alexandria for the entrance of the lovers, leaving the opening lines on 'our general' for Enobarbus to speak after their exit. In Irving's *Merchant of Venice,* Shylock had returned to his empty house and knocked pathetically on the door as the curtain fell. Tree's Shylock

> knocked again and again, thrust open the door--not locked, after all--cried "Jessica!" entered the house, ranged round its rooms (visible through lattice work and open windows), emerged, still crying hoarsely, saw a gondola pass on the horizon, flung himself to the ground in a paroxysm, rent

his garments, and poured ashes upon his head.[18]

In the cause of realism, Tree had live rabbits loose on stage in *A Midsummer Night's Dream;* real horses for *Richard II;* a complete ship rocking in a realistic sea for *The Tempest;* a terraced garden with real grass, fountains and box hedges for *Twelfth Night;* and a rural scene for *The Winter's Tale* with cottage, stream, waterfall, trees and a live donkey. Changes of sets--during which the principals took calls--occupied an unconscionable time: Crosse records that he measured these once, 'and found that altogether the audience sat gazing at the curtain for forty-five minutes while elaborate sets were built up or taken down behind it'. Consequently, 'cuts amounted to about a third of the play'.[19]

Tree believed that his endeavours followed the spirt and intention of his author, arguing that Shakespeare himself, who had apologized for an 'unworthy scaffold', would have welcomed scenic elaboration. In an article in the *Fortnightly Review,* July 1900, he contended that the spectacular and munificent staging of Shakespeare was not only according to public taste, but was also justified by the demands of the text and the probability that even in Shakespeare's time performances would have been lavishly dressed and often given against a rich background 'in the private houses and castles of the nobles'. The following month a letter from William Poel condemned Tree's arguments as 'unconvincing, and to the uninformed, misleading'. A further reply to Tree appeared in the September issue from W. Hughes Mallett, who took issue particularly with 'the disproportionately long waits between the acts' that were required by the 'georgeous mounting', and with the practice of rearranging scenes to reduce set changes: less time, energy and money spent on sets, he argued, could open the way to more productions.[20] Tree firmly believed in the theatre's duty to 'teach and delight', and in his own method of fulfilling that purpose through accurate, realistic and splendid revivals. He claimed 'that, worthily to represent Shakespeare, the scenic embellishment should be as beautiful and costly as the subject of the drama being performed seems to demand; that it should not be subordinate to, but harmonious with, the dramatic interest ... Every man should avail himself of the aids which his generation affords him'.[21] One of his strongest arguments was that audiences would not be attracted unless offered a 'plethora of scenic spectacle and georgeous costumes', and he supported his point with figures to show that between 1898 and 1900 his first three Shakespearian productions at Her Majesty's, *Julius Caesar, King John* and *A Midsummer Night's Dream,* had been attended by 242,000 people, 170,000 and 220,000 respectively. As G. Wilson Knight points out, on occasion Tree's interpretations could reveal 'a vein of Shakespearian ore' when, for example, he interpolated the interlude of bird-song into *Much Ado About Nothing,* where bird imagery is a 'characteristic element'.[22] Knight also draws attention to a sense of the miraculous, of 'spiritualized showmanship', in Tree's productions, where intensity and power went with the display: 'when Tree offended, it was through his own creative exuberance; he offended as an artist; and as a deeply Shakespearian artist'.[23]

Between 1905 and 1913, Tree supplemented his regular season offerings of Shakespeare with Annual Shakespeare Birthday Festivals at which, in addition to his own company, guest companies led by F.R. Benson, Arthur Bourchier and even William Poel were invited to perform. He thereby established His Majesty's as the London palace of Shakespeare in succession to the Lyceum, with himself as King plus an entourage of 'courtiers', as Shaw put it. The purists might cavil at his methods, but, at the expense of the few, Tree, like Irving, performed the inestimable service of commending Shakespeare to the many who otherwise would have neither seen nor read his plays.

What Irving and Tree were to London, F.R. Benson was to the Provinces. For thirty years he toured his company playing Shakespeare in repertory, sending out as many as four companies at a time, and producing thirty-five of the plays. (James Agate suggested that the most appropriate monument to Benson would be a statue on wheels!) His company, the 'Bensonians', included many of the best players of the time, and they owed much to his abilities as a teacher. It was said that he 'created more than one generation of actors'. The key to Benson's success both as performer (though he was not a great actor and tended to grimace too much) and as teacher, was his unbounded energy. In *My Memoirs* he recalls Henry Ainley saying to him: 'You made us work like blazes; you didn't spare us and you didn't spare yourself. You never said you were tired, so, of course, we couldn't. After rehearsal, you rushed us all to football, or cricket, or hockey. Perhaps, after all, this strenuous regime did sometimes save us from getting into trouble'.[24] Benson (who once advertised for a 'male juvenile lead, slow bowler or good batsman preferred'), exemplified his theory that a fit body was essential to make an actor quick, graceful, powerful, and natural on stage. Benson admits that he 'may have emphasized too much the athletic side in the various antics--weight carrying, toe-climbing, headlong descents down a rope from the flies, and the rest of it--but people on the whole were interested and entertained'.[25] Crosse recalls Benson's 'missing link' Caliban in which he would 'clamber nimbly up a tree and hang head downwards from a branch, chattering with rage at Prospero'.[26] But his performances combined skilful interpretation with the 'antics': for example, his Caliban also brought out a 'responsive devotion to music, songs and sweet airs that give delight and hurt not'.[27]

Benson did his best to carry the Lyceum style around the country, utilizing as full scenery as possible within the limitations of repertory touring, but never allowing spectacle to intrude upon the action or the poetry. He believed that no play should be adapted for the sake of one part, but in the nineteenth-century tradition, he took liberties with the text, especially in the tragedies where his preference for a slow pace necessitated substantial omissions. When he did do *Hamlet* in full, at the Lyceum in March 1900, it played six hours plus an hour and a half interval for dinner. His deliberate style could yield to a swifter mode, to the extent that Max Beerbohm reported that in *Henry V* at the Lyceum (February 1900), 'speech after speech was sent spinning to the boundaries'.[28] But the review is mainly critical for Max felt that the performance had neither the 'dignity' of the old school nor the 'subtle intelligence' of the new. Other London critics tended to find Benson's productions 'amateurish', but such dismissals cannot mar Benson's great achievements, which were to bring back an Elizabethan zest to the staging of Shakespeare and to apply his energies not only to his own performances but also to the provision of an invaluable workshop for tyros, and to the task of keeping Shakespeare alive in the Provinces through the demanding schedules of the circuits. Nor must it be forgotten that from 1886 to 1913, with the exception of the years 1889, 1890 and 1895, the Stratford Festivals, which had been inaugurated in 1879, were under Benson's direction.

The production of Shakespeare in the commercial theatres during the nineteenth century had followed the direction established by Macready and Kean towards spectacular realism, and nineteenth-century reforms had gone no further than the restoration of the original language. Webster's experiment with *The Taming of the Shrew* was forgotten, and the plays unmutilated were relegated to the reader's fireside imagination. Men of letters had accepted the view of Coleridge and Lamb that the plays could not really be *acted* because the theatre corrupted the sublimity of the poetry, and they stayed away in contempt from the theatre, which did little to allay their mistrust. But scholars maintained their interest in the authenticity of the texts, and in the summer of 1880 William Griggs published his facsimile edition of the first and second Quarto editions of *Hamlet* (1603 and 1604), with a foreword by Dr. F.J. Furnivall, President of the New Shakespeare Society. A few months later, Dr. Furnivall received an offer from a relatively obscure actor, a William Poel, to deliver a paper to the Society on the Acting Editions of Shakespeare. It was accepted, but before the lecture was delivered Poel made another offer: to stage *Hamlet* in the full 1603 version. Again, Dr. Furnivall accepted, and on 16 April 1881 Poel's first Elizabethan style production was given on a bare draped platform at St. George's Hall. Reaction ranged from enthusiasm on the part of some scholars to scorn from most critics, who, like Dutton Cook, found it 'wearisome and depressing'. Robert

Speaight acknowledges that 'the note of theatrical triumph was conspicuously absent ... [but] the performance was historical ... because it announced the birth of a new idea'.[29] From then on, Poel was a significant force in Shakespeare theatre, although, in Speaight's phrase, his theatrical career was destined to be 'a sublime failure'.

Poel was the son of Matilda and William Pole, a civil engineer with the not uncommon combination of mathematical and musical ability. William Junior inherited a musical sense, determination, and (unorthodox) religious fervour from his parents, who steered their son in his father's footsteps by apprenticing him to a firm of building contractors, where he served nearly six years before committing himself to the theatre in 1876 by leaving London and joining Charles Mathews' company at Bristol. 'It was the genius of the poet-dramatist Shakespeare', he declared in 1916, 'and of the actor Salvini who so finely interpreted some of his characters, which urged me to labour in the cause of the theatre'.[30] Looking back on this era, Poel (who had retained the misprint of his name from his first Bristol programme) recalls:

> As regards Shakespeare's plays, the traditions and the conventions of the eighteenth century were still in use. There were the same "readings," "business," and division of the dialogue into scenes, the same mutilation of the text and transposition of incidents although Garrick's and Colley Cibber's perversions of the text had been given up. The chief drawback lay in the English actor's want of imagination, and in his inability to appreciate the swiftness and ease with which the dialogue was spoken on the stage by Elizabethan actors.[31]

He also came to the conclusion that the proscenium arch and realistic scenery were incompatible with Elizabethan drama, and dedicated himself to freeing it from all trammels of convention. In 1879 he formed The Elizabethans, a small company of 'professional ladies and gentlemen whose efforts [were] specially directed towards creating a more general taste for Shakespeare'.[32] They toured performing in rooms, small halls and schools where they were entirely dependent on the text for effects. After the seminal *Hamlet* in 1881, he managed the Royal Victoria Coffee Hall (later the Old Vic) for Miss Emma Cons for two years, stage managed for F.R. Benson for a season, then formed his Little Comedies Company in 1885 for the presentation of drawing-room entertainment--mostly one-act plays, several of which he wrote himself--at soirées and for charities. He returned to his consuming passion when he became instructor for the Shakespeare Reading Society, which had been founded by students at University College, London. At first the Society gave unacted recitals, then performed in costume but without scenery. Poel drew upon the resources of this group when he mounted a full-scale production of *The Duchess of Malfi* for J.T. Grein's Independent Theatre at the *Opéra Comique* in October 1892. In 1893 he produced *Measure for Measure* for the Society at the Royalty, which he converted for the occasion to reproduce the Elizabethan Fortune Playhouse, and in the following year he formed The Elizabethan Stage Society (E.S.S. hereinafter), which gave its first official programme, *Twelfth Night*, at Burlington Hall on 21 June 1895, again using the Shakespeare Society's wardrobe of Elizabethan costumes.[33]

A brochure issued in July 1896 declared that 'THE ELIZABETHAN STAGE SOCIETY is founded to illustrate and advance the principle that Shakspere's Plays should be accorded the build of stage for which they were designed'. It included in its aims the construction of 'a theatre specially built on the plan of the sixteenth century ... which could be used as a school-house for instruction in the poetic drama as well as for performances of Shakspere's plays in accordance with his original design'.[34] According to Poel, the object of the E.S.S. was to revive the Elizabethan masterpieces 'so as to represent them as nearly as possible under the conditions existing at the time of their first production--that is to say, with only those stage appliances and accessories which were usually employed during the Elizabethan period'.[35] The E.S.S. functioned as a non-profit, subscription society, and relied upon Poel's purse for financial subsidies as well as upon his genius for direction. It mounted thirty productions between 1895 and July 1905 (see Appendix E), when it was dissolved officially, and its costumes, properties and model of the platform stage of the Fortune were auctioned off.[36] Its name continued to be associated with Poel's productions and actually occurs on several programmes between 1911 and 1913, although there appears to be no record of a formal revival.

The majority of performers in E.S.S. productions were amateurs, for Poel found them more malleable than professionals, and on many occasions he used women in men's roles, a reversal of Elizabethan practice which he introduced largely because women were more available than men for the long hours of rehearsal that he demanded, for Poel's reforms concerned more than the structure on which the plays were presented. He held that the atmosphere of Elizabethan drama was not created, as in modern theatre, through the eye, but through the ear. Lewis Casson, one of many professional actors who acknowledge a debt to Poel, recalls that

> his first step was to cast the play orchestrally ... for the first three weeks of a month's rehearsal the company sat round a table, as in a school class-room, and 'learnt the tunes' from him by endless repetition in a strongly marked exaggerated form; so that at the end of, say, two weeks the whole play had become as fixed in musical pattern as if written in an orchestral score.[37]

Poel's technique of swift and musically inflected speech placed the emphasis on 'key-words' for sense and on the 'tunes' for poetic effect. The result was that he was able 'to keep the exquisite rhythm and cadence of the verse even whilst the drama was hurtling along its swift tempestuous course',[38] each scene flowing unbrokenly into the next. This pattern confused and shocked many contemporaries, who dismissed Poel as a dictatorial eccentric, and even William Archer denounced him as 'a non-scenic Beerbohm Tree'. Archer regarded Poel's attempts to recreate the Elizabethan theatre as spurious and retrogressive, maintaining that Poel's other reforms were already in the air and would have come about without him; but as Speaight points out, such arguments are beside the point because 'it was Poel who set this work afoot'.[39] He was still ahead of his time when he died in 1934 because it was not until the second half of this century that it became fashionable to stage Shakespeare in the full Elizabethan style, with a proper thrust stage. In fact, Poel's productions were usually mounted on a reconstructed Elizabethan stage set within the modern box stage; a picture of an Elizabethan stage seen through the frame of the proscenium arch, and consequently lacking in the actor-audience intimacy that characterized Elizabethan performances. Although Poel built an apron over the orchestra pit for *The Two Gentlemen of Verona* at His Majesty's in 1910, it was not until July 1927, when he produced Samuel Rowley's *When You See Me You Know Me* at the Holborn Empire, that he mounted a production on a full Elizabethan thrust stage by constructing a platform over the stalls. The chief general criticism against Poel and the E.S.S. was summed up by A.B. Walkley: 'these efforts have their place in an educational curriculum, but none in the catalogue of pleasures. Reconstitute the Elizabethan stage as you may, you cannot restore the Elizabethan frame of mind'.[40]

The majority of critics may have been hostile to Poel's endeavours, but many performers recognized their value, especially with respect to his methods for revitalizing poetic speech. Granville Barker, who played the lead in the E.S.S. 1899 production of *Richard II*, declared in a letter to Poel: 'You shook all my previous convictions by showing me how you wanted the first lines of *Richard II* spoken'.[41] Basil Dean learnt from Poel 'the secret of rhythmic speech, the value of the operative word, and the magic of Shakespeare when it is spoken both musically and intelligently',[42] and Edith Evans declared: 'I first learnt to play Shakespeare under a very great man, William Poel ... [who] taught me how to look for life in the lines. He also showed me that blank verse was for pace, for speed'.[43] Lillah McCarthy acknowledged that she had come to understand 'the essential of drama--harmonious movement' through Poel, and admitted: 'the discipline of William Poel's rehearsals sometimes wore me down. But I emerged from it knowing something'.[44] Lillah McCarthy played

Gwendolin in Poel's E.S.S. production of Swinburne's *Locrine* in 1899, one of the longest roles for women; Gwendolen's rival, Estrild, was played by Elsie Fogarty, who passed on many of Poel's techniques to 'several generations of English actors' through her Central School of Speech Training and Dramatic Art.[45] Poel's role as 'the Father of the Puritan Revolution in the theatre' (Bridges-Adams' title), and importance as a counter to commercial trends, was well stated by Edward Garnett in 1913:

> he alone has reversed the "traditional" practice of bringing Shakespeare's art down to our level by mutilations, by guillotining it with "drop scenes," and by cramping the swing and balance of its effects behind the "proscenium arch." He alone has restored the Elizabethan stage itself with the precise conditions under which our supreme dramatist practised and developed his craft.[46]

Before Poel's influence affected the commercial stage, another maverick force made itself felt--Edward Gordon Craig. As a young actor, Craig played many Shakespearian roles, including Hamlet for Ben Greet at the Olympic in 1897, but by the end of the century he had turned away from acting to stage design. Little of his early work reached stage production, except in amateur performances, but his ideas were contagious, spreading from London to Berlin and Moscow. An invitation from Beerbohm Tree to do the stage designs for *Macbeth* resulted in a nasty dispute after Tree consulted Joseph Harker, his scene painter, who advised him that Craig's three-dimensional scenes 'painted with light' were impractical. Craig's attempts to work with Otto Brahm and Reinhardt on Shakespeare and other productions also failed, but he was more successful in working with Stanislavsky at the Moscow Art Theatre on a production of *Hamlet* which after three years preparation finally opened on 8 January 1912 (see Chapter Eight). Craig's designs for *Hamlet* typify his style: gaunt perpendicular blocks, manufactured from adjustable folding screens, capture the atmosphere and mood of the play through a combination of line, mass and colour, dwarfing the figures. Not surprisingly, Poel objected to Craig's approach:

> the central interest of drama is human, and it is necessary that the figures on the stage should appear larger than the background, or let the readers of Shakespeare remain at home. To see Mr. Craig's "rectangular masses illuminated by a diagonal light" while the poet's characters walk in a darkened foreground is not, I venture to think, to enjoy 'the art of the theatre' ... there is no room for man in Mr. Craig's world.[47]

Nevertheless, the two men shared a common desire to escape from cluttered realistic spectacles towards a more elemental theatre. But where Craig saw the setting as an integral element equal in importance to the acting and dialogue, Poel relegated it (and its designer) to a secondary, supportive role.

The impact of both Poel and Craig on the West-End was negligible until Granville Barker and Lillah McCarthy mounted their notable Shakespeare productions at the Savoy in 1912-14. Poel and Craig had been revolutionaries, opposing the orthodoxies of their time. At first sight Barker appears to be another, but a recognition of the eclectic nature of his Savoy experiments indicates that in fact he was evolutionary. Lillah McCarthy recognized that in their productions they 'used Poel's methods, not strictly in accordance with the Elizabethan stage, but most of the scenes were played on an apron stage, and the delivery of the verse was given in accordance with Poel's methods'.[48] Bridges-Adams points out that as well as profiting from the schooling of Poel and pleasing his disciples, Barker pleased Craigites with 'massive pylons and bare expanses'; Reinhardt admirers with 'a touch or two borrowed from the *Deutsches Theatre'*; balletomanes with 'colouring that even the Russians could hardly surpass'; devotees of Dolmetsch with 'a consort of viols'; scholars with an 'unmutilated text'; and 'former *habitués* of the Court ... with the athletic utterance that Shaw had imposed'.[49] The problem was, as Barker declared, 'that a new formula has to be found. Realistic scenery won't do, if only because it swears against everything in the plays, if only because it's never realistic ... We shall not save our souls by being Elizabethan. It is an easy way out, and, strictly followed, an honourable one', but requires an audience that is 'historically sensed'.[50] The Savoy attempt at a solution was to be 'decorative, therefore, not realistic and cumbrous'. In the words of Bridges-Adams, Barker had to 'out-Poel Poel, and out-Tree Tree, in a single gesture'. The result was three controversial productions, *The Winter's Tale, Twelfth Night* and *A Midsummer Night's Dream,* which found a third way in a 'post-impressionist' approach that combined faithfulness to the full, original text, with simple, almost abstract settings in the manner of Gordon Craig that were as spectacular in their way as Tree's, beautiful to the eye, and complementary to the mood of the action. Barker followed Poel's example in keeping close to Elizabethan staging, abandoning the picture-frame stage in favour of a three-tier structure (as opposed to the two levels favoured by Poel), the lowest of which was formed by an apron twelve foot deep thrust out over the orchestra pit. He also banished the footlights and lit the forestage from a battery of projectors mounted in front of the dress circle (as Poel had done for *The Two Gentlemen of Verona)*. Barker allowed a free hand to his stage designer, Norman Wilkinson, whose decor, which tended to the bizarre, blazed with exotic colour, and was matched by the costumes--designed by Albert Rutherston for the first play and by Norman Wilkinson for the others. Draped curtains formed the background for *The Winter's Tale:* for example, a startling gold for Leontes' palace, offset by white pilasters. A stark shepherd's cottage for the rural scene was condemned by the *Times'* critic as 'a model bungalow from the Ideal Homes exhibition', but he found the production 'very startling and provocative and audacious'.[51] Similar effects were achieved in *Twelfth Night* (which the *Morning Post* critic, like many of his colleagues, found 'less curiously and distractingly perverse' than *The Winter's Tale)*, where Orsino's palace was set with twisted barley-sugar pillars in a pink, black and silver setting, and the exterior of Olivia's house had golden gates set in white walls.

In these productions, Barker 'swept shadows from the stage as if they were germs', but in *A Midsummer Night's Dream* he softened the lighting to provide a fantastic wood:

> at its centre was a rough green velvet mound, white flowered. Above it hung an immense terra-cotta wreath of flowers which depended a light gauze canopy where fireflies and glow-worms flickered. In the background were curtains lighted in various changing tones of green, blue, violet, and purple, with a backcloth of green rising to a star-spangled purplish-blue. The plan was to set the midnight wood of the Immortals apart from the more or less realistic Palace scene in black and silver, with its white silk curtains.[52]

There was no Mendelssohn, but Elizabethan airs by Cecil Sharp. Barker was more faithful to the texts than William Poel, whose omissions often seemed inconsistent with his principles, cutting only six lines from *The Winter's Tale* and none from *Twelfth Night* or from *A Midsummer Night's Dream*. Except for two short intervals in *Twelfth Night,* and only one fifteen minute break in each of the other two plays, he maintained a continuous action, eliminating much conventional stage business, constantly playing forward to the audience, and delivering the lines with a rapidity that bewildered those accustomed to either the old declamatory style or to the more recent natural mode. W.A. Darlington, who later became a drama critic for the *Daily Telegraph,* had been brought up on the 'Academic' approach to Shakespeare, but like many others, had all his 'preconceived notions' changed by the Savoy productions:

> it was as if I had been looking at a wax figure in a glass case, when Barker came and whisked away the glass to show me that what I had mistaken for a cleverly moulded dummy was in fact a living and breathing man. The Shakespeare I had been brought up on, the dead-and-gone classic literary

> figure who had expressed himself in dramatic form and must therefore be given his meed of ritual worship in the theatre, had vanished; and in his place was a man who had written for the theatre because he had loved it and understood it, whose plays were as vital as if they had just left his pen.[53]

The Winter's Tale opened on 21 September 1912, but despite enthusiastic audiences it sustained heavy losses, and was replaced on 15 November by *Twelfth Night,* which enjoyed a successful run, as did *A Midsummer Night's Dream* which followed on 6 February 1913. Preparations were under way for productions of *Macbeth* and *Antony and Cleopatra,* but these and further experiments were cut short by the outbreak of war. However, enough had been done to throw out a firm challenge to convention and tradition not in obscure society productions, but in a commercial theatre in the heart of the West-End: 'even the fantastic draperies that took the place of Tree's front cloths and Poel's traverse curtains, came down with a defiant flop', declares Bridges-Adams, 'as if Barker himself had hurled them at us from the flies, saying "There! What do you think of that?"'[54] There were the inevitable objections to artistic change, particularly against the rapid delivery, but the majority of audiences, performers and directors recognized that Barker's fusion of decor, costume and vital speech with ensemble playing of the highest order, had completed the transition from Victorian to modern by transforming the staging of Shakespeare in a manner that was both closer to the original mode and appropriate to the twentieth century.

NOTES

1. In 1836 Tieck and Gottfried Semper made a reconstruction of Henslowe's Fortune Theatre; see Robert Speaight, *Shakespeare on the Stage: An Illustrated History of Shakespearian Performance* (Little, New York, 1973), p. 106.
2. George Odell, *Shakespeare from Betterton to Irving* (Constable, London, 1921), vol. 2, p. 247.
3. Henry Morley, *The Journal of a London Playgoer from 1851-1866* (George Routledge & Sons, London, 1866), p. 98.
4. Allardyce Nicoll, *A History of English Drama 1660-1900* (Cambridge University Press, Cambridge, 1959), vol. 5, p. 38. See also Nicoll, *Development of the Theatre* (George G. Harrap & Sons, London, 1958), ch. XI.
5. Nicoll, *History,* vol. 5, p. 40.
6. Austin Brereton, *The Life of Henry Irving* (Longmans, Green, & Co., London, 1908), vol. 2, p. 329.
7. Edward Gordon Craig, *Henry Irving* (Dent, London, 1930), p. 1.
8. Odell, vol. 2, p. 398.
9. *Times,* 29 December 1888.

10. Laurence Irving, *Henry Irving. The Actor and His World* (Faber & Faber, London, 1951), p. 439.
11. Odell, vol. 2, pp. 439-40.
12. William Archer, *The Theatrical World of 1897* (Walter Scott, London, 1898), p. 152.
13. Clement Scott, *The Drama of Yesterday and Today* (Macmillan, London, 1899), vol. 2, p. 412.
14. 'Stanley Jones' (Leonard Merrick), *The Actor and His Art: Some Considerations of the Present Condition of the Stage* (Downey & Co., London, 1899), p. 123. First published in *Tomorrow*, 1896-98.
15. Gordon Crosse, *Fifty Years of Shakespeare Playgoing* (Author, London, 1941), p. 43.
16. G.B. Shaw, 'The Dying Tongue of Great Elizabeth', *Saturday Review*, 11 February 1905, p. 171. Included in *Shaw on Theatre*, ed. E.J. West (MacGibbon & Kee, New York, 1958), p. 103.
17. Crosse, p. 44.
18. J.C. Trewin, *Shakespeare on the English Stage 1900-1964. A Survey of Productions* (Barrie & Rockliff, London, 1964), p. 41.
19. Crosse, p. 45.
20. H. Beerbohm Tree, 'The Staging of Shakespeare', *Fortnightly Review*, N.S. vol. 68 (July 1900), pp. 52-66; Poel's Letter (August 1900), p. 355; W. Hughes Mallett's 'Reply' (September 1900), pp. 504-12.
21. H. Beerbohm Tree, *Thoughts and After Thoughts* (Cassell, London, 1913), p. 56.
22. G. Wilson Knight, *Shakespearian Production* (Faber & Faber, London, 1964), p. 210.
23. Ibid., p. 213.
24. Benson, p. 312.
25. Ibid., p. 298.
26. Crosse, p. 31.
27. Benson, p. 298.
28. Max Beerbohm, *Around Theatres* (Rupert Hart Davis, London, 1953), p. 62.
29. Robert Speaight, *William Poel and the Elizabethan Revival* (William Heinemann, London, 1954), p. 51. Biographical information also from this volume.
30. Poel's Diary, quoted by Speaight, p. 26.
31. William Poel, *Monthly Letters* (T. Werner Laurie, London, 1929), pp. 2-3.
32. Quoted in Speaight, p. 46.
33. Two years later the E.S.S. revived *Twelfth Night* in the Old Hall of the Middle Temple where it had been first performed in 1602. This production may have owed something to Elizabeth Robins, whose request to do the same thing in 1891 had met with a rebuff from the Benchers after the event had been announced prematurely in the press.
34. Brochure in the Enthoven Collection.

35. William Poel, *Shakespeare in the Theatre* (Sidgwick & Jackson, London, 1913), pp. 203-4.

36. Perhaps its most notable revival was not Shakespearian, or even Elizabethan, but medieval: *Everyman,* in 1901, which received universal plaudits, was repeated countless times and launched a wave of miracle and morality revivals.

37. Lewis Casson, 'William Poel and the Modern Theatre', *Listener,* 10 January 1952, p. 58. See also Stephen C. Schultz, 'Two Notes on William Poel's Sources', *Nineteenth Century Theatre Research,* vol. 2, no. 2 (Autumn 1974), pp. 85-92, for Poel's debt to the elocutionist and reciter, Samuel Brandram, and to the *Comédie Française*.

38. Lillah McCarthy, *Myself and My Friends* (Thornton Butterworth, London, 1933), p. 28.

39. Speaight, p. 274.

40. A.B. Walkley, *Drama and Life* (Methuen, London, 1907), pp. 137-8.

41. Quoted by Speaight, p. 149.

42. *Stratford Dossier,* quoted by Speaight, p. 96.

43. Edith Evans, *Listener,* 10 February 1937, p. 261. Part of a BBC Shakespeare Series January to March 1937.

44. L. McCarthy, p. 30.

45. Speaight, p. 146.

46. Edward Garnett, 'Mr. Poel and the Theatre', *The English Review,* July 1913, p. 592.

47. Poel, *Shakespeare,* p. 223.

48. Lillah McCarthy, Lecture to Royal Institute, 27 January 1934 (Enthoven Collection).

49. W. Bridges-Adams, 'Granville Barker and the Savoy', *Drama,* N.S. vol. 52 (Spring 1959), p. 30.

50. H. Granville Barker, 'The Golden Thoughts of Granville Barker', letter to the Editor, *Play Pictorial,* vol. 21, no. 126 (1913), p. iv.

51. *Times,* 23 September 1912, p. 7.

52. Trewin, p. 58.

53. W.A. Darlington, *Six Thousand and One Nights* (George G. Harrap & Co., London, 1960), p. 65.

54. W. Bridges-Adams, *The Lost Leader* (Sidgwick & Jackson, London, 1954), p. 10. See also: *Listener,* 30 July 1953, pp. 173-5; *A Bridges-Adams Letter Book,* ed. with a Memoir by Robert Speaight (Society for Theatre Research, London, 1971), p. 91; and Karen Greif, '"If This were Play'd Upon a Stage": Harley Granville Barker's Shakespeare Productions at the Savoy Theatre, 1912-1914', *Harvard Library Bulletin,* vol. 28, no. 2 (April 1980), pp. 117-45, which includes some interesting illustrations.

Chapter Eight

EDWARD GORDON CRAIG: ARTIST OF THE THEATRE

> Here is the work. Who, greater than his age
> Will use this work to consecrate the stage?
>
> John Masefield, Preface to *Scene*

At first glance, Edward Gordon Craig does not appear to fit in the context of this book because he had nothing to do with the new drama and little immediate influence on the English stage. However, regarded in the light of his rebellion against the established, commercial modes of Victorian theatre, he is an essential transitional figure who must take his place alongside Shaw, Granville Barker, William Poel and the others who, one way or another, sought to bring about changes in the established theatre.

Craig was born on 16 January 1872, and his roots were firmly in the theatre. His mother, Ellen Terry, the most celebrated English actress of her day, came from a theatrical dynasty, and his father, Edward William Godwin, though an architect by profession, was continuously involved in theatrical pursuits from costume and set design to production. Godwin's direct influence on Craig was small, because by the time the boy was three, he and Ellen Terry had gone their separate ways.[1] Later, Craig came to regard Henry Irving as his 'father'; nobody could have had one so dedicated to the theatre, and throughout his life Craig looked up to Irving with a respect and admiration deeper than that of one artist for another.

Craig's first stage appearance was at the age of six when he entered among a crowd of villagers in *Olivia*, an adaptation of *The Vicar of Wakefield*, in which his mother was playing at the Court Theatre. His first appearance in an Irving production was two days before his thirteenth birthday while in Chicago, visiting his mother on tour. Largely to please Ellen Terry, Irving gave him a small part as a gardener's boy in *Eugene Arram*, and subsequently he appeared in crowd scenes in several other plays during the tour. After an erratic schooling during which he showed on aptitude for nothing except art, he was given his first job in the Lyceum production of *The Dead Heart*. His development was strongly influenced by four actors: J.L. Toole and William Terriss, who gave him worldly advice; Walter Lacy, who provided elocution lessons; and, above all, Henry Irving, whose example at rehearsals taught him theatrical technique and methods. In the summer of 1890 he toured with the Haviland and Harvey Company; the following years saw him touring with the Shakespeare Company of W.S. Hardy and with Sarah Thorne's Company, and playing for Irving both on tour and in London. He performed in a variety of roles, including lead parts in several Shakespeare productions, scoring a notable success as Hamlet for Ben Greet at the Olympic in May 1897.

Acting for Craig during the 'nineties was more a necessity than a vocation. In 1893 he had married May Gibson, and their increasing family--four children by 1898--imposed an unwelcome burden upon him and a demand for money that his mother was prepared to meet only sparingly. His first inclination was towards theatre production. Having watched Irving shape a play and bring it to life on stage, he hankered to do the same, and experimented with *Henry IV* and Browning's *A Blot in the 'Scutcheon*. His first opportunity came by chance through the invitation of the local vicar to mount a charity production at the Uxbridge Town Hall. He decided to put on de Musset's *On ne badine pas avec l'Amour (No Trifling with Love)*, aiming at perfection in detail in the Lyceum manner. Although he was given the free assistance of the Lyceum wardrobe and props departments, costs ran up and there was little profit for charity, but Craig had enjoyed his first taste of control over a complete production. He might then have progressed further in that field, but the friendship of the 'Beggarstaff Brothers', James Pryde and William Nicholson, who introduced him to the world of form, line and colour, turned his enthusiasm in the direction of the graphic arts, particularly wood engraving, in which he soon became expert. In 1896, chafing under the bonds of family responsibilities, he found personal freedom by taking up with an old friend, Jess Dorynne, whom he rediscovered on joining Sarah Thorne's company at Chatham. She shared his artistic interests, and helped him produce *The Page*, a monthly art magazine he founded that survived, somewhat erratically, for three years, and she hand-coloured most of the woodcuts in *Gordon Craig's Book of Penny Toys* (1899).

A more important influence at this time was the musician Martin Shaw, who revealed the magic and power of music to him. Shaw led Craig back to the theatre by inviting him to be stage-director for an amateur production by the Purcell Operatic Society, which Shaw had founded, of *Dido* and *Aeneas* at the Hampstead Conservatoire (later the Embassy Theatre) 17-18-19 May 1900. By this time, Craig said he was 'beginning to see on a distant horizon a new conception of the theatre. Nothing to do with archaelogy--no realism--but something nearer to poetry'.[2] Directing the opera enabled Craig to combine the meticulous methods of the Lyceum with concepts of stage production that he had first encountered ten years earlier at the private theatre in Bushey of Hubert von Herkomer, realistic portrait painter turned theatre experimenter. Rebelling against the static realism of conventional *mises en scéne,* Herkomer had amazed audiences with artistic stage effects of moonlight, misty mornings, sunrises, and other phenomena, using electric lights and painted gauzes to recreate nature's mobile and atmospheric moods. Craig, too, rejected historical or descriptive realism and, as Stanislavsky was to recognize years later, required the spectator to become an 'active creator' in the production through the response of his imagination to the stimulating harmonies of colour, light, music, movement and design. Seven months of painstaking preparation were rewarded by wide praise from the critics and the satisfaction of proving what could be achieved by having control in the hands of a single director who was both artistic and experienced in the theatre. For *Dido and Aeneas* Craig dispensed with conventional painted sets, 'painting' with coloured materials and light. Two cloths, one ultramarine and one grey, which were moved like sails with block and tackle, formed the background, and the only moveable structures were Dido's throne and four trellis walls covered with grape-laden vines. The lighting played an important role, and was innovative in the absence of footlights and substitution of overhead lights, sidelights, and two spotlights mounted in the rear of the auditorium. The setting and lighting were combined with groupings and stage effects aimed at exploiting to the full the art of symbol and suggestion and at providing an appropriate context for the action. Haldane Macfall, an art critic who believed that 'it is through man's imagination that he reaches the Realities', recognized that *Dido and Aeneas* 'was the first step of a new movement which is destined to revolutionise the production of the poetic drama'. There was 'no attempt at presenting a series of realistic pictures, done from photographs taken upon the spot', but simplicity and 'a haunting impression of glowing colour' that sustained the note of tragedy throughout, especially in the last scene where 'the woe-begone figure of Dido, wrapped in her black robes, reclines amidst the sombre black cushions of her throne ... [against] the great lilac background that springs in one broad expanse straight upwards to the heavens'.[3] Finally, a rain of pink paper rose petals descended on Dido as the set deepened into darkness.

Although a deficit of £180.15.0 had been incurred and met out of the pockets of friends, the artistic success of the production encouraged Shaw, Craig and the Society to stage another Purcell opera, *The Masque of Love,* and to revive *Dido and Aeneas* at the Coronet Theatre the following March. To help draw audiences, Ellen Terry and a small company performed *Nance Oldfield* as a curtain raiser, but the productions succeeded again on their own merits. A third season was held in March 1902 offering Handel's *Acis and Galatea*. When this was announced, a critic in the *Saturday Review* wrote a condemnation of the Purcell Society which drew a letter of rebuke from W.B. Yeats, who declared perceptively:

> Last year I saw *Dido and Aeneas* and *The Masque of Love* ... and they gave me more perfect pleasure than I have met with in any theatre these ten years. I saw the only admirable stage scenery of our time, for Mr. Gordon Craig has discovered how to decorate a play with severe, beautiful, simple, effects of colour, that leave the imagination free to follow all the suggestions of the play. Realistic scenery takes the imagination captive and is at best but bad landscape painting, but Mr. Gordon Craig's scenery is a new and distinct art. It is something that can only exist in the theatre. It cannot even be separated from the figures that move before it. The staging of *Dido and Aeneas* and *The Masque of Love* will some day, I am persuaded, be remembered among the important events of our time.[4]

Another poet who admired Craig's work was Laurence Housman. He invited Craig to produce his new play, *Bethlehem*, which had music by Joseph Moorat, and he agreed to give Craig a free hand. This Craig used rather ruthlessly--especially with the music where he substituted excerpts from the classics--according to his growing conviction that the producer must overrule all others, including the author, in the cause of theatrical effectiveness. Craig was now forming a concept of an Art of the Theatre: as the artist in the plastic arts had to have complete mastery and control over his materials, so the 'stage-manager' or producer, the 'master of the science of the stage', must have the same basis of skill and experience in all phases of theatrical work, and the same control over all elements of the final production. This principle of artistic control was particularly important in an evocative mode of theatre where dialogue, movement and design--down to the very colour and texture of the costumes--were fused to create a unified aesthetic impression, a mood that conveyed emotion.

Such authoritarian control worked in the amateur theatre, given a dedicated group of performers and assistants, but how would it succeed in the commercial theatre where the competing demands of author, actor, designer, all the ancillary trades, and the box office manager had to be reckoned with? Craig soon discovered that the prevailing conditions in the commercial theatre militated against his ideal when he accepted his mother's invitation to design a production for her of Ibsen's *The Vikings of Helgeland*. He encountered the egoism of actors (which became, like realism, something of a *bête noire* with him) and the intransigence of the traditionalists and of the practical or less imaginative. Even his sister Edy, who was responsible for the costumes, like the discontented performers, was forced to appeal directly to Ellen Terry. 'All this produced an undercurrent of intrigue and subversion', writes Edward Craig, 'and the atmosphere in the theatre was electric with tension'.[5] The production opened on 15 April 1903 at the Imperial to a mixed reception. G.B. Shaw, whose conception of theatre was poles apart from Craig's, puts his finger on the problem in a letter to Ellen Terry in which he condemns Craig on two counts: 'matricide' in ruining his mother's role--she was miscast as the fierce warrior-wife, Hjördis--and 'treachery to the author' in sacrificing the play to

> clever effects ... what he aimed at was so well done that he has bowled over all the critics who have any artistic perception; and they have forgotten to tell him that his business was to bring out Ibsen's qualities and not his own. If he did that to a play of mine, I would sacrifice him on the prompter's table before his mother's eyes.[6]

Craig had rejected Ibsen's authentic settings, which he stylized, staging much of the action in semi-darkness to intensify the tragic mood, but thereby angering Shaw and other critics. However, many admired the grim rocky slope and mist-encircled, inky sea of the first act; the effective circular banqueting table of the second act, with its crown-like overhead wrought-iron circle bearing lights that shed a 'gloomy radiance'; and the simplicity of the final set with its single casement, dais and hard light. The artist William Rothenstein found *The Vikings* 'a drama singularly grand and lofty in spirit, the interpretation of which is more remarkable than any which I have seen in this, or any other country', and he praised Craig for proving 'that the particular qualities which excite our enthusiasm in other arts may also be brought upon the stage'.[7] But lack of support forced the withdrawal of the piece after three weeks, and *Much Ado About Nothing* took its place. Despite only two weeks in which to prepare this production, Craig mounted some effective sets which were inspired by Sebastiano Serlio's *Five Books of Architecture* (1545). Particularly impressive was the church scene (iv.1) where he created his atmosphere mainly through vertical lines with sunlight shafting through an unseen stained glass window to cast a multi-coloured pool of light on the floor.

These early experiments indicate that unlike the advocates of the new drama, who were prepared to compromise with the established theatre and wanted some share in the total enterprise rather than complete control, or Granville Barker, who, as has been recognized, was evolutionary rather than revolutionary, Craig rebelled totally against the theatre of his time. Realism in any form--new or old, for the sake of spectacle or in the cause of truth--was anathema to him: where

Shaw was iconoclastic in ideas, but not in his dramaturgy, Craig would gladly have sacrificed Shaw--and all his ideas--on the prompter's table in the cause of artistry in the theatre. Although the two productions for Ellen Terry helped to make Craig's name more familiar in theatrical circles, his revolutionary technique and approach were guaranteed not to endear him to anyone in the commercial theatre, and it is not surprising that recognition was accorded him not from the world of theatre but from that of art, where his work was becoming known through one-man exhibitions (of which there were thirty between 1901 and 1914).[8]

In May 1903, through his friend William Rothenstein, the artist, he became an original member of the Society of Twelve with whom he exhibited six times in the next twelve years. Rothenstein also introduced him to an important patron of the arts, Count Harry Kessler, a member of the Court at Weimar, who invited him to produce a play there. Despite the frustrations and disappointments of the venture with his mother, and the financial losses and consequent worries resulting from the Purcell Society productions, Craig had lost neither his theatrical ambitions nor his ideals; therefore, he would not accept Kessler's offer unless his conditions were met. In a letter to William Rothenstein, he declared:

> I can do nothing talking to Dukes and Grand Duchesses & Poets with a court actress or two thrown in--
>
> I have had so much experience of these *discussions* about a production.
>
> If only he [Kessler] or the duke would make me a definite offer I would make them a definite answer.
>
> As I have told him I can do nothing without first reading the play--secondly, I can do nothing unless he can assure me that absolute power will be given me over *play, actors & actresses,* scenery costume & every detail in the production.[9]

This matter lapsed, but Kessler was persistent, and Craig agreed to send some of his work to Germany, the result of which was an invitation from Otto Brahm to come to Berlin for a 'trial period'. The manner of invitation angered Craig, but eventually he agreed to go--a decision that was to transform his life. The immediate project was designs for a production of Hofmannstahl's translation of Otway's *Venice Preserved* for the Lessing theatre, but the collaboration failed and Craig's designs were mutilated. After a forlorn attempt to work for Reinhardt, he moved on to Weimar where he revelled in an artistic environment in which his ideas could flourish. Among those he met were two modern architects, the Belgian Henry van de Velde and the Austrian Joseph Hoffman, who encouraged him to construct a model of his ideal theatre and influenced the architectural direction of his thinking, already inspired by Serlio and by Manfred Semper's *Handbuck der Architectur*, which he had discovered in Berlin when seeking ideas for *Venice Preserved*. 'I wish to remove the *Pictorial Scene'*, he wrote in his Daybook, 'but to leave in its place the *Architectonic Scene'*. [10]

An exhibition of his stage designs and book engravings, sponsored by Kessler, toured Germany and was shown in both Vienna and London. In the introduction to the catalogue, Kessler wrote: 'the *Gesammtkunstwerk* that Wagner thought to found on the basis of music and poetry will soon, perhaps, be re-created by Craig or under his influence, from painting, dance and gesture'.[11]

The mention of dance indicates the appearance of a new influence in Craig's life: Isadora Duncan. They met in Berlin in December 1904, and immediately formed a passionate relationship from which they drew mutual artistic inspiration. His genius fanned the flame of her art, and in return he derived from her a concept of the essence of abstract movement and what it could convey: 'by means of suggestion in movement', he wrote a few years later, 'you may translate all the passions and the thoughts of vast numbers of people, or by means of the same you can assist your actor to convey the thoughts and the emotions of the particular character he impersonates'.[12] Here Craig had gone beyond what Isadora had taught him the body in motion could achieve, and had extended her concept of expressive movement to include the supporting background. From their first encounter Craig's feelings were 'a mixture of overwhelming admiration and furious resentment--admiration for what had been to him the greatest artistic experience of his life, resentment that this revelation should come from a woman'.[13] Within a few weeks of their meeting, an inevitable battle had begun, she wrote, 'between the genius of Gordon Craig and the inspiration of my Art'.[14] Both were egocentrics, consumed by love of their art, to which all else would be sacrificed. At the very time of their affair, Craig was sacrificing Elena Meo, whom he had met in 1900: she was back in London with their two children, and he was to return to her unwavering devotion more than once. As his notebook reveals, he was perplexed by the concurrence of a fierce attraction for one woman and an abiding love for another. But, as he confessed in a letter to Martin Shaw, through Isadora he felt 'alive again (as artist)', and his mind teemed with ideas.

One of the first concrete results of this fermentation was a book which he wrote in one week while in Berlin in 1905. The difficulties of finding outlets for his ideas in the regular theatre had already directed his attention to the possibility of spreading his message through the printed word. He had written his first article in 1902, and was discovering a fascination in the magic and power of language. *The Art of the Theatre* (1905) is a Socratic dialogue between a Stage-Director and a Playgoer in which the former is spokesman for Craig's new concepts of 'The Art of the Theatre', which

> is neither acting nor the play, it is not scene nor dance, but it consists of all the elements of which these things are composed: action, which is the very spirit of acting; words, which are the body of the play; line and colour, which are the very heart of the scene; rhythm, which is the very essence of dance. (p. 138)

He propounds three new unities, action, scene and voice:

> And when I say *action,* I mean both gesture and dancing, and prose and poetry of action.
>
> When I say *scene,* I mean all which comes before the eye, such as the lighting, costume, as well as the scenery.
>
> When I say *voice,* I mean the spoken word or the word which is sung, in contradiction to the word which is read, for the word written to be spoken and the word written to be read are two entirely different things. (pp. 180-1)

The aim of unity imposes as a necessity the supremacy of one man, the 'stage-manager', now elevated to the rank of 'Artist of the Theatre', whose concept of the play dictates every aspect of acting, setting, movement and design, and whose control is exercised over every phase of production.

Despite his principles, he agreed to work on designs for a production of *Elektra* by the great Italian actress, Eleanora Duse. This project was abandoned by Duse, and consequently it required a great deal of persuasion from Isadora to get him to agree to design the scenes for Duse's 1906 production of Ibsen's *Rosmersholm* in Florence. Again, he did not have control over the whole production, but he did insist on an absolutely free hand with the scene. He incarcerated himself in the theatre with a few workmen assistants, and did not allow anyone else in until he had finished. When Duse, accompanied by an apprehensive Isadora, saw what he had achieved, she embraced Craig and swore to devote herself to showing the world his art. Gone was the heavy, conventional drawing-room, and in its place 'a vision of loveliness', enthused Isadora:

> through vast blue spaces, celestial harmonies, mounting lines, colossal heights, one's soul was drawn toward the light of [a] great window which showed beyond, no little avenue, but the infinite universe ... Was this the living room of Rosmersholm? I do not know what Ibsen would have

> thought. Probably he would have been as we were--speechless, carried away.[15]

An objective, independent report was given by the designer Enrico Corradini, who saw a 'completely transformed' stage:

> the usual wings were gone. Here was a new architecture of great height, ranging in colour from green to blue. It was simple, mysterious, fascinating, and a fitting background to the complicated lives of Rosmer and Rebecca West; it portrayed a *state of mind*. [16]

Unfortunately, collaboration between Craig and Duse ended abruptly when he saw his *Rosmersholm* sets cut down to fit the stage at Nice Casino. He flew into a rage, blaming Duse--who was innocent of the crime--and she ordered him out of the door and out of her life.

This experience drove a further wedge between Craig and the commercial theatre, while the success of his book, which had appeared in German, English, Dutch and Russian, sent him in pursuit of another dream: the establishment of a new theatrical magazine that would provide an outlet for his ideas and for those of all who were striving for a revitalized, artistic theatre. After restlessly following Isadora around Europe designing the décors for her dances, he retreated to Florence, where he established a base from which the first issue of *The Mask* was published in March 1908. Craig was again fortunate in his personal contacts, finding an ideal secretary-assistant in Dorothy Nevile Lees, an authoress in her own right, who not only took on most of the secretarial and administrative tasks, but also contributed articles to the magazine. *The Mask* appeared monthly the first year, then quarterly more or less regularly, except for suspension during the war, until 1929. It was almost entirely written by Craig himself, who used well over sixty false initials or pseudonyms, including that of 'John Semar' the editor, to disguise his identity and give the impression of a large body of contributors.[17] *The Mask* sought to be an 'art' rather than a 'trade' journal, dedicated to the promotion of one 'IDEA'--the movement 'Towards a New Theatre' that would re-establish the 'nobler traditions' of European theatre and take its rightful place among the Fine Arts. *The Mask* was eclectic in preserving or rediscovering the best of the past, virulent in condemning realism and 'the parody of the theatre' offered at the time, suspicious of revolutionary new movements, and idealistic in its aim for 'the theatre of the future'. It reprinted a great variety of extracts from earlier works on theatre and costume, and its pages were decorated with woodcuts showing old Venetian costume, *Commedia dell' Arte* characters, and stylized figures, masks and scenes by Craig, all aimed at drawing on the past to inspire the future. Among the evils which it attacked were:

> Realism, Vulgarity, Commercialism and the trade spirit, Pedantry, Theatricalism, the aggressive personality of the actor, the star system, badly built theatres, the invasion of the theatre by other artists, the system of actor managers, the representation of ugliness, the acceptance of mere "effectiveness" as a substitute for thoroughness in all branches of the profession, the selfish apathy and cowardice which would oppose all progress or reform lest it should militate against personal prosperity and personal ease.[18]

Such a catalogue places Craig firmly in the ranks of the opponents of the established theatre such as Jones, Archer, Shaw and Granville Barker, all of whom, despite their differences, would have subscribed to most of its principles although, of course, in most instances, Craig's remedies would have been regarded as more painful than the evils they purported to cure.

The Mask conducted several Symposia on such questions as 'Realism', 'A National Theatre' and 'The Position of the Theatre', soliciting answers to questionnaires sent all over Europe. Its international status was maintained by articles on the theatre in various countries and regular 'Foreign Notes' covering theatrical events from New York, Moscow, London ('home', of course, was Florence), and elsewhere. The tone of the articles, particularly those by Craig, was prophetic. A typical rhetorical outburst is entitled 'Motion. Being the Preface to the Portfolio of Etchings by Gordon Craig', which envisions the rebirth of Beauty in the mould of Craig's ideal theatre:

> for the fulfilment of this most superb dream must first come the union of the three Arts...The Arts of Architecture, Music and Motion. These three Arts bring to the Religion of Truth three vital needs. The First brings the Place.......The Second the Voice.......The Third reveals the Event.......The Temple.......The Hymn....... The Balance. Without Architecture we should have no Divine Place in which to praise. Without Music no Divine Voice with which to praise. Without Motion no Divine Act to perform. Architecture.......Music.......Motion.......These are the great Impersonal Arts of the Earth.......and together form the mysterious link between Now and the Hereafter. For the fulfilment of our most superb Life, these three must be again united from one end of the Earth unto the other.[19]

The journal was attractively printed on hand-made paper, and although its circulation appears never to have exceeded one thousand, its advocacy of the 'IDEA' stimulated thought in advanced theatrical circles throughout the world. Writing in

1945, Jacques Coupeau declared that *The Mask*,

> which initiated us so nobly and guided us so helpfully is by no means out of date. Today, when we turn the pages inside its handsome vellum binding, we realize more clearly than ever that it linked up the theatre with all the great forms of art and tried to rescue it from every kind of rut. There is not an artist of our day whose entire universe has eluded his [Craig's] influence.[20]

Some of the best and most important of Craig's articles from *The Mask* were collected in *On the Art of the Theatre* in 1911. In an Introduction, Dr. Alexander Hevesi, director of the Budapest State Theatre, identifies the twin evils Craig fought and the essence of his approach:

> for more than two hundred years there have been two men working on the stage, spoiling all that is to be called Theatrical Art. These two men are the Realist and the Machinist. The Realist offers imitation for life, and the Machinist tricks in place of marvels. So we have lost the truth and the marvel of life--that is, we have lost the main thing possessed by the art. The Art of the Theatre as pure imitation is nothing but an alarming demonstration of the abundance of life and the narrowness of Art ... True Art is always discovering the marvel in all that does not seem to be marvellous at all, because Art is not imitation, but vision. (pp. xvii-xviii)

The original dialogue, *The Art of the Theatre*, forms the nucleus of the new book, which also contains the notorious essay 'The Actor and the Über-Marionette'. Craig drew part of his inspiration for this essay from a statement--reprinted frequently in *The Mask*-- made by Duse to Arthur Symons:

> to save the theatre, the theatre must be destroyed, the actors and actresses must all die of the plague. They poison the air, they make art impossible. It is not drama that they play, but pieces for the theatre. We should return to the Greeks, play in the open air; the drama dies of stalls and boxes and evening dress, and people who come to digest their dinner.[21]

Seizing on this, Craig argues that

> acting is not an art. It is therefore incorrect to speak of the actor as an artist. For accident is an enemy of the artist. Art is the exact antithesis of pandemonium, and pandemonium is created by the tumbling together of many accidents. Art arrives only by design. Therefore in order to make any work of art it is clear we may only work in

> those materials with which we can calculate. Man is not one of these materials. (pp. 55-6)

He goes on to assert that actors 'must create for themselves a new form of acting, consisting for the main part of symbolical gesture' (p.61). He then declares that 'the actor as he is now must go, and in his place comes the inanimate figure--the Über-marionette we may call him, until he has won for himself a better name' (p.81). Because the egoism of the actor interferes with the projection of the character he is playing, he must not attempt to identify himself with that character as in realistic theatre, but must stand outside his role, in complete control of himself, acquiring the virtues of the marionette:

> the über-marionette will not compete with life--rather will it go beyond it. Its ideal will not be the flesh and blood but rather the body in trance--it will aim to clothe itself with a death-like beauty while exhaling a living spirit. (pp. 84-5)

In a Preface added in 1925, Craig denied wanting to eliminate the actor in favour of a wooden puppet: 'the über-marionette is the actor plus fire, minus egoism: the fire of the gods and demons without the smoke and steam of mortality' (pp. ix-x). Craig declared later that only Henry Irving approximated this ideal of an actor in complete technical control of himself. In a manner that looks forward to Brecht, but in a prophetic rather than a didactic mode, Craig sought a 'noble artificiality' from actors in conscious control of their gestures and movements: 'today they *impersonate* and interpret; tomorrow they must *represent* and interpret [the Brechtian phase]; and the third day they must create' (p.61). Reaching for an understanding of these ideals, G. Wilson Knight saw that

> for Craig the human drama is not only shadowed but itself interpenetrated by spirit-powers. That is why his actors must be able to perform in exact physical obedience to, or unison with, the over-ruling design ... acting is an art which demands a perfect fusion of spirit and body; and it is because, in his fallen state, man has lost this unity that Craig, at the limit, demands the 'über-marionette,' which is his symbol of perfection.[22]

In a companion essay from *The Mask*, 'Plays and Playwrights Pictures and Painters in the Theatre', the same sense of prophecy and evangelism that informs so much of Craig's writing reappears to condemn the writer, musician and painter as 'utterly useless' in the theatre:

> let them keep to their preserves, let them keep to their kingdoms, and let those of the theatre return to theirs.

> Only when these last are once more re-united there shall spring so great an art, and one so universally beloved, that I prophesy that a new religion will be found contained in it. That religion will preach no more, but it will reveal. It will not show us the definite images which the sculptor and the painter show. It will unveil thought to our eyes, silently--by movements--in visions. (p.123)

Such utterances were not the mere dreams of a Utopian theorist, but the earnest vision of a man whose belief was 'also in the necessity of daily work under the conditions which are today offered us' (p.53), and whose constant concern was with practical designs and working models: indeed, the motto of *The Mask* was 'after the practice, the theory'. In 1907, infused with the idea of movement, and inspired by diagrams in Book Two of Serlio's *Five Books* showing 'a floor divided into squares from which seemed to emerge a simplified architectural structure',[23] Craig set about constructing a stage that could itself express movement through the manipulation of volume and plane by the raising and lowering of blocks:

> I wanted a *'scene'* so mobile, which (within rules) might move in all directions--tempos--in all things under the control of the one who could dream how to move its parts to produce *'movements.'* And shortly after this I found in the 3 and 4 leaved screen (each leaf the width of each side of the floor squares) the solution of my question.[24]

Eight years later he described his 'Screens. The Thousand Scenes in One Scene' in *The Mask:*

> The Scene is made up usually of four, six, eight, ten, or twelve screens ... Each part or leaf of a screen is alike in every particular except breadth, and these parts together form a screen, composed of two, four, six, eight, or ten leaves. These leaves fold either way and are monochrome in tint.
>
> The height of all these screens is alike.
>
> These screens are self-supporting and are made either of a wooden frame covered with canvas, or of solid wood ... Sometimes a flat roof is used with these screens, at other times the space above the top line is shown.[25]

A limited number of additions, such as a flight of steps or a balcony, and essential properties were allowed. Ideally, these screens should move during a performance to complement the natural flow of the action, and he discovered that the alteration of a screen's angle or the variation of light upon it could transform the mood or expression of the scene. In this manner he managed to fuse his admiration for permanent scenes, like the Greek *skene,* Roman *frons scaenae,* medieval church and

Elizabethan playhouse, with his passion for movement and plasticity. The artistic value of his invention, he claimed, was that it became 'a living thing ... capable of all varieties of expression ... The Scene always remains the same while incessantly changing', like a human face.[26] As a working model could be at the fingertips of the director and actor for experiment, there was also the practical advantage of economies in time, labour and money. To support his claims, Craig prefaced his account with quotations from Yeats, to whom he had given a model, who declared:

> Henceforth I can all but "produce" my play while I write it, moving hither and thither little figures of cardboard through gay or solemn light and shade, allowing the scene to give the words and the words the scene.
>
> I am very grateful for he [Craig] has banished a whole world that wearied me and was undignified and given me forms and lights upon which I can play as upon some stringed instrument.[27]

Craig also included a letter to the actor Giovanni Grasso from Filiberto Scarpelli, who had seen Craig's model Scene in action in Florence. 'Craig is a great painter, a great architect, a great poet', Scarpelli declared: 'he paints with light, he constructs with a few rectangles of cardboard, and with the harmony of his colours and of his lines he creates profound sensations'.[28]

The screens were first used on the stage of the Abbey Theatre, Dublin, for Lady Gregory's *The Deliverer* and Yeats' *The Hour Glass* on 12 January 1911. By this time Craig was close to seeing his screens in action under his own direction. Stanislavsky had encountered Craig's work in *The Mask* and had caught Isadora Duncan's enthusiasm for the man, so had invited him to direct a play of his own choice in Moscow. Craig accepted, naming *Hamlet;* and he decided to use his screens. He made his first visit to Moscow in October 1908. Stanislavsky agreed to give him complete artistic freedom and every assistance he required. They had four weeks of discussions, after which Craig returned to Florence to work out details. The following April he returned to Russia for three months of further discussions, which were extensively recorded by the interpreters, Ursula Cox in English and Michael Lykiardopoulos in Russian.[29] On 28 February 1910, he returned to Moscow, records Stanislavsky,

> with a complete plan for the production of "Hamlet." He brought with him the models of the scenery and the interesting work began. Craig supervised everything and Sulerjitsky and I became his assistants ... In one of the rehearsal rooms which had been given over entirely to Craig, there was built a large model reproduction of our

> stage. This was lit by an electric system that was an exact copy of what the production would have on our real stage, not a single detail of any effect being overlooked.[30]

Craig placed models of his screens on the model stage, and using figures of wood representing the actors 'moved the figures on the stage with the help of a long stick and actually demonstrated all the movements of the actors on the stage' (p. 512). At this time, Stanislavsky was beset by doubts concerning his realistic techniques, especially with respect to classic drama, and he welcomed the opportunity to experiment with a stylized production in collaboration with a fellow-artist who sought 'the same naturally born creative principles'. But when Craig returned to Florence at the end of April and left him to realize on stage the 'scenic dream' of another artist, Stanislavsky encountered considerable practical difficulties both with his actors and with the screens. Problems with the former were never resolved to the satisfaction of either man, for the actors failed to achieve the 'noble simplicity', 'grand assurance' and 'masterful restraint' desired, and those with the latter led to a compromise in which the screens had to be constructed not out of solid material, as Craig wished, but out of unpainted canvas secured on light wooden frames. A further disappointment over the screens was in store because they collapsed 'like a house of cards' just as the audience was entering the theatre on the first night, 5 January 1912, so for safety's sake unwanted curtain drops had to be made to conceal the shifting of the screens, which should have taken place in the course of performance. Craig later 'realized that he should never have attempted to use his screens for the play at all',[31] and regretted the expenditure of time which could have been employed more usefully on his theatre studies.

Nevertheless, the Moscow *Hamlet* was a significant production and gave a very useful boost to Craig's reputation because he did achieve an impressive synthesis of interpretation and design. It was based, declared Stanislavsky, on the concept of Hamlet as 'the best of men, who passed like Christ across the earth and became the victim of a cleansing sacrifice', and the action was designed to be seen from Hamlet's perspective as 'he looked deep into earthly life in order to solve the mystery and meaning of being' (p. 513). The first scene exemplified this approach, comprising:

> Mysterious corners, passages, strange lights, deep shadows, moon rays, court sentries, unfathomable underground sounds at the rise of the curtain, choruses of variegated tonalities becoming one with underground blows, the whistling of the wind, and a strange, far-off cry. (pp. 517-18)

The following scene presented the Court through Hamlet's eyes, as, placed on the forestage, he looked back where

> the King and Queen sat on a high throne in golden and brocaded costumes, among the golden walls of the throne room, and from their shoulders there spread downwards a cloak of golden porphyry, widening until it occupied the entire width of the stage and fell into the trap. In this tremendous cloak there were cut holes through which appeared a great number of courtiers' heads, looking upward at the throne. The whole scene resembled a golden sea with golden waves. But this golden sea did not shine with bad theatrical effect, for Craig showed the scene by dimmed lights, under the slipping rays of projectors that made the gold glitter in places with terrible and threatening glow. (pp. 514-15)

Despite the difficulties and disappointments in the final result felt by both Craig and Stanislavsky, and a generally unfavourable reception from Russian critics, the production received considerable attention from the European press. That Craig had in large measure achieved what he had set out to do is indicated by the report of the special correspondent of the *Times*, Terence Philip, who reported that

> Mr. Craig has the singular power of carrying the spiritual significance of words and dramatic situations beyond the actor to the scene in which he moves. By the simplest of means he is able in some mysterious way to evoke almost any sensation of time or space, the scenes even in themselves suggesting variations of human emotion ... the production is a remarkable triumph for Mr. Craig, and it is impossible to say how wide an effect such a completely realized success of his theories may have on the theatre of Europe.[32]

Craig's visits to Moscow revived his long-standing desire to institute a theatre school. He had experienced one form of 'school' under Irving at the Lyceum, but his concepts were closer to those of Herkomer whose pupils engaged in stage, costume and programme design as well as in acting. Craig began to conceive the idea of a school of his own in 1903, and received reinforcement from Isadora Duncan, whose career was largely directed towards maintaining her dancing school. The 'Second Dialogue', written in 1910 for *The Mask* and included in *On the Art of the Theatre,* declares admiration for the theatre-school combination of the 'Constan Art Theatre' in Moscow, and when *Hamlet* was produced he asked Stanislavsky to help finance a project that would supplement the Russian work, but Stanislavsky had plans of his own. On 16 July 1911 Craig had been honoured by 150 of his çompatriots at a dinner at the

Café Royal--those of the arts noticeably predominating over those of the theatre. This honour and the reception of *Hamlet* encouraged him to believe that support for his school could be found, so he formed two committees to launch it:

> an International Committee which represented England, France, Germany, Russia, Austria-Hungary, Italy, and Japan, and included an impressive array of distinguished names, and an English Advisory Committee, of which the Chairman was William Rothenstein, and most of its members those who had promoted the dinner in Craig's honour the year before.[33]

However, money was not readily forthcoming until Elena Meo, who had taken it upon herself to raise the funds, persuaded Lord Howard de Walden to pledge a subsidy of £5,000 for the first year and £2,500 for the following two years. Craig chose 27 February 1913, his mother's birthday, to announce the foundation of his school, which was to be based not in England but in Florence at the Arena Goldoni where he had been conducting his theatre experiments since 1908. 'My proposal', he wrote in *The Mask*, 'is to discover or rediscover the lost Art of the Theatre by a practical expedition ... into the realms where it lies hidden'.[34] 'The Second Dialogue' looked forward to 'a college of experiment in which to study the three sources of art--Sound, Light and Motion' *(Art,* p. 240), and these three formed the basis of the school's curriculum, which dealt with all aspects of stagecraft except acting, although mime and movement were given great emphasis. Subjects for study ranged from theatre history to handicrafts, which of course included the manufacture and manipulation of masks, models and marionettes. Craig drew up rules with an almost paranoiac concern for secrecy, and the first 'pupils-*cum*-assistants' arrived in the summer of 1913. Craig's happiness at having fulfilled a cherished ambition was short-lived: 'it came in 1913; it went in 1914', he sighed, 'for the war swept it away and my supporter did not see the value of keeping the engine fires "banked!" So the fires went out'.[35]

After the war the fires were not relit, and although Craig continued to promote his ideas for the rest of his life, the bulk of his creative work had been completed by 1914. The degree of his influence is debatable and, to a large extent, conjectural. His ideas certainly had very little immediate effect on the Edwardian theatre except in the area of poetic drama where Yeats and Arthur Symons acclaimed him as their prophet. As early as 1902, Symons saw in Craig's work 'the suggestion of a new art of the stage, an art no longer realistic, but conventional, no longer imitative, but symbolical',[36] and he recognized Craig's distinctive style in the designs for Masques, notably those for the 'Masque of London', which were

> built up definitely between the wings of the stage ... there are always the long straight lines, the sense of height and space, the bare surfaces, the subtle significant shadows, out of which Mr. Craig has long since learned to evoke stage pictures more beautiful and more suggestive than any that have been seen on our stage in our time.[37]

William Rothenstein suggested to Beerbohm Tree that he should employ Craig: 'Tree needed some persuasion', but he agreed, and invited Craig to do the designs for a production of *Macbeth*. Craig accepted, duly presented Tree with designs and models, and suggested 'that Tree should leave London and himself in charge of his theatre!'[38] Tree's response to this proposal is, unfortunately, unrecorded, but he did show Craig's work to the scene painter, Joseph Harker, who 'vigorously attacked [it] as being unpractical in every way'.[39] The collaboration collapsed, and London lost the chance of seeing a unique combination of great showmanship and great artistry. An awareness of Craig's ideas undoubtedly influenced Granville Barker's Savoy productions, especially his Shakespeare--but the main impact was abroad, where Adolphe Appia had been working along similar lines. The two men appear to have influenced each other very little: Craig was not aware of Appia's work until 1908, and they did not meet until 1914. They shared both a dislike of realism and a belief in symbolical representation, but Appia was music-oriented, his ideas having stemmed from Wagner, and Craig began from the standpoint of the actor-producer. More importantly, where Craig was a revolutionary who sought a unique art of the theatre, Appia was a reformer who envisioned an integration of the separate arts, with the *mise en scène* providing a sculptural background in which the necessary 'plasticity' to dramatize the action was provided by light and shadow. Both men sought the elemental and essential, what Jacques Rouche termed Craig's 'simplicité grandiose'. It was unfortunate that the Craig-Reinhardt collaboration attempted in 1905 dissolved in disagreement. After their meeting, says Denis Bablet, Reinhardt's

> work bore the stamp of the influence thus absorbed. His *Winter's Tale* and *King Lear* were among the first of what were rightly called 'Craigische Vorstellungen' (Craigish productions), with their simplification of the visual element, the three-dimensional architecture of their scenery, and their use of lighting to stimulate the imagination.[40]

Craig was not without his detractors. Typical is Lee Simonson, the American stage designer, who admired Appia for his aesthetic doctrine but condemned Craig for being a 'day-dreamer', an 'exalted mountebank' who 'ignored technical problems altogether' and never achieved anything on the real stage.[41] Conversely, Sheldon Chaney praised him as 'the prophet who directed a thousand artists towards a different future ... the great stimulating force behind the modernistic effort'.[42] Denis Bablet claims that Craig's ideas 'affected some utterly dissimilar forms of theatrical activity'.[43] Among these he includes those of Jouvet and Barrault in France; Tairov and Meyerhold in Russia; Oskar Schlemmer and the Bauhaus group in Germany; and, also in Germany, the expressionists and Brecht. A glance through the plates in Fuerst and Hume's *XXth. Century Stage Decoration* (1929; rpt. 1967), despite the authors' tendency to disparage Craig's work, confirms the range of his influence, as do the plates in Léon Moussinac's *The New Movement in the Theatre* which show his work coming to life in the 'twenties in Paris, Berlin, Prague, Zagreb, Moscow, New York and London. In his Introduction to *The New Movement,* R.H. Packman declares that the new theatre was characterized by 'the mask, improvisation, the collective spectacle, and the imaginative collaboration of the spectator',[44] with echoes of the Commedia dell' Arte--all derived in some measure from Craig's teaching--and when he quotes from Jacques Copeau and Louis Jouvet, who both advocate a dramatic architecture and a theatre free from the trammels of realism, the inheritance in both ideas and rhetoric is undeniable.

Despite Craig's motto--'after the practice, the theory'--there is much truth in Simonson's accusation that he lacked practicality, and the fact must be faced that he achieved very little in the live theatre during his lifetime. His air of the genius *manqué* could be viewed as a mask for intellectual and artistic inadequacy--compensated for by a flamboyant life-style. However, his impact on the English theatre has to be seen in generalities rather than specifics. As Nicoll points out in his evaluation of Craig, the tradition of 'the English stage, from the times of Burbage and Shakespeare onwards, has derived its strength from the words created by its dramatists and interpreted by its long line of distinguished actors and actresses'.[45] Therefore, Craig's ideas, with their elevation of the director to supreme control and tendency to minimize the role of the actor, were sown on infertile ground in his own country, although they flowered abroad. Subsequently, the fruit was re-imported when continental ideas inspired by Craig, as indicated above, returned as part of the international exchange that has characterised twentieth-century theatre. Although Packman is not alone in declaring that 'in Gordon Craig we possess the originator of today's new conception of the theatre',[46] the value of his contribution remains controversial: his main achievement was as prophet and propagandist, inspirer and stimulator, whose potency came from his faith in the theatre as art. His aesthetic approach differs considerably from that of most figures discussed in this book, but he clearly belongs with them in a shared perception of the established theatre as moribund and corrupted by commercialism, and in a shared aspiration to vitalize it with new ideas, new forms and new conceptions for a new century.

NOTES

1. She was unable to marry because her first husband, the painter George Frederick Watts, who was forty when she married him at the age of sixteen, gave her a separation only, not a divorce. Biographical information is mainly from Edward Craig, *Gordon Craig. The Story of His Life* (Gollancz, London, 1968), identified as *Story* below.

2. *Story*, p. 111.

3. Haldane Macfall, 'Some Thoughts on the Art of Gordon Craig', *The Studio*, vol. 23, no. 102 (September 1901), pp. 255-6.

4. *The Letters of W.B. Yeats*, ed. Allan Wade (Macmillan, London, 1954), p. 366.

5. *Story*, p. 170.

6. G.B. Shaw, *Collected Letters 1898-1910*, ed, Dan H. Laurence (Max Reinhardt, London, 1972), p. 325.

7. Letter to *Saturday Review*, 9 May 1903, p. 588.

8. Full details of exhibitions are given in *Edward Gordon Craig: A Bibliography*, ed. Ifan Kyrle Fletcher and Arnold Rood (Society for Theatre Research, London, 1967), pp. 96-111.

9. Quoted in William Rothenstein, *Men and Memories 1900-1922* (Faber & Faber, London, 1932), p. 55.

10. Quoted in Denis Bablet, *Edward Gordon Craig*, tr. Daphne Woodward (Theatre Arts Books, New York, 1966), p. 123.

11. Ibid., p. 74.

12. Edward Gordon Craig, *On the Art of the Theatre* (William Heinemann, London, 1957), p. 27. Subsequent quotations from Craig in parentheses refer to this volume, unless otherwise indicated.

13. *Story*, pp. 191-2.

14. Isadora Duncan, *My Life* (Gollancz, London, 1928), p. 199. Craig's account is given in *Index to the Story of My Days* (Hulton, London, 1957), pp. 256-91.

15. Duncan, p. 217.

16. Quoted in *Story*, p. 219.

17. An alphabetical list is given in Fletcher and Rood's *Bibliography*, p. 62.

18. Edward Gordon Craig, *A Living Theatre* (Author, Florence, 1913), p. 13.

19. *The Mask*, vol. 1, no. 10 (December 1908), p. 186.

20. Quoted in Bablet, p. 99.

21. Arthur Symons, *Studies in Seven Arts* (Constable, London, 1906), p. 336.

22. G. Wilson Knight, *Shakespearian Production* (Faber & Faber, London, 1964), p. 221.

23. *Story,* p. 233.
24. Quoted in *Story,* p. 235.
25. *The Mask,* vol. 7, no. 2 (May 1915), p. 147.
26. Ibid., p. 147.
27. Ibid., p. 139.
28. Ibid., p. 160.
29. For a complete chronicle of the relationship and events, including Ursula Cox's transcription, see Laurence Senelick, 'The Craig-Stanislavsky "Hamlet" at the Moscow Art Theatre', *Theatre Quarterly,* vol. 6, no. 22 (Summer 1976), pp. 56-122.
30. Constantin Stanislavsky, *My Life in Art,* tr. J.J. Robins (Geoffrey Bles, London, 1962), pp. 510-11. Subsequent page numbers in parentheses.
31. *Story,* p. 272.
32. *Times,* 9 January 1912, p. 8.
33. *Story,* p. 280.
34. *The Mask,* vol. 5, no. 4 (April 1913), p. 288.
35. Edward Gordon Craig, *The Theatre Advancing* (Constable, London, 1921), p. xxvii.
36. Symons, p. 349.
37. Ibid., pp. 355-6.
38. Rothenstein, pp. 151, 152. Craig attributes Tree's interest to Frederick Whelen: see *Story,* p. 245.
39. *Story,* p. 254.
40. Bablet, p. 84.
41. Lee Simonson, *The Stage Is Set* (Harcourt Brace & Co., New York, 1932), p. 344.
42. Sheldon Cheney, *Stage Decoration* (1928; rpt. Blom, New York, 1966), pp. 73-4.
43. Bablet, p. 111.
44. R.H. Packman, intro. to Léon Moussinac, *The New Movement in the Theatre* (B.T. Batsford Ltd., London, 1931), p. 15.
45. Allardyce Nicoll, *English Drama 1900-1930. The Beginnings of the Modern Theatre* (Cambridge University Press, Cambridge, 1973), pp. 109-10.
46. Packman, p. 18.

Chapter Nine

CONCLUSION

'Without Contraries is no progression.'

William Blake

In 1889, despite the fact that the term 'renaissance' was in the air, the English theatre offered its audiences much the same as it had provided fifty years earlier. There were differences, of course, notably in the general manner of presentation, which had become more refined--at the cost of some vigour--but the staple fare remained melodrama, sentimental comedy and farce. Increasingly, the drama had focused on everyday life, and had dealt with domestic and commercial themes that reflected the daily concerns of its audiences, but by-and-large the characters remained stereotypes, and the treatment of moral and social issues was superficial and conventional. Even such competent dramatists as Taylor, Robertson, Jones and Pinero, despite having higher aims for the drama, succeeded in doing little more than introducing a modicum of social criticism into plays that were in all other respects well-crafted, conventional melodramas or 'well-made' comedies. The public wanted to be entertained and to have its emotions exercised--it certainly did not want to be required to think--and with few exceptions, managers catered to that demand with little or no concern for a 'higher' drama. The economic conditions of the theatre, where a steady flow of money from the box office is essential to pay for rents, scenery, lighting, stage crews, theatre personnel, actors, and even authors, place the dramatist at the mercy of the manager or entrepreneur to an extent unknown in the other arts; and what is worse, their aims may be antithetical, the one concerned with artistic integrity, the other with making a cash profit, with the added disadvantage to the former that the latter, who pays, calls the tune. This familiar economic squeeze was particularly tight in the closing years of the nineteenth century when the actor-manager system prevailed in the London theatres, and although the occasional experiment was made in the commercial theatre--such as that of the Charringtons in 1889 and of Elizabeth Robins with her Ibsen productions--it was the subscription society, notably J.T. Grein's Independent Theatre and the Stage Society, that began to break new ground by introducing the new drama to English audiences.

The arrival of Ibsen's plays in the last decade of the century put the English 'renaissance' into perspective and provided the impetus for a more radical change in the theatre, a change towards the 'new' that was very much alive in other fields of artistic and social endeavour as the 'old' century ran out its course. However, the era remained essentially conservative as the radicals, although voluble, were relatively few in number and were opposed by a well-entrenched establishment. It is not surprising, therefore, that the struggle to bring about what many on both sides regarded as a revolution in the theatre was protracted, and that there were many casualties; but no battle is ever fought without them, and it would depreciate the struggle if one recognized only the successful and neglected to take into full account the contributions of those who tried and failed. The Independent Theatre was one of those casualties as it did not fulfill the hopes it aroused when formed, but the attention it received at the time--and since--is a measure of its importance as the first concerted effort to establish the new drama in England. Its true successor, the Stage Society--for the New Century Theatre never came to anything--fared better for several reasons: it built on the work and experience of the Independent Theatre; it was run by a committee with a wide range of ability and experience, and was not dependent, as its predecessor had been, on the initiative of one man; and it had the cooperation of the acting profession.

The success of the Stage Society in its first five years led directly to the launching of the Vedrenne-Barker management at the Royal Court, 1904-07, and to the explosion of Shaw onto the theatrical scene. For the first time, a commercial theatre was able to turn its back on the outdated, but persistent, formulas of the Victorian era, and introduce to a box-office audience a range of innovative and provocative plays new both in form and in content. The offerings were not entirely of the new drama variety which the Independent Theatre had advocated and the Stage Society had initially espoused, as many of the plays presented did not fit the category of realistic social drama that the term covered: it was, in Shaw's case, an adaptation of existing modes, but an adaptation that utilised existing forms, such as the melodrama and the well-made-play, and infused them with new life by turning the conventional moralities on their heads and by forcing audiences to think. The dramatists presented by the Court, in the words of Desmond MacCarthy quoted earlier, 'represented an aesthetic and dramatic movement of remarkably wide sympathies'; it was this range, of which the new drama was only part, that opened the theatrical imagination to new possibilities for a new era. Paradoxically, although the Court years were dominated by Shaw as author, they also demonstrated the effectiveness of having one producer or director in control of all aspects of production. This control was particularly important with respect to the acting, where all performers, including the stars, were obliged to function as part of an ensemble within the producer's overall conception. The day of the actor-manager was virtually over, as was the brief period in which the author challenged him for pride of place in the theatre.

The campaign to establish new modes of drama was not only against commercial interests, but also against the prejudices and taboos of a puritanical, middle-class society that was eminently satisfied with its own morality and mode of living, and suspicious of, or openly hostile to, innovations or new ideas, which it considered subversive. The censorship may have been in the hands of one arbitrary individual, but there is little doubt that the actions of the Examiner of Plays angered only a minority of intellectuals and met with the unquestioning approbation of the majority of the ruling and middle classes. The confrontations of dramatist and censor, therefore, were essential skirmishes in a battle for progress that was not confined to the theatre. Similarly, the desire to give the drama one outlet free from commercial control by establishing an endowed National Theatre, where both new plays and established classics could flourish in repertory, had social implications, for the recognition of the need for such an institution, on a par with libraries, schools and welfare services, and its funding (especially if out of the national treasury) would constitute public acknowledgement of the social role of the drama and its right to a free existence. As pointed out earlier, the fact that attempts to abolish the censorship and to establish a National Theatre were abortive does not reduce the significance of the campaigns because they played an important role in focusing public attention on the deficiencies of conventional dramatic fare and in educating the public to an awareness of serious drama as an alternative mode.

The process of evaluation and revaluation, ever speculative, will go on: at present there is a phase in which the tendency to dismiss the nineteenth century as a dark age in the annals of English theatre is being reversed, and those who condemned it--especially contemporaries--are perceived as misguided: perhaps the contraries of historical criticism are as necessary for progress as the contraries of change. There is no doubt that the Victorian theatre was vital and energetic, relevant for its audiences, and, above all, theatrical in the praiseworthy sense. On the other hand, there is no doubt that the era bequeathed very little by way of 'literature' to posterity; it did not grapple seriously with the issues of its day, and was hidebound by moral convention, dramatic formulas, conventional acting, and a system that militated against flexibility and change. Victorian audiences were not prepared to accept change, but between 1889 and 1914 the process of public education made significant gains, and many of the earlier limitations were shaken off. During this period Ibsen and the new drama came to be accepted in the commercial theatre, and realism was established as the dominant dramatic mode; an important channel of subsequent development was opened with the counter-movement of anti-realism in the work of Gordon Craig and in the parallel attempts to re-establish poetic drama; and Shakespeare's texts, cut and corrupted for over two centuries, were restored to the stage, and his plays, so often made mere vehicles for spectacular effects and grandiose, star-directed acting, were reinterpreted for the twentieth century in a manner that was both modern yet closer to the way in which they were presented on the Elizabethan stage. Furthermore, the producer had emerged as the dominant figure in the theatre, supplanting the actor-manager, and acting had attained a new level of sophistication; the repertory system might not have worked in London, but it had established itself in several important provincial centres; and the campaigns to abolish censorship and to establish a National Theatre, although unsuccessful at that time, had been hard fought and had established bridgeheads for later victory.

The frequent appearance in many of the foregoing chapters of the same names indicates that the achievements of the period were due primarily to the work of a few individuals who were dedicated to the task of raising the standards of English drama so that it could take its rightful place alongside the other arts in the cultural and social life of the country, on a par with the drama in the rest of Europe. Chief among these were: William Archer, whose sincerity, acumen and authority won over many sceptics; Henry Arthur Jones, a limited dramatist but indefatigable propagandist; the irrepressible J.T. Grein, who sustained his purpose despite discouragement and obloquy; Bernard Shaw, whose astonishing industry and joy in disputation added power and colour to the action; Granville Barker, who expressed his genius in so many roles--actor, dramatist, producer and advocate; William Poel, who helped to undo the damage done to Shakespeare over three centuries; and Gordon Craig, prophet of a new dimension in total theatre. Others played their supporting parts, but these were the principals whose charisma in the theatre of life brought about the dramatic process of transition, with its crises and reversals, that transformed the Victorian into the modern English theatre.

Appendix A

A British "Theatre Libre"
from *The Weekly Comedy*, Saturday, November 30, 1889

The historian who shall undertake the task of writing the annals of English literature for the decade that is now waning will be able, when he comes to the chapter devoted to the national drama, to sum up the tendency of the whole period in one comprehensive statement--We are advancing.

The days when the stage of England was fed on foreign fare are over. It is able now to live upon its own resources, and if our theatres continue to borrow from abroad it is because there still exists among our theatrical managers a want of confidence in native work, and because a foreign success frequently holds out the promise of equal success in England.

Theatrical managers in this country are nothing if not conservative. Their paramount aim is, and must be, to make both ends meet; and the first question with them is not, will this play prove an artisitic success, but--will it prove a financial one?

Therefore, they are unwilling to go outside the beaten track; they cling to the traditional, well-worn dramatic formula, which sends the public home in a satisfied mood; a formula in which reality, likelihood and possibility are thrown overboard in order to reach the happy ending, without which no play can hope--so they say--for financial prosperity.

There are many playwrights who are quite content with this state of things. They write down to the popular standard; they make money by doing so, and their works find a ready market.

But there is also a small and daily increasing number of younger authors, whose aim, in the first place, is not money, but art; whose ideals soar above the commonplace; whose notion of play-writing is not that it should merely cause tears to flow, or laughter to roar, but that real human emotion should be aroused by the presentment of real human life.

The position of these ambitious playwrights is at present unpromising, nay, hopeless, unless they can afford to test their strength at the doubtful trial of a matinée, that *"enfant terrible"* of the critical fraternity.

In France, where the rising tide was equally hampered by managerial conservatism and timidity, M. Antoine has opened fresh fields and pastures new to the coming men by founding a Théatre Libre, which, supported by the power of the Press, has become an important factor in the dramatic world, in spite of many injudicious selections and defective performances. And M. Antoine may boast to-day, that through his enterprise, so humbly begun, already more than one talent of promise has been drawn from obscurity, and been admitted to the boards of leading playhouses.

What has been done in France, cannot it be done, too, in England? Is not a British "Théatre Libre"--a theatre free from the shackles of the censor, free from the fetters of convention, unhampered by financial considerations--is not such a theatre possible? That is the question.

We do not doubt for one moment the possibility, the expediency, the ultimate success of a theatre on these lines.

For a British Théatre Libre would aim neither at fostering play-writing of a merely didactic kind, nor at introducing subjects of an immoral, or even unwholesomely realistic nature.

It would nurture realism, but realism of a healthy kind; it would strive to annihilate the puppets which have done yeomen's service for years and years, and would instead depict human beings bearing human characters, speaking human language, and torn by human passions.

It would nurture didatic *[sic]* drama to a certain extent, in so far as dramatic construction, delineation, and analysis of character are concerned.

But unlike the French Théatre Libre, the British Free Stage should banish all that is vulgar, low and cynically immoral.

Its chief ideal ought to be to admit all who have something new to say, who have the courage and the ability to cast aside banal sentiment, faulty construction, and useless padding, when writing for the stage.

As in France the initiation of a Free Stage must emanate from private enterprise. It must be founded by the cooperation of all who have the welfare of the drama at heart. In cases like this the individual is powerless; it is in the union of many that strength and the best chance of success lie. Single-handed proceedings create only envy and jealousy, and give rise to accusations of partiality. No formidable sum of money is needed to realise the plan of a Free Stage. A moderate capital (say £2,000) derived partly from honorary contributors, partly from earnest subscribers who have the leisure and feel inclined to devote their evenings to the performances, which ought not to exceed two a month, and lastly from the small fees to be levied on every play sent in, in order to check a too copious influx of manuscripts--is all that is needed to start a Free

Stage and to keep it going...

The main, the cardinal point, to ensure success, is the patronage under which the new venture is to be launched. In the first place, the united sympathy of the Press, which never withholds its aid when a good cause is at stake, is to be hoped for; in the second place, the valuable advice of novelists, such as Messrs. George Meredith and Thomas Hardy, whose romances reveal great dramatic ability, and of playwrights ranking as high as Messrs. Pinero and Jones is to be acquired; and finally the benefit of the assistance of old playgoers, of wealthy and disinterested friends of the drama, of artists, historians, and specialists of all kinds will not be vainly sought.

For all literary and artistic England is alive to the fact that the future of our advancing national drama will not depend upon the accuracy, the splendour, the taste of the mounting, nor upon the perfection of the acting, nor upon the quantity of our playwright's production.

No, there is only one way to attain excellence, to free our drama from the trammels of convention, and of the commonplace. That way is never to lose sight of the principal maxim, which casts all other considerations into the shade--The play's the thing.

And to help the play to become what it should be we cherish the thought of, and hope for sympathy on behalf of, the establishment of *a British Free Stage*.

We* have forwarded our "suggestion" for the foundation of a British "Free Stage" to many literary and dramatic authorities, and it is with infinite satisfaction and gratitude that we record the cordial response our appeal has met with. We shall publish week by week all the expressions of opinion which have reached us, whether favourable to our scheme or the reverse. This week we print the first batch which came to hand, but we may announce that up to the moment of going to press we have been favoured with the views of Messrs. Edw. Rose, W. Sapte, Jr., J.P. Hurst John Coleman, Percy Reeve, Cecil Howard, Dr. Aveling, Boyle Lawrence, and communications from Messrs. S. Grundy and Haddon Chambers, which we are compelled to hold over.

*i.e. the editors, J.T. Grein and C.W. Jarvis.

178

INDEPENDENT THEATRE PRODUCTIONS 1891-1897

Date	Author	Title	Theatre	Producer/Director
First Season 1891-1892				
13 March	Ibsen	*Ghosts*	Royalty	Cecil Raleigh
9 Oct.	Zola	*Thérèse Raquin*	Royalty	Herman de Lange
4 March	Th. de Banville	*The Kiss*	Royalty	Charles Hoppe
	A. Symons	*The Minister's Call*		
	Geo. Brandes	*A Visit*		
8 July	W.G. van Nouhuys	*The Goldfish*	*Opéra Comique*	Charles Hoppe
Second Season 1892-1893				
21 Oct.	Webster	*The Duchess of Malfi* (arr. William Poel)	*Opéra Comique*	William Poel and Paul M. Berton
9 Dec.	Shaw	*Widowers' Houses*	Royalty	Charles Hoppe
26 Jan.	A. Raffalovitch	*Roses of Shadow* (a duologue)	Athenaeum	Not known
	Ibsen	*Ghosts*		
21 Feb.	Geo. Moore	*The Strike at Arlingford*	*Opéra Comique*	Charles Hoppe
28 April	A. Benhan	*Theory and Practice* (a duologue)	Terry's	Herman de Lange
	Anon. (Mrs. Hugh Bell and Elizabeth Robins)	*Alan's Wife*		
2 June	H.M. Paul	*At a Health Resort*	Comedy	Herman de Lange
	'J. Holland'	*Leida*		

15 June	Browning	*A Blot in the 'Scutcheon*	*Opéra Comique*	Louis Calvert
10 July	E. van Goethem	*The Cradle*	St. George's Hall	Not known
	G.H.R. Dabbs and Ed. Righton	*Dante*		
	Mrs. Hugh Bell	*Jerry-Builder Solness* (parody)		

Third Season 1893-1894

27 Oct.	Michael Field	*A Question of Memory*	*Opéra Comique*	Herman de Lange
	F. Coppe	*Le Pater*		
8 Dec.	J.D. Vymer	*The Debutante*	*Opéra Comique*	Herman de Lange
	J. Todhunter	*The Black Cat*		
23 Feb.	Zola	*The Heirs of Rabourdin*	*Opéra Comique*	Herman de Lange
4 May	Ibsen	*The Wild Duck*	Royalty	Herman de Lange

Fourth Season 1895

4 Jan.	Anon. [Dorothy Leighton]	*Thyrza Fleming*	Terry's	Herman de Lange
15 March	J.C. de Vos	*A Man's Love*	*Opéra Comique*	Herman de Lange
	Mrs. O. Beringer	*Salvé*		
25 March	Ibsen	*Rosmersholm*)	Théâtre de	A.-M. Lugné-Poe
	Maeterlinck	*L'Intruse*)	l'Oeuvre at	
26 March	Maeterlinck	*Pelléas et Mélisande*)	*Opéra Comique*	
27 March	Ibsen	*Solness le Constructeur*)		

Fifth Season 1897

10 May	Ibsen	*A Doll's House*	Globe	Wilfred Beckwith
17 May	Ibsen	*The Wild Duck*	Globe	Wilfred Beckwith
24 May	Shakespeare	*Antony and Cleopatra*	Olympic	Louis Calvert
24 June	Ibsen	*Ghosts*	Queen's Gate Hall	Not Known

Sixth Season 1898

9 Dec.	Brieux	*Blanchette*	West Theatre (Albert Hall)	Conal O'Riordan

NOTE: For full production details for most of the above, see J.P. Wearing, *The London Stage 1890–1899*, 2 vols. (Scarecrow Press Inc., Metuchen, N.J., 1976).

Appendix C

THE STAGE SOCIETY PRODUCTIONS 1899-1914

Date	Author	Title	Theatre	Producer/Director
First Season 1899-1900				
26 Nov.	Shaw	*You Never Can Tell*	Royalty	James Welch
21 Jan.	Sydney Olivier	*Mrs. Maxwell's Marriage* *	Pr. of Wales	Janet Archurch
25 Feb.	Ibsen	*The League of Youth* (tr. Wm. Archer)	Vaudeville	Chas. Charrington
29 April	Fiona Macleod (Wm. Sharp)	*The House of Usna*	Globe	Granville Barker
	Maeterlinck	*Interior* (tr. Wm. Archer)		
	-"-	*Death of Tintagiles* (tr. Alfred Sutro)		
10 June	Hauptmann	*The Coming of Peace (Friedensfest)* (tr. Janet Achurch & Chas. E. Wheeler)	Vaudeville	Janet Achurch
1 July	Shaw	*Candida*	Strand	Chas. Charrington
Second Season 1900-1901				
4, 8 Nov.	Thomas Hardy	*The Three Wayfarers*	Strand & Gt. Queen St.	Chas Charrington
	W.E. Henley & R.L. Stevenson	*Macaire*		
16, 20 Dec.	Shaw	*Captain Brassbound's Conversion*	Strand & Criterion	Chas Charrington

Appendix C (contd.)

Second Season 1900–1901 (contd.)

24–25 Feb.	Gilbert Murray	*Andromache*	Strand & Garrick	Chas Charrington
31 March & 1 April	Hauptmann	*Lonely Lives (Einsame Menschen)* (tr. Mary Morison)	Strand	G.R. Foss
12–13 May	Ibsen	*Pillars of Society* (tr. Wm. Archer)	Strand & Garrick	Oscar Asche
16–17 June	L. Alma-Tadema	*The Unseen Helmsman*	Comedy	A.E. George
	W. Kingsley-Tarpey	*Windmills*		

Third Season 1901–1902

5–6 Jan.	Shaw	*Mrs. Warren's Profession**	New Lyric Club	Author
26–27 Jan.	Granville Barker	*The Marrying of Ann Leete*	Royalty	Author
16–17 March	François de Curel	*The New Idol* (tr. Maurice Durand and Hugh Stokes)	Royalty	Harvey Long
4–5 May	Ibsen	*The Lady from the Sea* (tr. Mrs. F.E. Archer)	Royalty	Chas Charrington
20 June	Maeterlinck	*Monna Vanna** (with A.-M. Lugné-Poe)	Victoria Hall	M. Cheron

Fourth Season 1902–1903

25–26 Jan.	Ibsen	*When We Dead Awaken* (tr. Wm. Archer)	Imperial	G.R. Foss
22–23 Feb.	W.Somerset Maugham	*A Man of Honour*	Imperial	A.E. George
15–16 Mar.	St. John Hankin	*The Two Mr. Wetherbys*	Imperial	Charles Rock

<u>Fourth Season 1902-1903</u> (contd.)

Date	Author	Play	Theatre	Producer
26-27 Apl.	Herman Heijermans	*The Good Hope* (tr. Christopher St. John. By Arrangement with J.T. Grein)	Imperial	Max Behrend
7-8 June	Ian Robertson	*The Golden Rose* or *The Scarlet Woman*	Imperial	Author
	S.M. Fox	*The Waters of Bitterness*		Granville Barker
	Shaw	*The Admirable Bashville* or *Constancy Unrewarded*		Author

<u>Fifth Season 1903-1904</u>

Date	Author	Play	Theatre	Producer
29-30 Nov.	Gorki	*The Lower Depths* (tr. Laurence Irving)	Royal Court & Gt. Queen St.Th.	Max Behrend
31 Jan. & 2 Feb.	Brieux	*The Philanthropists* (tr. by a Member of the Society)	King's Hall	Granville Barker
13-14-15 March	Browning	*A Soul's Tragedy*	Royal Court	Holbrook Blinn
	Frederick Fenn & Richard Pryce	*'Op o' me Thumb*		Nigel Playfair
15-16-17 May	R.O. Prowse	*Ina*	Royal Court	A.E. George
26-27-28 June	W.B. Yeats	*Where There is Nothing*	Royal Court	Granville Barker

Appendix C (contd.)

Sixth Season 1904-1905

Date	Author	Play	Theatre	Producer
18-19-20 Dec.	Leo Tolstoy	*The Power of Darkness** (tr. Louise & Aylmer Maude)	Royalty	Max Behrend
29-30-31 Jan.	G.S. Street	*Great Friends*	Royal Court	Clifford Brooke
12-13-14 March	Brieux	*The Three Daughters of M. Dupont** (tr. St. John Hankin)	King's Hall	J.G. Brandon
21-22-23 May	Shaw	*Man and Superman*	Royal Court	Granville Barker
25-26-27 June	L. Alma-Tadema	*The New Felicity*	Royalty	Author
	Joseph Conrad	*One Day More*		G.R. Foss

Seventh Season 1905-1906

Date	Author	Play	Theatre	Producer
26-27 Nov.	Hope Merrick	*Jimmy's Mother*	Scala	A.E. Drinkwater
	E.F. Benson	*Dodo: A Detail of Yesterday*		Thalberg Corbett
28-29 Jan.	Ibsen	*Lady Inger of Östråt*	Scala	Herbert Jarman
8-9-10 April	Brieux	*Maternité**	King's Hall	Madge McIntosh
13-14 May	Sudermann	*Midsummer Fires* (Faithfully rendered in English by Mr. & Mrs. J.T. Grein)	Scala	Hans Andresen
17-18 June	John Pollock	*The Invention of Dr. Metzler*	Scala	A.E. Drinkwater
	Gogol	*The Inspector-General* (Based on tr. of Arthur A. Sykes)		Charles Rock

Eighth Season 1906–1907

9–10 Dec.	Hauptmann	*The Weavers* (tr. Mary Morison)	Scala	Hans Andresen
10–11 Feb.	St. John Hankin	*The Cassilis Engagement*	Imperial	Madge McIntosh
24–25 Mar.	Brieux	*Les Hannetons* (The Incubus)* (tr. H.M. Clark)	Imperial	Janet Achurch
9–10 June	Wedekind	*Der Kammersanger (The Tenor)* (tr. by a Member of the Society)	Imperial	Frank Reicher
	Charles McEvoy	*David Ballard*		Author

Ninth Season 1907–1908

24, 26 Nov.	Granville Barker	*Waste**	Imperial	Author
26–27 Jan.	Arnold Bennett	*Cupid and Commonsense*	Shaftesbury	Frank Vernon
1–2 Mar.	Margaret M. Mack	*The Gates of the Morning*	Shaftesbury	Norman Page
5–6 Apl.	Edward Garnett	*The Breaking Point**	Haymarket	Frank Vernon
31 May & 1 June	Herman Heijermans	*Links* (tr. Howard Percy & W.R. Brandt)	Scala	William Haviland

Tenth Season 1908–1909

6–7 Dec.	St. John Hankin	*The Last of the de Mullins*	Haymarket	W. Graham Browne

Appendix C (contd.)

Tenth Season 1908-1909 (contd.)

21-22-23	Giuseppe Giacosa	*The Rights of the Soul* (tr. Miss F.M. Rankin)	Kingsway	William Haviland
	Turgénev	*The Bread of Others* (tr. J. Nightingale Duddington)		
28-29 Mar.	Margaret Mack	*Unemployed*	Aldwych	Norman Page
	George Calderón	*The Fountain*		
2-3 May	Arnold Bennett	*What the Public Wants* (10th. Jubilee and 50th. Production)	Aldwych	Norman Page
20 May	Gilbert Canaan	*Dull Monotony* (Performed at Jubilee Reception)	Hotel Cecil	Norman Page
6-7 June	H. Hamilton Fyfe	*A Modern Aspasia*	Aldwych	J. Fisher White

Eleventh Season 1909-1910

5-6 Dec.	Shaw	*The Shewing-Up of Blanco Posnet**	Aldwych	Irish National Theatre Soc.
	Yeats	*Kathleen Ni Houlihan*		
	Lady Gregory	*The Workhouse Ward*		
13-14 Feb.	Fred D. Barker	*A Lioness and her Whelp*	Shaftesbury	A.E. Drinkwater
	Lady Bell	*The Way the Money Goes*		E. Harcourt Williams
20-21 March	Felix Saltern	*Points of View: Three Plays*	Shaftesbury	
		1. *Count Festenberg* (tr. by a Member of the Council)		
		2. *Life's Importance* (tr.Hugh de Selincourt)		William Haviland
		3. *The Return* (tr. a Member of the Council)		

Eleventh Season 1909-1910 (contd.)

22-23 May	Ludwig Thoma	*Champions of Morality** (tr. H.A. Hertz and Frederick Whelen)	Aldwych	Norman Page
5-6 June	Ashley Dukes	*Civil War*	Aldwych	Frank Vernon

Twelfth Season 1910-1911

4-5 Dec.	John Masefield	*Pompey the Great*	Aldwych	E. Harcourt Williams
29-30 Jan.	Ashley Dukes	*Pride of Life*	Aldwych	Kenelm Foss
	George Calderón	*The Little Stone House*		
	Armin Friedmann and Alfred Pogar	*The Passing of Talma* (tr. H.A. Hertz)		
19-20 Mar.	G. Lowes Dickinson (John Goldie)	*Business*	Aldwych	Frank Vernon
28-29 May	Anton Tchehov	*The Cherry Orchard* (tr. Mrs. Edward Garnett)	Aldwych	Kenelm Foss
11-12 June	C.B. Fernald	*The Married Woman*	Aldwych	Kenelm Foss

Thirteenth Season 1911-1912

10-11 Dec.	George Moore	*Esther Waters*	New Princes	J. Clifford Brooke
4-5 Feb.	Norman McKeown	*Travellers*	New Princes	Author

Thirteenth Season 1911–1912 (contd.)

Date	Author	Play	Theatre	Producer
10–11 March	Hermann Bahr	*The Fool and the Wise Man* (tr. Mrs. F.E. Washburn Freund)	New Princes	Frederick Whelen
	August Strindberg	*Creditors* (tr. Ellie Schleussner)		
5–6 May	Jacinto Benavente	*The Bias of the World* (tr. Francesch de Ros and Beryl de Zoete)	New Princes	Allan Wade & Norman Wilkinson
16–17 June	P.R. Bennett	*Mary Edwards*	Aldwych	Stanley Drewitt
	Stanley Houghton	*Hindle Wakes* (Miss Horniman's Manchester Company)		Lewis Casson
8–9 Dec.	G.J. Hamlen	*The Waldies*	Haymarket	Norman Page
16–17 Feb.	Jacques Copeau and Jean Croué (from Dostoievski)	*The Brothers Karamazov* (tr. Christopher St. John)	Aldwych	Frederick Whelen
9–10 March	Arthur Schnitzler	*Comtesse Mizzi* (tr. H.A. Hertz)	Aldwych	Clifford Brooke
	–"–	*The Green Cockatoo* (tr. Penelope Wheeler)		Norman Page
22–23 June	George Moore	*Elizabeth Cooper*	Haymarket	Clifford Brooke

Fifteenth Season 1913–1914

Date	Author	Play	Theatre	Producer
7–8 Dec.	J.O. Francis	*Change* (By a visiting company of all-Welsh Players)	Haymarket	Tom Owen

Fifteenth Season 1913-1914 (contd.)

Date	Author	Play	Theatre	Producer
15-16 Feb.	Anatole France	*Au Petit Bonheur* (tr. Ashley Dukes)	Haymarket	Allan Wade and Ashley Dukes
	-"-	*The Comedy of the Man Who Married a Dumb Wife* (tr. Ashley Dukes)		
5-6 April	Frank Harris	*The Bucket Shop*	Aldwych	Norman Page
10-11 May	Anton Tchehov	*Uncle Vanya* (tr. Mrs. R.S. Townsend)	Aldwych	Guy Rathbone
14-15 June	C.E. Wheeler	*The Golden Fleece*	Haymarket	Lewis Casson

*Unlicensed at time of performance.

NOTE: Full production details for plays presented in regular London theatres given in J.P. Wearing, *The London Stage 1890-1899, 1900-1909* and *1910-1919* (Scarecrow Press Inc., Metuchen, N.J., 1976, 1981 and 1982).

Appendix D

TOAST AT STAGE SOCIETY DINNER, 17 MAY 1904

WHEN WE SLEEPING BEAUTIES AWAKEN
BY
OWEN SEAMAN

[With acknowledgements, for the Title, to the Master]

There was a time, as I am told,
Back in the dim Victorian Age,
When Antic Custom, dull and cold,
Wrapped like a pall the British Stage;
And some among the best "reporters" said:-
"Dramatic Art is practically dead!"

But ere they fixed the funeral site
A race of Thinking Men arose,
Clapped on the corpse a searching light
And found her simply comatose;
(The gentleman who took this fearless line
Started her cure in 1899).

Before the lapse of many days,
The Sleeping Beauty stirred in bed
And used the Tennysonian phrase:
"O love! thy kiss would wake the dead!"
From Frederick Whelen came that clarion sound;
His was the smack that brought the lady round.

They fed her up (for she was weak
And swelled with swallowing windy puffs)
On German, Belgian, French and Greek,
On Norse and even native stuffs;
With equal appetite the patient drank in
Essence of HAUPTMANN, HEIJERMANS and HANKIN.

Exotic fish and local fowl--
With these they plied her generous maw,
CUREL and BARKER cheek by jowl
And IBSEN jostling BERNARD SHAW;
(Thus, if *The Lady from the Sea* looked foreign,
For British Matrons there was *Mrs. Warren).*

Her mortal frame expanded, too,
On transcendental meat and drink;
Of thoughts that ranged quite near the blue
She caught the missing MAETERLINCK;
And after meals of more than earthly manna,
Inhaled the stiffish fumes of *Monna Vanna.*

Taught, in *The Good Hope's Crib,* to know
The salient signs of healthy growth,
With every second word or so
She wrapped you out a ribald oath;
Showing that, should her other powers go wrong,
Her language still could "suffer and be strong."

Such is her progress, large and free,
Whose nerve of late reduced to pulp,
I now and here propose that we
Should drink in one exhaustive gulp;
Long may her history, freed from hoary fossils,
Live in the Acts of You, her Young Apostles!

THE ELIZABETHAN STAGE SOCIETY PRODUCTIONS 1893-1913

Date and place given for first performances only of each production. In all cases, the productions were directed by William Poel.

Date	Title	Theatre
9 Nov. 1893	*Measure for Measure* (For Shak. Reading Society, but listed in final programme, 5 May 1905).	Royalty
21 June 1895	*Twelfth Night*	Burlington Hall
7 Dec. 1895	*The Comedy of Errors*	Gray's Inn Hall
2 July 1896	Marlowe - *Doctor Faustus*	St. George's Hall
28 Nov. 1896	*The Two Gentlemen of Verona*	Merchant Taylor's Hall
10 Feb. 1897	*Twelfth Night*	Old Hall, Middle Temple
9 July 1897	Scenes from *Arden of Feversham* and *The King and the Countess,* an episode from the play *The Raigne of King Edward the Third*	St. George Hall
5 Nov. 1897	*The Tempest*	Egyptian Hall, The Mansion House
11 Feb. 1898	Beaumont and Fletcher - *The Coxcomb*	Inner Temple Hall
5 Apl. 1898	Middleton and Rowley - *The Spanish Gypsy*	St. George's Hall
11 June 1898	Ford - *The Broken Heart*	St. George's Hall
23 July 1898	Jonson - *The Sad Shepherd*	Courtyard, Fulham Palace
29 Nov. 1898	*The Merchant of Venice*	St. George's Hall
24 Feb. 1899	Jonson - *The Alchemist*	Apothecaries' Hall
20 Mar. 1899	Swinburne - *Locrine*	St. George's Hall
15 May 1899	Calderón - *Such Stuff as Dreams Are Made of* (*La Vida es Sueño,* tr. Edward Fitzgerald)	St. George's Hall

3 July 1899	Kálidássa - *Śakuntalá*	Conservatory, Botanical Gardens
11 Nov. 1899	*Richard II*	Lecture Theatre, U. of London Burlington Gdns.
15 Dec. 1899	Molière - *Don Juan*	Lincoln's Inn Hall
21 Feb. 1900	*Hamlet* (First Quarto)	Carpenters' Hall
7 Apl. 1900	Milton - *Samson Agonistes* (First Production)	Lecture Theatre, V. & A. Museum
22 June 1900	Schiller - *The Death of Wallenstein* (tr. Coleridge) and scenes from *The Piccolomini*	Lect. Th., Burlington Gardens
1 Dec. 1900	Walter Scott - *Marmion*	Lect. Th., Burlington Gardens
7 July 1901	*Everyman* and *The Sacrifice of Isaac* (Chester Cycle)	The Master's Court, Charterhouse
21 Nov. 1901	*King Henry V*	Lect. Th., Burlington Gardens
11 July 1902	Jonson - *The Alchemist*	Imperial Theatre
23 Apl. 1903	*Twelfth Night*	Lect. Th., Burlington Gardens
10 Aug. 1903	Marlowe - *Edward II*	New Th., Oxford
23 Feb. 1904	*Much Ado About Nothing* (For London Schools Board - at seven schools)	
6 Apl. 1905	Poel - *The First Franciscans*	St. George's Hall
5 May 1905	*Romeo and Juliet* (Last production of the E.S.S. as an organized body)	Royalty

Autumn Tour, 29 Oct. to 10 Dec. 1904: alternated Marlowe, *Doctor Faustus* and *The Comedy of Errors* at London (1), Bedford (1), Cambridge (1), Coventry (1), Nottingham (3), Manchester (3),

Edinburgh (4), Glasgow (3), Aberdeen (3), St. Andrews (1), Newcastle (1), Durham (1), Leeds (3), Liverpool (3), Birmingham (3), Chester (2), Rugby (1), Oxford (2), Cheltenham (1).

The following are listed by William Poel as E.S.S. Productions in *Shakespeare In the Theatre*, but were produced after its dissolution and only those marked (E.S.S.) mention the society in their programme:

Aug. 1906	Goldsmith - *The Good-Natur'd Man*	New Th., Cambridge
30 Mar. 1907	Poel - *The Redemption of Agnes* (Published title: *The Temptation of Agnes)*	Coronet
11 June 1907	*The Merchant of Venice*	Fulham
11 Apl. 1908	*Measure for Measure*	Gaiety, Manchester
10 Nov. 1908	*The Bacchae of Euripides* (tr. Gilbert Murray)	Court
10 Dec. 1908	*Samson Agonistes* (Milton Tercentenary)	Lect. Th., Burlington Gardens
22 June 1909	*Macbeth*	Fulham
20 Apl. 1910	*The Two Gentlemen of Verona*	His Majesty's
6 Mar. 1911	*Jacob and Esau* and *The King and the Countess* from *Edward III* (The Ethical Stage Society in connection with the E.S.S.)	Little
11 Aug. 1911	Schiller - *The Death of Wallenstein* (tr. Coleridge) and scenes from *The Piccolomini* (E.S.S.)	New Th., Oxford
15 Dec. 1911	*The Alcestis of Euripides* (tr. Francis Hubback)	Grand Staircase, London University
1 Aug. 1912	Kálidássa - *Śakuntalá* (E.S.S.)	Examination Hall, Cambridge
10 Dec. 1912	*Troilus and Cressida* (E.S.S.)	King's Hall, Covent Garden

12 May 1913	*Troilus and Cressida* (E.S.S.)	Stratford Festival

NOTE: Full production details for plays presented in regular London theatres given in J.P. Wearing, *The London Stage 1900–1909* and *1910–1919* (Scarecrow Press Inc., Methuchen, N.J., 1981 and 1982).

Appendix F

LETTER TO THE EDITOR OF THE *TIMES*, 29 OCTOBER 1907, ON CENSORSHIP OF PLAYS

Sir,

The Prime Minister has consented to receive during next month a deputation from the following dramatic authors on the subject of the censorship of plays. In the meantime may these authors, through your columns, enter a formal protest against this office, which was instituted for political, and not for the so-called moral ends to which it is perverted--an office autocratic in procedure, opposed to the spirit of the Constitution, contrary to common justice and to common sense?

They protest against the power lodged in the hands of a single official--who judges without a public hearing, and against whose dictum there is no appeal--to cast a slur on the good name and destroy the means of livelihood of any member of an honourable calling.

They assert that the censorship has not been exercised in the interests of morality, but has tended to lower the dramatic tone by appearing to relieve the public of the duty of moral judgment.

They ask to be freed from the menace hanging over every dramatist of having his work and the proceeds of his work destroyed at a pen's stroke by the arbitrary action of a single official neither responsible to Parliament nor amenable to law.

They ask that their art be placed on the same footing as every other art.

They ask that they themselves be placed in the position enjoyed under the law by every other citizen.

To these ends they claim that the licensing of plays shall be abolished. The public is already sufficiently assured against managerial misconduct by the present yearly licensing of theatres, which remains untouched by the measure of justice here demanded.

George Bancroft
H. Granville Barker
J.M. Barrie
Florence Bell
Laurence Binyon
Gilbert Cannan
Comyns Carr
R.C. Carton
Egerton Castle
Haddon Chambers
Joseph Conrad
W.L. Courtney
John Davidson
Hubert H. Davies
H.V. Esmond
Fredk. Fenn
John Galsworthy
Edward Garnett
W.S. Gilbert
Cosmo Gordon-Lennox
St. John Hankin
Robert Harcourt
Thomas Hardy
Anthony Hope
Laurence Housman
Maurice Hewlett
Henry Hamilton
Basil Hood
Frederic Harrison
E.W. Hornung
Roy Horniman
W.H. Hudson
Ford Madox Hueffer
Laurence Irving
Henry James
Henry Arthur Jones
W.W. Jacobs
W.J. Locke
John Masefield
Robert Marshall
A.E.W. Mason
W.S. Maugham
Maarten Maartens
Desmond MacCarthy
Justin Huntly McCarthy
T. Sturge Moore
Arthur Morrison
George Meredith
Gilbert Murray
John Pollock
A.W. Pinero
H.M. Paull
(Mrs.) De La Pasture
L. March Phillipps
Cecil Raleigh
Elizabeth Robins
Morley Roberts
Ernest Rhys
G. Bernard Shaw
A. Sutro
Algernon Charles Swinburne
Arthur Symons
J.M. Synge
Edward Thomas
H.A. Vachell
H.G. Wells
Margaret Woods
Anthony Wharton
W.B. Yeats
I. Zangwill

Anon (William Archer and R.W. Lowe). *The Fashionable Tragedian: A Criticism* (G. Taylor, London, 1877)

Archer, Lt Col Charles. *William Archer: Life, Work and Friendships* (Allen & Unwin, London, 1931). Includes a Bibliography of Archer's writings

Archer, William. *About the Theatre* (T. Fisher Unwin, London, 1886)

_____ *The Theatrical World of 1893-1897* (5 vols., Walter Scott, London, 1894-98)

_____ *Playmaking: A Manual of Craftmanship* (Chapman Hall, London, 1912)

_____ *Old Drama and the New: An Essay in Re-valuation* (William Heinemann, London, 1923)

_____ and H. Granville Barker. *A National Theatre. Scheme and Estimates* (Duckworth, London, 1907)

Arnott, J.F. and J.W. Robertson. *English Theatrical Literature 1559-1900. A Bibliography* (Society for Theatre Research, London, 1970)

Bablet, Denis. *Edward Gordon Craig,* tr. Daphne Woodward (Theatre Arts Books, New York, 1966)

Baker, Henry Barton. *History of the London Stage and Its Famous Players (1576-1903)* (George Routledge & Sons, London, 1904)

Baker, Michael J.N. *The Rise of the Victorian Actor* (Croom Helm, London, 1978)

Barker, Harley Granville. 'The Coming of Ibsen', in *The Eighteen Eighties,* ed. Walter de la Mare (Cambridge University Press, Cambridge, 1930)

_____ *The Exemplary Theatre* (Chatto & Windus, London, 1922)

Becker, George J. (ed.) *Documents of Modern Literary Realism* (Princeton University Press, Princeton, N.J., 1963)

Beerbohm, Max. *Around Theatres* (Rupert Hart Davies, London, 1953)

_____ *More Theatres 1898-1903* (Taplinger Publishing Co., New York, 1969)

_____ *Last Theatres 1904-1910* (Taplinger Publishing Co., New York, 1970)

Benson, Sir Frank (Francis Robert). *My Memoirs* (Ernest Benn, London, 1930)

Booth, Michael R. *English Plays of the Nineteenth Century* (5 vols., Clarendon, Oxford, 1969-76)

_____ 'Shakespeare as Spectacle and History: The Victorian Period', *Theatre Research International,* vol. 1, no. 2 (February 1976), pp. 99-113

_____ *Victorian Spectacular Theatre 1850-1910* (Routledge & Kegan Paul, London, 1981)

Borsa, Mario. *The English Stage of Today,* tr. and introduction by Selwyn Britton (John Lane, London, 1908)

Byrne, M. St Clare. 'Fifty Years of Shakespeare Production 1898-1948', *Shakespeare Survey,* 2 (Cambridge University Press, Cambridge, 1949)

Conolly, L.W. and J.P. Wearing. *English Drama and Theatre 1800-1900: A Guide to Information Sources* (Gale Research Co., Detroit, 1978)

Craig, Edward. *Gordon Craig. The Story of His Life* (Gollancz, London, 1968)

Craig, Edward Gordon. *On the Art of the Theatre* (William Heinemann, London, 1911 and 1957)

_____ *Towards a New Theatre* (Dent, London, 1913)

_____ *Henry Irving* (Dent, London, 1930)

_____ *Index to the Story of My Days* (Hulton Press, London, 1967)

Crosse, Gordon. *Fifty Years of Shakespeare Playgoing* (Author, London, 1941)

Donaldson, Frances. *The Actor-Managers* (Weidenfeld & Nicolson, London, 1970)

Dukore, Bernard F. *Bernard Shaw, Director* (George Allen & Unwin, London, 1971)

Egan, Michael (ed.) *Ibsen. The Critical Heritage* (Routledge & Kegan Paul, London, 1972)

Ervine, St John Greer. *The Theatre in My Time* (Rich & Cowan, London, 1933)

_____ *George Bernard Shaw. His Life, Work and Friends* (Constable, London, 1956)

Filon, Pierre Marie Augustin. *The English Stage. Being on Account of the Victorian Drama,* tr. Frederic Whyte, introduction by H.A. Jones (John Milne, London, 1897)

Findlater, Richard. *The Unholy Trade* (Gollancz, London, 1952)

_____ *Banned! A Review of Theatrical Censorship in England* (MacGibbon & Kee, London, 1967)

Fletcher, Ifan Kyrle, and Arnold Rood. *Edward Gordon Craig: A Bibliography* (Society for Theatre Research, London, 1967)

Gaskell, Ronald. *Drama and Reality: The European Drama Since Ibsen* (Routledge & Kegan Paul, London, 1972)

Green Room Book; Or Who's Who on the Stage (London, 1906-09)

Greif, Karen. '"If This Were Played upon a Stage": Harley Granville Barker's Shakespeare Productions at the Savoy Theatre, 1912-1914', *Harvard Library Bulletin,* vol. 28, no. 2 (1980), pp. 117-45

Grein, Jacob Thomas. *Dramatic Criticism* (5 vols., Various, London, 1899-1905)

Grundy, Sydney. *The Play of the Future. By a Playwright of the Past* (Samuel French, London, 1914)

Henderson, Archibald. *George Bernard Shaw. Man of the Century* (Appleton Century Crofts, New York, 1956)

Howard, Diana. *London Theatres and Music Halls 1850-1950* (Library Association, London, 1970)

Hudson, Lynton (Alfred). *The English Stage 1850-1950* (Harrap, London, 1951)

Hughes, Alan. *Henry Irving, Shakespearian* (Cambridge University Press, Cambridge, 1981)

Hunt, Hugh. *The Live Theatre* (Oxford University Press, London, 1962)

_____ Kenneth Richards and John Russell Taylor. *The Revels History of Drama in English*, vol. VII, general editor T.W. Craik (Methuen & Co. Ltd. London, 1978)
Hynes, Samuel. *The Edwardian Turn of Mind* (Princeton University Press, Princeton, N.J., 1968)
Irving, Henry. *The Drama. Addresses* (William Heinemann, London, 1893)
Irving, Laurence. *Henry Irving. The Actor and His World* (Faber & Faber, London, 1951)
Jackson, Antony. 'Harley Granville Barker as Director of the Royal Court 1904-1907', *Theatre Research*, vol. 12, no. 2 (1972), pp. 126-38
Jackson, Holbrook. *The Eighteen Nineties. A Review of Art and Ideas at the Close of the Nineteenth Century* (Grant Richards, London, 1922)
James, Henry. *The Scenic Art. Notes on Acting and the Drama 1872-1901*, ed. Allan Wade (Rupert Hart Davies, London, 1949)
Jones, Doris Arthur. *The Life and Letters of Henry Arthur Jones* (Gollancz, London, 1930)
Jones, Henry Arthur. *The Renascence of the English Drama* (Macmillan, London, 1895)
_____ *The Foundations of a National Drama* (Lectures, etc., 1896-1912) (Chapman Hall, London, 1913)
'Jones, Stanley' (Leonard Merrick). *The Actor and His Art: Some Considerations of the Present Condition of the Stage* (Downey & Co., London, 1899). First published in *Tommorow*, 1896-98
Knight, G. Wilson. *Shakespearian Production* (Faber & Faber, London, 1964)
Knowles, Dorothy. *The Censor, the Drama and the Film 1900-1934* (George Allen & Unwin, London, 1934). Includes a detailed Bibliography of newspaper articles, letters, etc.
MacCarthy, Desmond. *The Court Theatre 1904-1907*, ed. Stanley Weintraub (University of Miami Press, Coral Gables, Florida, 1966. Originally published by A.H. Bullen, London, 1907)
MacQueen-Pope, W. *Carriages at Eleven* (Robert Hale, London, 1972)
Mazer, Cary M. *Shakespeare Refashioned: Elizabethan Plays on Edwardian Stages* (U.M.I. Research Press, Ann Arbor, 1981)
McCarthy, Lillah (Lady Keeble). *Myself and My Friends* (Thornton Butterworth, London, 1933)
McDonald, Jan. 'Continental Plays Produced by the Independent Theatre Society, 1891-8', *Theatre Research International*, vol. 1, no. 1 (October 1975), pp. 16-28
Meyer, Michael. *Ibsen: A Biography* (Doubleday & Co. Inc., Garden City, New York, 1971)
Miller, Anna Irene. *The Independent Theatre in Europe from 1887 to the Present* (1931; reprint B. Blom, New York, 1966)

Montague, Charles Edward. *Dramatic Values* (Methuen & Co. Ltd., London, 1911, revised 1925)

Morgan, Margery M. *A Drama of Political Man. A Study in the Plays of Harley Granville Barker* (Sidgwick & Jackson, London, 1961)

Nicoll, Allardyce. *A History of the English Drama 1660-1900* (6 vols., Cambridge University Press, Cambridge, 1959)

_____ *English Drama 1900-1930. The Beginnings of the Modern Theatre* (Cambridge University Press, Cambridge, 1973)

Northend, Marjorie. 'Henry Arthur Jones and the Development of Modern English Drama', *Review of English Studies*, vol. 18 (1942), pp. 448-63

Odell, George C.D. *Shakespeare from Betterton to Irving* (2 vols., Constable, London, 1921)

'Orme Michael' (Mrs. J.T. Grein). *J.T. Grein. The Story of a Pioneer 1862-1935* (John Murray, London, 1936)

Pallette, D.B. 'The English Actor's Fight for Respectability', *Theatre Annual* (1948-9), pp. 27-34

Paulus, Gretchen. 'Beerbohm Tree and the New Drama', *University of Toronto Quarterly*, vol. 27 (1957-8), pp. 103-15

Pearson, Hesketh. *The Last Actor-Managers* (Methuen & Co. Ltd., London, 1950)

_____ *Beerbohm Tree: His Life and Laughter* (Methuen & Co. Ltd., London, 1956)

Pinero, Sir Arthur Wing. *The Collected Letters*, ed. and introduction by J.P. Wearing (Minneapolis University Press, Minneapolis, 1974)

Poel, William. *Shakespeare in the Theatre* (Sidgwick & Jackson, London, 1913)

_____ *What Is Wrong with the Stage? Some Notes on the English Theatre from the Earliest Times to the Present Day* (Allen & Unwin, London, 1920)

Purdom, C.B. *Harley Granville Barker. Man of the Theatre, Dramatist and Scholar* (Rockliff, London, 1955)

Reynolds, Ernest Randolph. *Modern English Drama. A Survey of the Theatre from 1900* (G. Harrap, London, 1949). Contains useful appendices and bibliography

Robins, Elizabeth. *Theatre and Friendships. Some Henry James Letters* (William Heinemann, London, 1932)

Rowell, George. *The Victorian Theatre. A Survey* (Oxford University Press, London, 1956)

_____ (ed.) *Victorian Dramatic Criticism* (Methuen & Co. Ltd., London, 1971)

_____ 'Tree's Shakespeare Festivals (1905-1913)', *Theatre Notebook*, vol. 29, no. 2 (1975), pp. 74-81

Salmon, Eric. *Granville Barker: A Secret Life* (Heineman Educational Books, London, 1983)

Schmidt, Hans. *The Dramatic Criticism of William Archer*, Cooper Monographs, no. 9 (Francke, Berne, 1964)

Schoonderwoerd, N.H.G. *J.T. Grein. Ambassador of the Theatre 1862-1935: A Study in Anglo-Continental Theatrical*

Relations (Van Gorcum & Co., Assen, 1963)

Shaw, George Bernard. *The Quintessence of Ibsenism* (Hill & Wang, New York, 1957)

_____ *Our Theatre in the Nineties* (3 vols., Constable, London, 1932)

_____ *Bernard Shaw's Letters to Granville Barker*, ed. C.B. Purdom (Phoenix House Ltd., London, 1956)

_____ *Shaw on Theatre*, ed. E.J. West (MacGibbon & Kee, New York, 1958)

_____ *Collected Letters 1874-1897* and *1898-1910*, ed. Dan H. Laurence (Max Reinhardt, London, 1965 and 1972)

_____ *An Autobiography 1856-1898* and *1898-1950*, selected by Stanley Weintraub (Max Reinhardt, London, 1969 and 1970)

Simon, Elliott M. *The Problem Play in British Drama 1890-1914* (Universitat Salzburg, Salzburg, 1978)

Speaight, Robert. *William Poel and the Elizabethan Revival* (William Heinemann, London, 1954)

_____ *Shakespeare on the Stage: An Illustrated History of Shakespearian Performance* (Little Brown & Co., New York, 1973)

Sprague, Arthur Colby. 'Shakespeare and William Poel', *University of Toronto Quarterly*, vol. 17, no. 1 (October 1947), pp. 29-37

Stephens, John Russell. *The Censorship of British Drama 1824-1901* (Cambridge University Press, Cambridge, 1980)

Stokes, John. *Resistible Theatres: Enterprise and Experiment in the Late Nineteenth Century* (Elek Books, London, 1972)

Stratman, Carl J. (ed.) *Britain's Theatrical Periodicals 1720-1967* (New York Public Library, New York, 1972)

Stromberg, Roland N. (ed.) *Realism, Naturalism and Symbolism* (Macmillan, London, 1968)

Symons, Arthur. *Plays, Acting and Music* (Constable, London, 1909)

Taylor, John Russell. *The Rise and Fall of the Well-Made Play* (Methuen & Co. Ltd., London, 1967)

Tree, Sir Herbert Beerbohm. *Thoughts and After Thoughts* (Cassel & Co. Ltd., London, 1913)

Trewin, J.C. *Benson and the Bensonians* (Barrie & Rockliff, London, 1960)

_____ *Shakespeare on the English Stage 1900-1964. A Survey of Productions* (Barrie & Rockliff, London, 1964)

_____ *The Edwardian Theatre* (Rowman & Littlefield, Totowa, N.J., 1976)

Walkley, Arthur Bingham. *Drama and Life* (Methuen & Co. Ltd., London, 1907)

Weales, Gerald. 'Edwardian Theater', in *Edwardians and Late Victorians*, ed. Richard Ellmann (Columbia University Press, New York, 1960)

Wearing, J.P. *The London Stage 1890-1899, 1900-1909* and *1910-1919* (Scarecrow Press Inc., Metuchen, N.J., 1976, 1981 and 1982)

West, E.J. 'The London Stage 1870-1980', *University of Colorado Studies*, Series B, no. ii (1943), pp. 31-84

Whitworth, Geoffrey. *The Making of a National Theatre* (Faber & Faber, London, 1951)

Who's Who in the Theatre (London, 1912, et seq.)

Wilson, Albert Edward. *Edwardian Theatre* (Arthur Baker, London, 1951)

INDEX